Get the eBook FREE!

(PDF, ePub, Kindle, and liveBook all included)

We believe that once you buy a book from us, you should be able to read it in any format we have available. To get electronic versions of this book at no additional cost to you, purchase and then register this book at the Manning website.

Go to https://www.manning.com/freebook and follow the instructions to complete your pBook registration.

That's it!
Thanks from Manning!

Modern Angular

ALSO COVERS SIGNALS, STANDALONE, SSR, ZONELESS, AND MORE

ARMEN VARDANYAN

MANNING
SHELTER ISLAND

For online information and ordering of this and other Manning books, please visit
www.manning.com. The publisher offers discounts on this book when ordered in quantity.
For more information, please contact

Special Sales Department
Manning Publications Co.
20 Baldwin Road
PO Box 761
Shelter Island, NY 11964
Email: orders@manning.com

Manning Publications Co.
20 Baldwin Road
PO Box 761
Shelter Island, NY 11964

Development editor: Ian Hough
Technical editor: Santosh Lalchand Yadav
Review editor: Dunja Nikitović
Production editor: Deirdre Blanchfield-Hiam
Copy editor: Kari Lucke
Proofreader: Keri Hales
Technical proofreader: Tanya Wilke
Typesetter: Dennis Dalinnik
Cover designer: Marija Tudor

ISBN: 9781633436923
Printed in the United States of America

Dedicated to my sister, Marina, who bought for me all my laptops except the one I used to write this book

contents

preface

When I started my career in the spring of 2016, Angular, as we know it today, did not yet exist; instead, I used to be an Angular.js developer—a long-forgotten framework that has now reached its end of life. While it offered interesting features and an opportunity to build more organized web apps, it did have some glaring flaws. This brings us to September 2016, when Angular 2 or, as it is known now, simply Angular was released.

This was huge! Everything changed at a moment's notice: we now had TypeScript, classes everywhere, strict organizational rules, and, soon enough, even a dedicated CLI tool to manage over applications. Of course, this was overwhelming at first; however, upon further research, it was revealed that the framework is actually very solid and an immediate upgrade upon anything we had prior, and that was the moment when many frontend developers, including myself, fell in love with it.

Of course, this new Angular, like any other tool, wasn't without flaws either: so began the process of continuous improvements upon the framework that we know and love. In the few first versions the framework stabilized, then in versions 8 and 9, we got a new rendering engine, and now we get a new phase of massive improvements that are often referred to (even by the Angular core team itself) as the "Angular renaissance."

I was always very involved with the progress and in-depth characteristics of Angular in the sense of *documenting* them. I loved going to the Angular source code and trying to figure out how the most interesting features actually work, trying out the most challenging problems, and speaking to industry experts. What I discovered is that, for me, the best way to learn something is to write about it. I started writing articles about Angular, going to podcasts, and in 2019 even began public speaking. All of this in the end culminated in this book.

But why have this book at all? Well, when this first began, we as a community didn't know anything about the "Angular renaissance"—we just knew Angular had scheduled major releases every six months, and with every release, we got some small new interesting things. However, we noticed that the changes incrementally got more and more revolutionary, so to speak; it was useful to write articles about all the features or talk about them at podcasts and events, but it kept growing and growing, with more changes that necessitated a very thorough exploration. Then it became obvious that something more was necessary.

And that is how this book came to be: a book that is meant to help Angular developers who are excited about these new changes, or maybe frightened by them, to understand the new features, appreciate them, use them in their new projects, or even migrate older projects toward a more modern approach.

The book cannot possibly claim to be a *complete* guide to everything new in Angular; as I write these words, Angular keeps changing and growing. During the writing of the book, I had to go back and change some things that were no longer current; this is the nature of software development, and the only thing we can do is keep learning. I know I learned a lot while writing this book, and I hope it will help you learn a thing or two about modern Angular too.

acknowledgments

This book is a huge achievement for me, and there are lots of people who helped me, in different ways and forms, to accomplish it and who deserve this gratitude.

First, I want to thank my girlfriend Shahane, who helped and supported me throughout this huge endeavor.

Next, I would love to acknowledge my editors: development editor Ian Hough and technical editor Santosh Yadav. Ian did a tremendous job and helped me establish myself as a writer. Santosh was a huge inspiration for me for years before I even undertook writing a book and is probably the person with the most significant effect on my professional career ever. Thanks as well to all the people who worked on the production and promotion of this book at Manning—my copyeditor Kari Lucke, project editor Deirdre Blanchfield-Hiam, as well as the rest of the team—working with all of you was a delightful experience!

I also want to acknowledge my friend Lars Gyrup Brink Nielsen for encouraging me to write a book, serving as a big inspiration, and helping in the initial stages of writing, as well as my colleagues Nune and Arsen, for helping me grow professionally and being so enthusiastic about the book.

Of course, I must thank the entirety of the Angular core team and everyone who loves and contributes to our favorite framework.

Finally, thanks to all the reviewers: Al Pezewski, Andy Robinson, Anooplal Hariharan, Aurélien Marocco, Betsegaw Lemma Amersho, Daniel McAlister, Dieter Jordens, Duncan McRae, Enrique Carro García, Eric Anderson, Frantisek Krul, Giuseppe Catalano Javid Asgarov, Jeff Smith, Juan Luis Barreda, Junaid Ramzan, Kiran

Krishnamurthy, Krishna Chaitanya Anipindi, Matteo Battista, Mitchell Fox, Peter Szabo, Rob Monhemius, Rodney A. James, Samuel Bosch, Simon Verhoeven, Steven Edwards, Tan Wee, and Tony Sweets. Your suggestions helped make this a better book.

about this book

Modern Angular is here to help understand and embrace the most recent changes to the Angular ecosystem, (starting from v12 up to v17), to either build new Angular applications from scratch or to migrate existing apps to these new versions. It does not function as a tutorial for Angular as a whole but rather helps Angular developers gain concrete knowledge about the new features while diving a little deeper into the base knowledge whenever necessary

Who should read this book

Modern Angular is meant to be utilized by people who are already familiar with Angular and have worked on projects before; it is good both for developers who just learned the important basics of the framework and those already very experienced with it. Additionally, it is useful to developers who maintain large legacy projects and look for strategies to bring their code up to modern standards.

How this book is organized: A road map

The book consists of 10 chapters, each covering a set of distinct new features. Each chapter first explores the old approach of doing things, then dives into the new approach by utilizing it in a brand-new project, and finally shows ways and strategies to help migrate existing codebases.

- Chapter 1 discusses modern Angular as a whole, why the changes are happening, how to set up a project from scratch using the recent Angular versions, and what structure these new projects have.

- Chapter 2 discusses standalone Angular building blocks, why we want them, how to perform all common tasks with standalone components, and how to migrate module-based components to become standalone.
- Chapter 3 dives into Angular's dependency injection mechanism, discusses the `inject` function, how it changed developers' approaches to dependency injection, and what building blocks were affected by this change.
- Chapter 4 explores various small new additions and improvements, like the optimized image loader, improved component inputs, better debugging options, and more.
- Chapter 5 discusses RxJS and how it works with Angular as of now and the new built-in interoperability library, tying in dependency injection improvements from chapter 3 to new approaches with RxJS.
- Chapter 6 introduces signals, explains why they are necessary, and provides high-level knowledge about all of their features.
- Chapter 7 dives deep into signals, explaining how they can improve application performance and how to approach some advanced tasks like state management and RxJS interoperability with them.
- Chapter 8 discusses unit testing in modern Angular applications and some new useful tools that can help with the task.
- Chapter 9 talks about server-side rendering, how it can enhance application performance, and how to build applications that utilize service-side rendering and web page prerendering.
- Chapter 10 discusses future prospects of the Angular framework like zoneless change detection and completely signal-based applications, and also explores some experimental new features that are already available like the new template syntax and deferred loading of components.

Readers are expected to read the book from start to end; however, after reading the first two chapters, developers can feel free to read the chapters on topics that interest them the most.

About the code

This book contains many examples of source code both in numbered listings and in line with normal text. In both cases, source code is formatted in a `fixed-width font` `like this` to separate it from ordinary text. Sometimes code is also **in bold** to highlight code that has changed from previous steps in the chapter, such as when a new feature adds to an existing line of code.

In many cases, the original source code has been reformatted; we've added line breaks and reworked indentation to accommodate the available page space in the book. In rare cases, even this was not enough, and listings include line-continuation markers (➥). Additionally, comments in the source code have often been removed from the listings when the code is described in the text. Code annotations accompany many of the listings, highlighting important concepts.

Please note: in chapter 10, we take a different route by exploring some experimental features on the code we already built; to have access to both versions, readers can use the source code repository and switch to the branch named "chapter-10" to review the other version.

The complete code for the examples in the book is available for download from the Manning website at https://www.manning.com/books/modern-angular, and from GitHub at https://github.com/Armenvardanyan95/modern-angular-hrms.

liveBook discussion forum

Purchase of *Modern Angular* includes free access to liveBook, Manning's online reading platform. Using liveBook's exclusive discussion features, you can attach comments to the book globally or to specific sections or paragraphs. It's a snap to make notes for yourself, ask and answer technical questions, and receive help from the author and other users. To access the forum, go to https://livebook.manning.com/book/modern -angular/discussion. You can also learn more about Manning's forums and the rules of conduct at https://livebook.manning.com/discussion.

Manning's commitment to our readers is to provide a venue where a meaningful dialogue between individual readers and between readers and the author can take place. It is not a commitment to any specific amount of participation on the part of the author, whose contribution to the forum remains voluntary (and unpaid). We suggest you try asking the author some challenging questions lest his interest stray! The forum and the archives of previous discussions will be accessible from the publisher's website as long as the book is in print.

about the author

ARMEN VARDANYAN is a Google Developer Expert for Angular and a frontend team lead with eight years of experience. He writes articles about Angular, TypeScript, RxJS, NgRx, and other related technologies and sometimes appears as a speaker at conferences.

about the cover illustration

The figure on the cover of *Modern Angular*, "Jeune Fille Armenienne," or "Young Armenian girl," is taken from a four-volume set by Auguste Wahlen, published in 1843.

In those days, it was easy to identify where people lived and what their trade or station in life was just by their dress. Manning celebrates the inventiveness and initiative of the computer business with book covers based on the rich diversity of regional culture centuries ago, brought back to life by pictures from collections such as this one.

Welcome to modern Angular

This chapter covers

- Our expectations of and goals for reading this book
- A general overview of common problems in previous versions of Angular apps
- New solutions for those problems provided by recent versions of Angular

Angular, one of the most popular frontend development frameworks, is at a crossroads. The framework has seen years of improvements in performance, user experience, and new features, like the introduction of the Ivy rendering engine, which reduced bundle sizes and improved run time. These developments have put the framework in a beneficial position.

Now, the community can focus on more than just improving the visible parts of the framework and, instead, work on the parts that directly affect user experience. Importantly, attention can also be directed toward aspects that affect the developer experience, such as better scalability and composability, among other aspects. These aspects are even more valuable for developers who work with the framework. Versions of the Angular framework have improved both the user and developer experiences, and more enhancements will continue to be added in future versions.

1

With this goal in mind, the Angular team has delivered several important updates in recent versions (starting in v13 and v14), which have become essential breakthroughs, putting Angular on a path of almost revolutionary changes. By the time this book is in print, Angular v19 will be live as the latest iteration of Angular, packed with an arsenal of modern tools built for various problems. We will cover all features, however minor, in recent releases (v12–v18) in rigorous depth, with examples, practical guides, and exercises.

1.1 What to expect

Before discussing what's new in Angular, let's first define who this book might be useful for, what skills and knowledge will be minimally required to grasp the concepts fully, and how the book is structured. Let's begin with the learning subjects.

1.1.1 Who will benefit from reading this book?

In light of the recent changes to Angular, several groups of developers who will need to understand the new features will find this book very useful:

- *New adopters of Angular*—Developers may either come from other frameworks or just have adopted Angular and want to learn about the latest features in more detail (assuming a base level of expertise)
- *Seasoned Angular developers*—Even the most experienced Angular developers can benefit from this book, as it provides a comprehensive overview of all the new features and changes introduced in Angular v12–v18.
- *Developers using an older version of Angular*—This book can help those using an older version of Angular to understand the benefits of upgrading to the latest version—and how to do it quickly and smoothly. In addition to covering the new features and changes introduced in recent versions, we'll discuss other relevant topics, such as changes that have been backported.

1.1.2 What do we need to know before getting started?

Certain knowledge is required to maximize the amount of information digested from this book. It is important to understand that this book is *not* an Angular tutorial, which would explain everything from scratch, but rather a guidebook of new features for developers already familiar with Angular and seeking more in-depth knowledge of modern approaches and tools. If you are unfamiliar with some concepts, see *Pro Angular 16* by Adam Freeman (Manning, 2024; https://www.manning.com/books/pro-angular-16), which follows a tutorial-based approach and has helpful explanations of more basic concepts. You can keep *Pro Angular 16* as a reference for this one; sometimes, I will reference it to help explain some concepts.

This book will explain (albeit briefly) some more advanced concepts necessary for the narration. Besides those explanations, the book assumes basic-to-intermediate knowledge of Angular, TypeScript, and HTML. Table 1.1 provides details of the minimally required knowledge.

Table 1.1 Minimally required knowledge

Technology	Level of Expertise	Details
TypeScript	Basic	Knowledge of what TypeScript is; how to declare types of variables, functions, and objects; and knowledge about generic types. Anything more sophisticated will be briefly explained in the book whenever necessary.
Angular	Intermediate	Because Angular itself is the main focus of the book, basic knowledge is sometimes not enough. The book assumes familiarity with the building blocks of an Angular application (components, directives, etc.) and knowledge about Angular's built-in packages like Http, Routing, and so on. Some minor advanced concepts will be explained as necessary, or a reference to *Pro Angular 16* will be provided.
RxJS	Basic	Only the most basic knowledge of RxJS (mainly observables, operators, and subscriptions) is necessary.
HTML	Very basic	The most entry-level knowledge of HTML tags and attributes is enough to understand the book's materials.
CSS	Very basic	Knowledge of CSS selectors is enough. The book does not focus on styling, and examples of components usually will not have CSS code.

1.1.3 How is the book structured?

As previously mentioned, many types of developers with various tasks will find this book useful. To best accommodate all of them, the book follows a certain pattern of explaining these new features. First, we will establish a problem that Angular developers experienced in previous versions and then cover solutions that the framework offered in those earlier versions (or note the absence of such prior solutions). We will then discuss the new tools available to solve that feature's particular problem in a new, modern Angular application. Finally, I will explain how developers can smoothly migrate their existing Angular applications to use the new feature.

All practical examples are structured in a brand-new Angular application. We will create this application from scratch, using the latest Angular version and the newest Angular features. The application will perform practical, real-life functions to maximize the practicality of the examples. We will set up this application later in this chapter.

Now that we have set prerequisites, we can define our starting point by understanding what Angular looked like before these revolutionary changes and what problems those changes try to address.

1.2 How Angular was

Before discussing the most recent versions, let's identify the framework's most important features that have been subjected to changes with the latest versions and the approach we'll take to building an Angular-based application.

1.2.1 *Angular's core features*

Next, we will talk about some, but not all, of the important parts of the Angular framework. I mainly focus on the features undergoing a transformation via the latest releases.

OBJECT-ORIENTED PROGRAMMING

Object-oriented programming (OOP) was long seen as a signifier of large enterprise projects, heavily popularized by languages like Java and C#. It was the go-to approach for managing complex applications. Angular itself has a rather complex and intertwined relationship with OOP.

Most Angular building blocks, like components, pipes, directives, guards, and many more, have historically been authored with OOP. All building blocks are represented by a class, data inside of them is stored as a property, and their behavior is described via methods. In the next chapters, especially chapters 3 and 10, we will see that some of those building blocks do not have to be classes; in fact, representing some of them as classes could be confusing for developers, especially those coming from other popular frontend frameworks like React, where functions reign supreme. We will see how this reality is about to change.

DEPENDENCY INJECTION

Dependency injection (DI) has been a very important and appealing part of the Angular framework, and it is hard to find a developer who hasn't utilized it in an Angular project. Until recently, DI was completely coupled with classes and OOP: to have DI, you needed to have a class with the `@Injectable` decorator; you could not use an instance of a service, a config, or anything else from the DI-tree in a function unless it is explicitly passed as an argument. Of course, this constraint denied us some composability. With the addition of the new `inject` function, this constraint has evaporated, opening a new era of composability and reusability.

MODULE-BASED ARCHITECTURE

Before v14, all Angular applications were built around `NgModules`, an Angular-specific concept. `NgModules` comprise a class that encapsulates all other building blocks and makes them work together. `NgModules` were used to build application architecture, share functionality, and more. However, many Angular developers experienced various problems with `NgModules`. Now, Angular allows developers to build applications without `NgModules`, a new practice known as "standalone."

RxJS

RxJS, the reactive extensions library for JavaScript, most likely plays a huge part in sharing the state between different parts of an Angular application. For instance, authentication and authorization events (access granted/revoked) are, at the very least, propagated through it. However, many applications either build some relatively simple state management mechanism via a service with a subject or use an existing state management solution like NgRx, which also relies on RxJS. New features have dramatically increased the interoperability between Angular applications and RxJS.

CHANGE DETECTION

Change detection, the mechanism by which Angular propagates the changes in a component's data to the UI, is a pretty complex and somewhat suboptimal algorithm. It relies on a third-party library (zone.js), with developers anxious to find solutions for building applications without this overhead. In later chapters, we will learn how to accomplish that and dive deep into the change detection mechanism.

1.2.2   *What is an Angular application?*

After the very first Angular release, multiple approaches to building Angular-based applications emerged. Monorepo tools like Nx, static site generators, and different builders have become fairly prominent and grown in communities. However, we will examine the most "classic" Angular projects—those built purely on Angular CLI—using the most popular (for the better or worse) approaches. In other words, we'll look at the types of applications you are more likely to encounter in the wild.

Let's imagine an Angular application around which our discussion will evolve. We will make a series of assumptions about this app:

- It uses Angular v12, which does not include the modern features of more recent versions.
- It does not use a dedicated state management library like NgRx or Akita. Instead, as with many Angular projects, it gradually reinvents state management in the form of services with a subject.
- It uses a modular architecture, not specific patterns like library-based or micro-frontends.
- It uses a third-party UI library (Angular Material, among others). The specific library is not important; we will just assume that dependency exists.

While these assumptions might feel a bit restrictive, they describe a large chunk of existing Angular apps.

Let's pose some important questions about this application:

- What are its main parts?
- How do those parts interact, and what is the glue that bonds them?
- On an architectural level, what are the most important and frequent challenges developers face?
- What are some challenges at the code level?
- How easy is it to onboard someone into an existing project?

With these questions in mind, let's briefly discuss the business and unique cases of the actual application. In our scenario, we will describe an HRMS (human resources management system) application where the entire workflow of an HR department is handled. It has several key parts:

- *Employees*—All the data about a company's employees, their profiles, accessible both for the HR personnel and employees themselves

- *Recruitment*—Data about the recruitment process, interviews, and admissions, accessible to the HR personnel and certain employees (usually the ones conducting technical interviews)
- *Time off*—A feature where employees can request time-offs and managers can approve them. Accessible to everyone
- *Work*—Data about the projects the company is working on, who reports to whom, submitting feedback, and so on. This has granular access, and some employees can see all of the pages, some can see only the parts of the pages, and so on.
- *Integrations*—Communications with third-party apps, like email or calendar. For example, we might want the person who is going to conduct a technical interview to receive an email invitation, the event added to their calendar, and also to allow them to see an integrated, personalized calendar in their "work" section profile. This could mean working with third-party services like Outlook, Google Calendar, or more.

Figure 1.1 shows a visual diagram of the application. As we can see, the application, even on a superficial level, appears to have multiple interconnected features. This means that the app will most certainly utilize RxJS, have performance issues (partially related to the change detection mechanism), have multiple services and reusable components/directives that require careful maintenance and structuring, and have multiple `NgModules`. It quickly becomes obvious that all the features we mentioned in the previous section will be significantly affected by the latest changes in Angular.

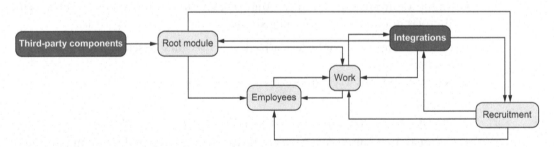

Figure 1.1   The relations between different parts of the application, with arrows representing relations between different modules, like shared components or services

To examine this application, we will do two distinct things. First, we will begin building this very application from scratch. Next, in every chapter, as previously promised, we will examine scenarios in which this app already exists on an older version of Angular so we can understand how to migrate it to use the latest features. For now, let us begin building this application by doing a basic setup so we can build upon it in subsequent chapters.

1.3 Let's start a modern Angular app

There are different ways of starting a new project with Angular, including different custom and third-party builders, bundlers, and other tools. However, those tools, while doubtlessly useful, are out of scope for this book; be mindful that through the entire course of the book, we are going to use the official Angular CLI and the official Angular CLI only.

If you do not have the Angular CLI on your machine, use the official Angular documentation page (https://mng.bz/PNEY) for proper installation; if you have an older version of Angular CLI, please install at least v16.0.0; if you have already done those steps, then proceed with this chapter, as we explore what a modern Angular application looks like.

1.3.1 Using the Angular CLI

The Angular CLI has a bunch of different commands and custom schematics. In this book, we will gradually encounter different (some quite new) scripts that would allow us to build using specific settings, generate environment files, migrate existing code, and so on. For now, we will focus on the probably most well-known command, ng new, which is used to create new projects.

ng new has several customization options for a newly created project, and the dedicated section of the Angular documentation explains them quite well. Here, however, we will focus on six of them, as outlined in table 1.2.

Table 1.2 Important parameters for creating a new Angular project

Parameter	Description	Default value
--strict	Enables strict type-checking in both templates and TypeScript files	True
--inline-template	Makes component templates inline by default. With the rise of stand-alone components, this approach has become very popular. Throughout the book, we will show whole components with inline templates to ensure maximum readability, but this is not considered either a good or bad practice and depends on developer preference.	False
--minimal	Creates a project without any testing-related files. This is good for learning, but we are not going to use it, as we also cover unit testing in this book; if you want to see a simplified version of the project tree, feel free to use this option.	False
--package-manager	Allows us to select which package manager to use (if we do not like npm for whatever reason) in the project. Angular CLI commands like ng add or ng update will use this option under the hood to install and update dependencies. We will stick to the default in this book, but you are welcome to explore other options.	npm
--standalone	This option is the most important for us, as it creates an application without NgModules by default, as it does with modern-day Angular apps. We will use this one outright.	True

Table 1.2   Important parameters for creating a new Angular project *(continued)*

Parameter	Description	Default value
-defaults	Skips the prompt questions and uses default values without asking. For example, it will generate an Angular routing, use CSS for styles, and so on.	False

1.3.2   *Creating a new project*

Now, as we have familiarized ourselves with several command options, let us go forward and finally create a new application. If you are using Angular v16, you will have to manually specify that you want a standalone component-based application. In v17 and higher, you can skip this parameter.

Navigate to a folder/directory of your preference and run the following command:

```
ng new hrms --defaults --standalone --routing
```

> **NOTE**   Depending on your CLI version (v16 or lower), you might see a warning that says, "Standalone application structure is new and not yet supported by many existing `ng add` and `ng update` integrations with community libraries." This statement mostly applies to using third-party libraries and is not very relevant to our application, so you can safely ignore it.

After all the installations are done, we should be able to see our new project. Let's open it with our chosen editor and explore the folder structure first. Most probably, the application looks something like this:

```
└── hrms/
    ├── src/
    ├── angular.json
    ├── package.json
    ├── tsconfig.app.json
    ├── tsconfig.json
    └── tsconfig.spec.json
```

Note that there can be several other files not mentioned here, like Git-related files, editor-specific autogenerated files, a README.md file, or more.

Let's pay attention to three important changes, as opposed to what we used to have in older versions:

- *No environments folder*—Environment files are used to store application configuration data like API URLs or third-party API configurations that might differ from environment to environment. Starting from Angular v15, environment files are not generated by default and can be added via a separate command. We will talk more about environments and builds/deployments in chapter 9.
- *No explicit polyfills.ts file*—Polyfills are used to support older browsers like IE11 or prior. Previously, an Angular project had this file by default from the very

beginning of the project, but now it is no longer autogenerated. This can also be added manually if necessary to support older browsers.

- If we open the angular.json file, we will notice it is far shorter than we used to have in older projects.

1.3.3 What changed?

Now, let us open the most interesting folder, src, and see what it contains:

```
.
└── hrms/
    └── src/
        ├── app/
        │   ├── app.component.css
        │   ├── app.component.html
        │   ├── app.component.spec.ts
        │   ├── app.component.ts
        │   ├── app.config.ts
        │   └── app.routes.ts
        ├── assets/
        ├── index.html
        ├── main.ts
        └── styles.css
```

Here, we can see another three differences from what we are used to:

- *No app.module.ts file*—The application is fully standalone and does not utilize modules for its architecture
- *app.routes.ts file instead of app.routing.module.ts*—This is again because we chose standalone
- *app.config.ts file*—This file will contain global configurations for our app, like providers, routing initialization, and more.

Now, let's start exploring the file contents themselves. app.component.html contains a predefined welcome page, app.component.spec.ts contains some boilerplate unit tests, and app.component.css is empty, so we will skip them. Let us now review the contents of app.component.ts.

> **Listing 1.1** `AppComponent`, **the root component of the project**

```
import { Component } from '@angular/core';
import { CommonModule } from '@angular/common';
import { RouterOutlet } from '@angular/router';

@Component({
  selector: 'app-root',
  standalone: true,
  imports: [CommonModule, RouterOutlet],
  templateUrl: './app.component.html',
  styleUrls: ['./app.component.css']
})
```

```
export class AppComponent {
  title = 'hrms';
}
```

This code looks like a fairly common Angular component, but it has two important distinctions:

- `standalone: true` marks this component as standalone and not belonging to any `NgModule`
- The `imports` array is used to import dependencies, like other modules and standalone components/directives/pipes, as this component is standalone and does not rely on an `NgModule` to locate its dependencies and instead imports them directly. Note that in v16 it imports `CommonModule`, to be able to use built-in directives and pipes, but those things are now also standalone and can be imported directly. That is, we can write `NgIf` in the imports array and import only itself instead of bringing the entire `CommonModule`. In v17+, `CommonModule` is not imported by default.

This is how a standalone component typically looks like, but of course, there is much more to it, as we will discuss in the next chapter. Now let's see the app.routes.ts file.

Listing 1.2   Default empty route definitions

```
import { Routes } from '@angular/router';
export const routes: Routes = [];
```

We can see that it is also simpler, as it does not use the `RouterModule` to register routes. Instead, those routes are only defined here and registered in the app.config.ts file, which we will now review.

Listing 1.3   Application configuration

```
import { ApplicationConfig } from '@angular/core';
import { provideRouter } from '@angular/router';

import { routes } from './app.routes';

export const appConfig: ApplicationConfig = {
  providers: [provideRouter(routes)]
};
```

Again, two important things to note here:

- The `ApplicationConfig` interface has one property, `providers`, which is used to provide DI tokens, as we previously did in `NgModules` with the property that shared the same name.
- Routes are registered with a special new function called `provideRouter`, which also accepts an array of our route definitions instead of `RouterModule` `.forRoot(routes)`.

Now it seems we have reviewed all of our files because, as mentioned previously, we do not have an app.module.ts file in a standalone setup. So, if we do not have that file, how is our application being initialized and bootstrapped? Well, this logic fully moved to the main.ts file.

Listing 1.4 main.ts

```
import { bootstrapApplication } from '@angular/platform-browser';
import { appConfig } from './app/app.config';
import { AppComponent } from './app/app.component';

bootstrapApplication(AppComponent, appConfig)
  .catch((err) => console.error(err));
```

As we can see, main.ts now uses a special bootstrapApplication function instead of the previous platformBrowserDynamic().bootstrapModule(AppModule) and directly bootstraps the AppComponent instead of an AppModule. In modern Angular apps, we do not need an NgModule, and this new function can directly create our application using one root component and the application configuration.

So far, we have seen changes relating to standalone components and how dependencies are provided (DI). We will cover those topics in the next two chapters fully before proceeding to other changes. Now, let's briefly discuss all of those changes to have our road map for learning.

1.4 What's new in Angular?

Before we begin a slightly more hands-on acquaintance with the latest and hottest features in Angular, let's discuss how the Angular team identifies issues and decides on the solutions so we can understand the reasoning behind all these new features.

1.4.1 How does Angular evolve?

Angular is an open source framework with a vibrant community of contributors and users. As such, very often, certain wishes of the general audience eventually materialize into actual features and improvements in the framework code. Let's see the process behind this; it would be helpful to understand how certain decisions are made and possibly participate in the process itself. For a certain idea to become a concrete feature in the Angular framework, it has to pass through rigorous steps, as shown in figure 1.2.

As we can see, this is quite a long process marked with lots of milestones; also noteworthy is the fact that there are other internal processes we are unaware of, mostly related to upkeep. But the public process is what makes Angular (to an extent) democratic; while the core team retains the final word on changes and API structure, fairly often contributors from the wider community either suggest changes or code directly (via pull requests), and that is how lots of features that we are going to discuss in this book came to life. Let's discuss the first step in this process in more detail.

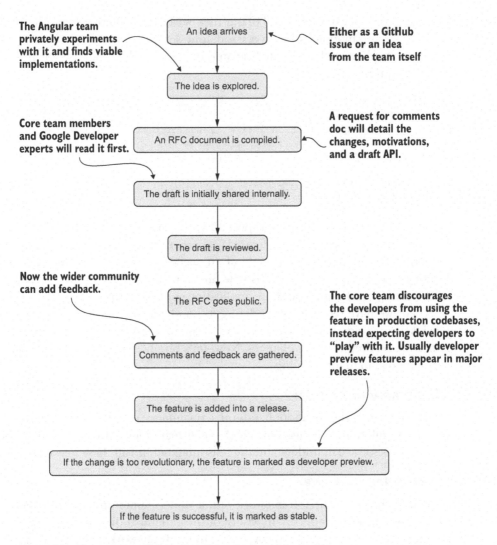

Figure 1.2   The process of integration of new features into Angular

1.4.2   *How does Angular recognize problems?*

As previously described (and, of course, what common sense tells us), the first step in adding a new feature to the framework is to identify a common and popular demand or a pain point for developers (maybe one of those we discussed previously). The process uses several methods—namely, internal research by the core team, an exploration of changes in the Web standards, GitHub issues submitted from the wider community, and direct pull requests contributed by community members. Finally, the Angular Developer Survey (https://mng.bz/w5q2) is an annual survey sent out to all interested Angular developers, where they can answer common questions, write about things they think need to change, and more.

After those things are gathered, discussions are often started, where contributors and users can vote on issues they find particularly appealing to them; this is yet another instance of democratic decision-making in the framework and yet another proof of how Angular is very feedback-driven and does, very often, listen to the developer community and adapt to new challenges.

However, it is very important to know that though the democratic process drives a lot of innovation in Angular, the core team still makes the ultimate decisions. Sometimes a highly requested feature may not be implemented, mainly because it conflicts with some core values the team has (e.g., backward compatibility, nonalignment with Web standards, and others we already discussed). Keeping all of this in mind, let us see the way Angular forges its path into the future.

1.4.3 *Current goals*

An important source of information on how Angular chooses its direction is the official Angular road map (https://angular.io/guide/roadmap), a detailed list of the features Angular is going to address in future releases. We can see a large number of topics there, but we are not going to explore any of them right now, as most of them are speculative anyway. However, familiarizing ourselves with the road map can give us an understanding of what we might expect in the future.

Instead, we will explore some current core goals—significant short-term changes that either improved the developer experience or laid a foundation for more radical changes. Those changes will reflect something already existing in the newer versions of Angular and are not speculative. We will examine those goals in the context of the previously mentioned HRMS enterprise application to understand what parts of such an application might improve.

EASE OF ADOPTION

Another famous (and at least partially correct) stereotype about Angular is that it is hard to learn or switch to. This is mainly related to the sheer number of features that Angular provides out of the box, including a very specific template syntax and other purely Angular-related concepts that the framework introduced like directives, pipes, and so on. Another important goal for the core team is to make the framework newcomer-friendly, either through improved documentation or directly by simplifying core concepts.

INCREASED COMPOSABILITY/REUSABILITY

Some Angular building blocks can be hard to reuse or repurpose. For instance, we can have multiple routing guards or interceptors that essentially do the same thing (like checking for certain roles or permissions, as mentioned) in different contexts and have problems being generalized, which can result in loads of copy-pasting and easily preventable bugs. It also severely affects the ability to refactor the codebase: changing one routing guard may mean changing all of them. We might also want to apply this reusability to directives that handle business logic to make our templates more dynamic.

REDUCED BOILERPLATE CODE

In general, Angular is considered a bit boilerplate-heavy compared to other frontend frameworks, so one of the goals of the core team (albeit not the most important one) is reducing the amount of code necessary to get up and running with Angular. In our application, we may have lots of boilerplate code to make some core functionality work, such as defining pipes and reusable components, providing services and environments, sharing state, creating routing guards, and other handlers.

IMPROVED TYPE SAFETY

As Angular is already built on top of TypeScript, we enjoy a lot of type safety with it. However, when we dive deeper, we discover that many parts of the framework itself contain a bunch of `any`s, which can and will make our apps less safe in terms of strict typing. Most prominent are the reactive forms, which, in an enterprise application dealing with a lot of user-generated data, can possibly be very important and widely used.

IMPROVED REACTIVITY

We saw many interconnected components and application parts in Figure 1.1, and there's a high possibility of connecting those elements via RxJS through Angular services. These connections introduce complexity and a higher probability of glitches and bugs. Simplifying that process would be of great benefit to larger apps and make them more accessible to newcomers.

1.4.4   New features

Starting from Angular v13, interesting and sometimes drastic improvements have been added, all addressing the topics we discussed previously. As this book is entirely dedicated to the modern state of Angular, we will not dive too deep into it in this chapter, but we will familiarize ourselves with a general overview of these additions.

STANDALONE BUILDING BLOCKS

We already encountered a standalone component when bootstrapping our HRMS application. Starting from v14, having `NgModules` is no longer required: Angular building blocks can now be standalone, meaning they do not require an associated `NgModule` to be used in an app. In v15, this new capability was marked as "stable" and is already widely used in many production-ready apps. We will discuss this new approach and all of its benefits (and some new pitfalls) in the next chapter.

THE INJECT FUNCTION

Until v14, it was only possible to inject dependencies in classes marked with one of Angular's decorators: `@Component`, `@Pipe`, `@Directive`, and, of course, `@Injectable`. It was impossible to use an instance of some DI value in a function (rather than a class) unless it was passed directly via an argument. With this new function, we can overcome this limitation and build a composable, reusable function that can be easily shared between components with the simplest approaches. This small change (essentially, the already-existing `inject` function was just exposed publicly by Angular) made huge waves through the Angular community, changing approaches, allowing for never-before-heard-of composability, and even resulting in the official deprecation of some previously widely used tools. We will dive deep into new DI patterns in chapter 3.

TYPE-SAFE REACTIVE FORMS

Reactive forms have long been a source of type-related bugs, and developers resorted to various (sometimes quite dirty) solutions to overcome these limitations. Again, from v14, new typed reactive forms have been introduced, which are now marked as "stable," that quickly replaced the previous ones (which have been renamed to *untyped reactive forms* to simplify migration). We will talk more about them in chapter 4.

DIRECTIVE COMPOSITION API

A new `hostDirectives` property has been added to the component/directive metadata object, which allows the automatic addition of other directives, essentially allowing us to build directives from other directives. This is a huge step up for composability, which was previously built with other (not always really suitable) solutions like OOP inheritance or pure DI. We will see how it simplifies both the directive/component code and the template in chapter 4.

BETTER COMPATIBILITY WITH RxJS

An entirely new package, rxjs-interop, has been added to Angular, which will help developers integrate RxJS code seamlessly into Angular apps. The new reactive primitive allows for switching from signals to observables, and vice versa, and the package has an easier, built-in way of unsubscribing from streams. We will explore this new package in chapter 5.

SIGNALS

Probably the most effective addition to Angular ever, signals are a new reactive primitive that is called to solve common problems we face with RxJS. Signals transform and significantly improve the change detection mechanism, bringing it to a new, more granular level instead of the current top-down checks system. We will talk about signals in great detail in chapters 6 and 7.

NEW TEMPLATE SYNTAX

Starting from v17, a new template syntax is available that is projected to replace `ngIf`, `ngSwitch`, and `ngFor` directives. This syntax allows for more readable templates and compiler optimizations. In v18, this syntax is already stable. We will talk about these new commands in chapter 10.

DEFERRED LOADING OF PARTS OF A TEMPLATE

Another addition to the new template syntax allows for deferred loading of a part of a template based on a condition or an event. This can help us build more performant applications while also reducing the final bundle size. We will cover this approach extensively in chapter 10.

NEW TOOLS FOR UNIT TESTING

The addition of a new unit testing framework, support for new APIs (like the previously mentioned `inject` function), and the emergence of AI tools have significantly affected how we view and write unit tests, allowing for a faster authoring experience and less time spent mocking data. In chapter 8, we will dive deep to understand how unit tests are driving modern Angular development.

SERVER-SIDE RENDERING HYDRATION

The server side has long been one of the weakest points of Angular, only supporting the most basic full rerender of the page, but recent developments have added long-awaited features—namely, full hydration. Full hydration greatly improves the performance of SSR apps, allowing for the reuse of the existing application state and DOM. In chapter 9, we will review this feature and familiarize ourselves with development experience improvements and a new experimental bundling system.

VARIOUS GRANULAR IMPROVEMENTS TO PERFORMANCE

Different small tools that improve the loading of the page and its different parts, like the loading of images, have emerged and are already stable. We will encounter such additions in different chapters, but mostly in chapter 3.

DEVELOPER EXPERIENCE IMPROVEMENTS

Better error messages, debugging, stack traces, and much more are already in Angular, with more improvements underway. We will examine these features in various chapters.

FINAL THOUGHTS

As we can see, these changes are a very large addition to the framework and can very well be hailed as "revolutionary." Sometimes developers refer to this as "Angular 3" as a reference to AngularJS being "Angular 1," the framework we had before v12 being "Angular 2," and now these new changes are marked as "Angular 3."

However, these names are confusing and do not correspond with reality. The Angular team has not made any statements referring to an entirely new framework. Although these changes are somewhat drastic, all of them are iterative, easily adoptable, and, for the most part, backward compatible. AngularJS to Angular was a full rewrite of the framework from scratch, with new concepts and approaches.

These updates are in no way an overhaul of the entire framework (although it would be fair to say that the difference between, let's say, Angular v18 in the future and Angular v12 will be very significant). So, we will refrain from calling it "Angular 3" or whatever other label some might conceive; instead, we treat it as "modern Angular" as in the current state of this framework.

1.4.5   *What about the future?*

Before moving on, let us briefly touch on two other related questions that may arise with the readers—namely, "What can we possibly expect next?" and "What will definitely stay the same?"

Let's start with the future prospects (see table 1.3). Note that these aren't speculations of preference-based fantasies but rather some experimental things already available in the framework for developer preview or already public RFCs (request for comments).

We won't discuss them in length in this book, but they're worth knowing about, and it's helpful to understand the motivations behind the changes already present.

Table 1.3   Prospects of new features in future versions of Angular

Change	Description	Version
Zoneless applications	Zone.js has been a required part of Angular since its very conception. However, it increases the bundle size and is not very efficient for change detection. With the new reactive primitive, the Angular team is exploring possibilities for allowing completely zone-free apps. They are possible currently with some adjustments as an experimental API but are not there by default.	v18
Alternative component authoring formats	As previously discussed, some building blocks (like route guards and resolvers) that have only been possible with classes previously are now available (and preferable) to be authored as functions. It is possible that the Angular team might also allow for functional pipes, directives, and even components, or maybe even a completely different authoring format.	Unknown
Partial hydration and resumability	We will discuss full-app hydration in chapter 9, as full hydration is already a stable part of the framework; however, the core team will also explore partial hydration of pages in SSR and application resumability.	Possibly v19
A let keyword for templates	This new keyword will allow developers to declare variables inside templates, simplifying the addition of complex logic to templates. These variables will only be available inside templates.	Possibly v18.1

The second question is of no less importance. The following is a list of things that we can treat as very stable, and that won't change in any significant way:

- *DI mechanisms*—While some minor improvements to DI will be present in the future (like being able to provide an InjectionToken at the root of the app), the DI framework itself has passed the test of time and remains one of the most beloved features for Angular developers.
- *Previous component authoring formats*—While functional components might be a possibility, class-based components are not going anywhere, at least in the foreseeable future.
- *RxJS support*—While Angular introduced a new reactive primitive, we will see in this book how integration with RxJS will become even smoother, and even if some developers might opt to use less RxJS in favor of signals, the core tenet of working well with RxJS will remain.
- *Routing*—After the introduction of the functional guards and other minor improvements, no significant changes are planned to the Angular routing.
- *HTTP client, animations, and other optional tools*—These tools are some parts of the framework that have definitely stood the test of time.

The future of Angular looks very bright, but to understand and be better prepared for it, we need to examine its present state.

1.4.6   *The learning process*

As we saw, each chapter of this book will revolve around one (or more) new concepts and will explore their real-life applications. In this context, each chapter will be loosely structured according to the paradigm we set out earlier: exploring a topic and the theory behind the changes, applying it with code examples, and then challenging the reader to code. All the solutions will be included in the GitHub repository, but I recommend they be implemented manually to increase the reader's skill proficiency.

I hope that this process will be both entertaining and informative and that the abundance of practical coding will help cement your knowledge of Angular. So, starting here, we begin our deep dive to explore each new feature one by one while building our modern Angular application.

Summary

- Angular has a rich history and keeps evolving.
- The community has identified a number of outstanding problems with the framework.
- The core team constantly proposes and implements new approaches to address those problems.
- A huge set of new concepts has already arrived, such as new dependency injection, standalone building blocks, signals, type-safe forms, functional building blocks, and more.
- New projects are now created using a standalone approach.

A standalone future

This chapter covers

- Using Angular components, directives, and pipes without `NgModules`
- Structuring applications without `NgModules`
- Routing and lazy-loading of standalone components
- Migrating existing applications to standalone

In the previous chapter, we learned about recent developments in Angular and laid out a learning plan for this book. We also created a project and already encountered standalone components. Now it is the time to explore one of the new capabilities of modern Angular, building applications without `NgModules`, colloquially known as *standalones*, and understand both the benefits and shortcomings of this approach. To do so, we first need to examine the reasons why teams are making a switch away from `NgModules` in a more profound way.

2.1 Why abandon NgModules?

As we know, before Angular v14, all Angular applications used NgModules to be able to run. It was the very first Angular concept new developers learned about, and it was the glue that held Angular applications together; components, in contrast, were specifically *not* that glue. In this context, NgModules were a fundamental part of the framework. So what changed? Why change so drastically? It turns out not everyone was happy with NgModules.

Before we move on, we need to understand several key points about both modules and standalones:

- NgModules still exist and are supported, and they have not deprecated. Actually, deprecation is yet to be discussed.
- Standalone building blocks interop with NgModules just fine; you can have a module-based project with some standalone components in it, or vice versa, and you can use NgModules inside your standalone components.
- The goal is to make NgModules optional rather than getting rid of them completely (at least for now).
- Developers seem to love standalone setups, and it becomes more and more likely that we, as developers, will encounter more standalone projects in the future.
- The core team itself seems to favor standalones, which makes future deprecation more likely.

Now, let's cover all the reasons why developers do not like NgModules.

2.1.1 Hard to learn, hard to explain

NgModules are difficult, both to learn for yourself and to teach or explain to others. To understand this argument, let's imagine two scenarios: one in which we are a new adopter of Angular and another in which we are maintaining an Angular project onboarding a new member.

LEARNING ANGULAR

We are students of Angular: we just finished learning JavaScript, read some things about TypeScript, and are now ready to take the Angular world by storm! Here comes the very first lesson: a concept called NgModules. What are they? Well, the official explanation from the documentation states: "NgModules configure the injector and the compiler and help organize related things together" (https://angular.io/guide/ngmodules).

Not super helpful. What's an injector? What compiler? It turns out that to understand NgModules, we first need to learn a bunch of other concepts that are considered (rightfully so) pretty complex for a beginner. So what now? We can examine the main.ts file, which is apparently the first entry point of our application, and see roughly what is shown in the following listing.

Listing 2.1 main.ts file in an `NgModule` setup

```
import { enableProdMode } from '@angular/core';
import { platformBrowserDynamic } from '@angular/platform-browser-dynamic';

import { AppModule } from './app/app.module';
import { environment } from './environments/environment';

if (environment.production) {
  enableProdMode();
}

platformBrowserDynamic().bootstrapModule(AppModule)
  .catch(err => console.error(err));
```

With NgModules, we needed to enable production mode to disable some checks and assertions.

We can only bootstrap an NgModule, not the AppComponent directly; only then the module will create the component.

Our application, with all of its building blocks, is declared inside the `AppModule`, which makes sense, so let's see what goes on inside it.

Listing 2.2 `AppModule`

```
@NgModule({
  declarations: [
    AppComponent,
  ],
  imports: [
    CommonModule,
  ],
  providers: [
  ],
  bootstrap: [AppComponent]
})
export class AppModule { }
```

Well, this one is weird. What is the `CommonModule`? What does `bootstrap: [App-Component]` even mean? And why is this class empty? Of course, all of those questions have logical answers, but they introduce even more complexity for us. So essentially, for now, we just need to understand that modules "declare" stuff, let the app work, and go on learning about our building blocks. This process makes the learning path a bit nonlinear, where we will have to revisit concepts later to really understand them, which can be discouraging for beginners.

TEACHING ANGULAR

Now let us explore the second scenario: we are a seasoned senior developer, and a new team member just joined our team. We are onboarding them by explaining our project step by step. Here are several questions we might hear from a new team member:

- "Why is the app structured the way it is?"
- "Do you have a shared module? Oh, you have two?"
- "Why is there both a core module and a shared module?"
- "Why are shared modules on lazy-loaded modules?"

Of course, many other questions may arise. We spend a lot of time managing NgModules, and each team working on a different project has its own view on how NgModules should be structured, whether there should be a shared module, etc. These nuances all become quite tedious to explain to a newcomer, and every time someone switches to a new (existing) Angular project, it feels like a very new experience where things need to be explained all over again.

We also have another layer of confusion, as TypeScript and JavaScript already have a concept of a module: we call files that export something a *module*; in NodeJS, we write module.exports, and in TypeScript, we use export and import statements to use functions, classes, and variables from other files. Why have a module concept on top of this? What's the difference between those concepts?

In Angular, NgModules are used to group functionality and hold all the dependencies (like pipes, directives, and other components) together in a place called the *compilation context*. The claim is that NgModules simplify this process and help us structure our applications, but it is important to understand that this can be done in other ways, too—ways that do not involve a high-level framework concept and can result in poorly structured code anyway.

As we can see, this discussion comes into the scope of one of the main goals of the Angular team—to make Angular and projects built with it more approachable. If we remember that this was one of Angular's main goals, the scenarios in this chapter alone would be reason enough to make the idea of at least optional NgModules very appealing to both the core team and the wider community. But wait, there's more!

2.1.2   *Indirectness and boilerplate*

When we write code, we tend to split it into different parts and then assemble them as needed. For instance, we can split a large function into smaller ones, name them appropriately, and call them whenever necessary in the larger one, making the latter much more readable. This method also allows for the reuse of the same functionality. In Angular, we split code into its brand building blocks: components, directives, pipes, and injectable services. Because injectable services are not related to the template, we will focus on the first three. Each building block usually lives in its own separate file to keep things nice and clean. So, to use, say, a child component in another component, we need to import it. However, the import process is not direct (e.g., just importing another component into our component's file) and involves a more complex mental model.

Let's see an example of a component from our HRMS application that uses a child component in its template on a use case of a list of employees that renders individual employee tiles.

Listing 2.3   Component used in a parent component

```
import { Component, Input } from '@angular/core';
import { Employee } from '<path-to-type>';
```

```
@Component({
  selector: 'app-employee-list',
  template: `
    <div class="employees-container">
      <app-employee *ngFor="let employee of employees"
      [employee]="employee"></app-employee>
    </div>
  `,
})
export class EmployeeListComponent {
  @Input() employees: Employee[];
}
```

As we can see, this component receives a list of employees as `Input` and renders `app-employee` components in a `for` loop. Obviously, it uses another component, so it must import it somehow, right? But if we look at this component file's import statements, we won't see any imports of that component being used. Of course, if we have worked with Angular previously, we will understand this works because a module exists somewhere that does the following.

```
import { EmployeeComponent } from '<path-to-component>';
import { EmployeeListComponent } from <path-to-component>';

@NgModule({
  declarations: [EmployeeComponent, EmployeeListComponent ]
})
export class EmployeeModule {}
```

This approach makes it harder to determine the dependencies of a component. Hold on, it could be worse! `EmployeeListComponent` could use a component from an entirely different module. So, if we navigated to `EmployeeModule`, we would then need to find the module that exports the component we are looking for, which could have a vague name like `SharedModule`. This component must, in turn, add that component to an `exports` array, and so on. Modern developer tools (like the Angular Language Service; https://mng.bz/j07z) have mitigated this problem to an extent by providing IDE tools and extensions that help the developer navigate directly to a component/ directive/pipe from a template, but if we were trying to build a mental model of our component tree, app structure, or the flow of data, those tools would help us only incidentally. It will remain pretty hard to find where a certain dependency must be imported, and we would still have an unnecessary degree of complexity.

Also somewhat challenging are the providers of injectable services. `NgModules` do have a `providers` array, but with newer options becoming available, developers have increasingly chosen to just mark services as `providedIn: 'root'`, to avoid dealing with `NgModules` and have a clearer understanding of when and how the service is used. Services that are not marked as `providedIn: 'root'`, on the other hand, have to dwell inside a child route in the overall routing system but are not defined on the route, making it hard to understand when a service is first instantiated only by looking at the application architecture.

Building on what we already covered, it also becomes obvious that we need to write a lot of boilerplate code. We need pretty standard `NgModule` definitions all over the place and some conventions about them. Some `NgModules` can grow to several hundred lines of code. We are not going to provide an example of such an `NgModule`. As we have seen, `NgModules` solve a problem that apparently already has a solution while also introducing more complexity and boilerplate code. But again, there is even more.

2.1.3 *Other concerns with NgModules*

While we covered the main topics, several other problems also exist with `NgModule` implementations.

- *Scattered codebase*—With `NgModules`, it is fairly easy to have related application blocks inside completely different `NgModules`, which means they can't be used directly together. This is a problem in and of itself, and to mitigate it, developers come up with different solutions, increasing complexity yet again, or resort to having modules solely dedicated to sharing functionality.
- *The shared module*—To group interrelated functionality, lots of projects utilize the concept of a `SharedModule`, a module specifically designed to declare and export reusable components/directives/pipes. While this solves the problem from the previous bullet point, it introduces other concerns, like an overly large module file or too many scattered `SharedModules`. If developers decide to create multiple `SharedModules`, it creates another question of when such a module should be created and what it should hold. "Should every lazy-loaded feature module have its own `SharedModule`?" is a valid question with many different answers, each of which is not really wrong. As a result, we have an inconsistent codebase.
- *Circular dependencies and harder debugging*—In a codebase with many `NgModules`, it is fairly easy to introduce a circular dependency, which can become a very hard problem to solve. Debugging ability will also be somewhat limited, for instance, by making error messages harder to read, as everything in the Angular app is wrapped in another layer of abstraction.

All these factors may convince us that we want an alternative to `NgModules`. So, let's explore how we can reduce our dependency on them. But instead of going straight to standalone components, we will spend a bit more time on some solutions that the wider community has come up with in years prior to the rise of standalone.

2.2 *Previous solutions*

Standalone Angular components first became available in v14 as a developer preview and became stable in v15, meaning relatively recently. So, how did developers overcome the challenges we listed previously? Let's explore some approaches, and maybe we'll find a way to move to standalone with v16 and later versions more easily.

2.2.1   *Hierarchic shared modules*

As was already mentioned, it became common for developers to use specific "share-able" NgModules in their apps to help with code splitting and separation of concerns. Those shared modules were useful when certain building blocks did not exactly corre-spond to a feature inside of an application but were needed in several places at once. We used the most primitive approach to create a single SharedModule and import it everywhere, but we saw that it was a pretty painful approach. So instead of having one large SharedModule, what one can often encounter in Angular codebases prior to stand-alone is multiple SharedModules on feature levels of an application, each holding reus-able components related to only that feature, and one a bit larger SharedModule at the top that contains application-wide building blocks. Figure 2.1 is a diagram of how that approach would work on the HRMS application we described.

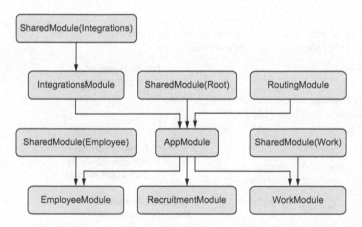

Figure 2.1   Diagram showing relations between modules in an HRMS application

As we can see, this process is fairly straightforward: each of those large submodules can have its own routed submodules, and to share functionality specific to a given fea-ture between those modules, a shared module is created. This approach makes a medium-sized application manageable and has worked well for multiple Angular proj-ects. However, it is hard to scale and notoriously hard to refactor: if something needs to be moved, it can quickly devolve into a mess, with components and other building blocks having difficulty finding their place in the app structure. So, for larger scenar-ios with multiple teams involved, other approaches have been created.

2.2.2   *Enter SCAMs*

SCAMs, or Single Component Angular Modules, is an approach to building applica-tion structures based on the principle of having a single module for every single declarable. For example, say we have a component that does not belong to some fea-ture module or a shared module but, instead, has a single NgModule dedicated to its declaration and the import of its dependencies. For instance, if we review our previous example (figure 2.1), we can see two components belonging to a feature module: `EmployeeComponent` and `EmployeeListComponent`, which are both declared inside `EmployeeModule`. With the SCAM approach, we would have modules specifically for both components that would be subsequently imported into other places where they are needed. Those specific SCAM modules are usually declared in the same file, as they serve as the point from which that component can be imported.

Listing 2.5   `EmployeeComponent` as a SCAM

```
import { Component, Input } from '@angular/core';
import { Employee } from '<path-to-type>';
import { EmployeeComponentModule } from '<path-to-component-scam-module>';

@Component({
  selector: 'app-employee-list',
  template: `
    <div class="employees-container">
      <app-employee *ngFor="let employee of employees"
      [employee]="employee"></app-employee>
    </div>
  `,
})
export class EmployeeListComponent {          ⟵  The declaration
  @Input() employee: Employee[];                  of the component
}                                                 itself

@NgModule({                                   Imports another
  declarations: [EmployeeListComponent]       component via its
  imports: [EmployeeComponentModule]      ⟵   own SCAM module
})
export class EmployeeModule {}             ⟵  The SCAM module of
                                              the parent component
```

Note that we name the approach Single *Component* Angular Module, and we have to do the same for directives and pipes: each will also have a dedicated `NgModule`. Also noteworthy is the fact that we do not add routing in these SCAMs, even if the component is a routed component (meaning there is a route somewhere that points to it), and these modules only serve as a place to declare the component/directive/pipe and import its dependencies.

This approach has a couple of benefits:

- *Easier to track dependencies*—They are listed in the same file.
- *Easier to refactor and move around an application*—We can just grab this file and move anywhere else.
- *Easier to unit-test*—We only have to mock the direct dependencies of this component, and we can use nonshallow rendering of the template (rendering the template as is).
- *Better code splitting*—We can lazy-load components themselves directly, making the application bundles very small and granular.

- *Easier to migrate to standalone*—A new hidden benefit of SCAMs emerged with the rise of standalone building blocks and the introduction of a migration schematic, which we will discuss in the subsequent sections of this chapter; in short, SCAMs make it very easy to run the schematic and get a fully standalone application without any problems.

Of course, these are very nice benefits, but some of the downsides of NgModules still remain:

- *Extra boilerplate code*—While the mental overhead of understanding the application structure is reduced, boilerplate code actually goes up; we now have an NgModule for everything.
- *Still somewhat hard to explain and approach*—Newcomers would still have to learn about NgModules, and onboarding into a project will be a bit more complicated if the new developer is unaware of the SCAM pattern.
- *Other modules can still be large*—For instance, we would still need to import the CommonModule to use directives like *ngIf or [ngClass] and possibly add lots of references to our bundles we do not use.

With all of these benefits and downsides in mind, developers were waiting for the opportunity to try to get rid of NgModules. Next, let's finally discuss the new standalone approach of authoring Angular building blocks.

2.3   Developing apps without NgModules

Before we begin, let's briefly examine what standalone will offer when we start developing with this approach:

- It is possible to build applications completely standalone, as with our new version of the HRMS app we initialized in the previous chapter. We will learn how all this functions without NgModules
- The standalone approach is backward compatible, so NgModules and standalone components can (and often do) coexist in the same codebase
- Many third-party tools and libraries still have not migrated away from NgModules, so there is full interoperability between standalone and modules. We will learn how to handle the connection between them.

We will start with building standalone components in a brand-new project, as we already have the standalone app in place, and then move over to show how this application is still fully compatible with other NgModules and how older tools that do not have standalone APIs can be integrated with standalone building blocks. Let's get started!

2.3.1   Creating our first standalone component

In every enterprise application (and a number of non-enterprise ones), the user's journey begins at one starting point: the proverbial login page. Let's build one for our HRMS application. We'll use template-driven forms (as they are fairly simple) and make an HTTP call if the form is deemed valid. First, let us create the component itself.

CREATING THE COMPONENT

Let's start by creating a folder named pages inside the src/app directory, so we can put our routed components inside it, including this first one. Don't worry about architecture or folder structure right now: we will refactor and reorganize stuff down the line. For now, let's create a file named login.component.ts inside this folder and put the component inside, as shown in the following listing.

Listing 2.6   Standalone `LoginComponent`

```
@Component({
    selector: 'app-login',
    template: `
        <div class="login-container">
            <h1>Login</h1>
            <form>
                <input type="text" name="email" placeholder="Email">
                <input type="password" name="password"
                    placeholder="Password">
                <button type="submit">Login</button>
            </form>
        </div>
    `,
    standalone: true,
})
export class LoginComponent {
    credentials = { email: '', password: '' };
}
```

Seems to be a fairly simple component, but with one key difference: in its metadata, we can see `standalone: true`, which indicates that this component is standalone and is not part of any `NgModule`. Therefore, we cannot declare it any `NgModule`, and anything related to this component (e.g., what other components or directives it imports) lives in this class.

IMPORTING NgMODULES INTO STANDALONE COMPONENTS

One very obvious question that will arise is that for this component to truly be a login component, we need to add some interactivity to it. That is, when the user enters something in the inputs, we want the credentials property to be updated. One of the popular approaches to achieve this is with a `ngModel` directive, but here is the catch: this component is not a part of any `NgModule`, so how does it import the `FormsModule` to be able to use `ngModel`? Well, when we mark a component as standalone, we can add a special `imports` property to its metadata that will list all the component's dependencies. Let's go on and update the component.

Listing 2.7   Standalone component importing a module

```
@Component({
    selector: 'app-login',
    template: `
```

```
      <div class="login-container">
          <h1>Login</h1>
          <form>
              <input type="text" name="email"
                  placeholder="Email"
                  [(ngModel)]="credentials.email" />
              <input type="password" name="password" placeholder="Password"
                  [(ngModel)]="credentials.password">
              <button type="submit">Login</button>
          </form>
      </div>
  `,
  standalone: true,
  imports: [FormsModule],
})
export class LoginComponent {
  credentials = { email: '', password: '' };
}
```

> **Uses the ngModel directive**

> **Imports the FormsModule directly into the component via its own metadata**

As we can see, the imports property on the component's metadata acts exactly like it does in `NgModules`: it allows us to import `NgModules` with components/directives/pipes that our component needs to function. We talked about the interoperability of the standalone component, `NgModule`, and here we see it at play: a standalone component can act as its own `NgModule` and work with `NgModules`. But wait, there is more. Let us now add a validation message that will be shown as long as one of the required inputs is not filled in.

Listing 2.8 Using `*ngIf` in a standalone component

```
template: `
    <div class="login-container">
        <h1>Login</h1>
        <form>
            <input type="text" name="email" placeholder="Email"
                [(ngModel)]="credentials.email">
            <input type="password" name="password" placeholder="Password"
                [(ngModel)]="credentials.password">
            <button type="submit">Login</button>
        </form>
        <span class="warning" *ngIf="!credentials.email ||
    !credentials.password">
            Please fill in all the required fields
        </span>
    </div>
  `,
```

IMPORTING STANDALONE DIRECTIVES INTO STANDALONE COMPONENTS

Now, we need a way to tell our component what `*ngIf` is. Of course, we could just add the `CommonModule`, which, as we know, contains the `NgIf` directive, to the `imports` array of our component, as we did with `FormsModule`, and it will certainly work. But this will cause the import of all other components and directives that `CommonModule` contains, like `JsonPipe`, or `NgClass`, and we do not need them in this component.

So how can we fix this problem? Well, the Angular team has us covered: from v15, all entities from the `CommonModule` are standalone, so we can dispose of the module and import whatever we need directly into our components. Let's bring the `NgIf` directive into the login component:

```
imports: [FormsModule, NgIf],
```

Now, our component will know what `*ngIf` means, match with the directive selector, and let it run, displaying the warning until the user fills in the necessary data. If we recall what we learned in the previous section about the SCAM approach, this can feel eerily similar. Essentially, we do what we did with the SCAM module, but with the added capability of just writing the previously module-related metadata directly into the component. This is why we mention that having SCAMs in place makes it super easy to migrate to standalone automatically.

PROVIDING SERVICES IN STANDALONE COMPONENTS

Now we move to our final concern: let's make the component a real login component by adding an HTTP call to an authentication API. For this purpose, we'll create a services folder under the app directory and add an auth.service.ts file in it, as shown in the following listing.

> **Listing 2.9   Authentication service**

```
import { HttpClient } from '@angular/common/http';
import { Injectable } from '@angular/core';

@Injectable()
export class AuthService {
    constructor(private http: HttpClient) { }

    login(credentials: { email: string, password: string }) {
        return this.http.post('/api/auth/login', credentials);
    }
}
```

This is pretty self-explanatory; the question is, how do we let the login component know about this service? As with `NgModules`, we can add this service to the `providers` array of the standalone component and then just use it. The following listing provides the full component code with the HTTP call in place.

> **Listing 2.10   Final version of the standalone `LoginComponent`**

```
import { Component } from '@angular/core';
import { NgIf } from '@angular/common';
import { FormsModule } from '@angular/forms';

import { AuthService } from '../services/auth.service';

@Component({
    selector: 'app-login',
```

```
    template: `
        <div class="login-container">
            <h1>Login</h1>
            <form>
                <input type="text" name="email" placeholder="Email"
                [(ngModel)]="credentials.email">
                <input type="password" name="password"
                    placeholder="Password" [(ngModel)]="credentials.password">
                <button type="submit" (click)="submit()">Login</button>
            </form>
            <span class="warning" *ngIf="!credentials.email ||
    !credentials.password">
                Please fill in all the required fields
            </span>
        </div>
        `,
    standalone: true,
    imports: [FormsModule, NgIf],
    providers: [AuthService],
})
export class LoginComponent {
    credentials = { email: '', password: '' };

    constructor(private authService: AuthService) {}

    submit() {
        if (this.credentials.email && this.credentials.password) {
            this.authService.login(this.credentials).subscribe();
        }
    }
}
```

We might notice that while the component is functional, it doesn't do much, as it is not routed or connected from anywhere to the application; it just exists by itself. Next, let's connect it to our application via routing and see it live.

2.3.2 *Routing standalone components and providing dependencies*

We already discussed how routing used to work with NgModules and discovered how it is supposed to be defined in a standalone setup. Now, let's figure out how to connect our injection dependencies (DIs) and make our component routable.

Let's begin by remembering how DI works in Angular. We will not dive too deep, as the next chapter is already dedicated to fully understanding DI, but we will examine the two core principles: how a dependency is provided and how it is injected. We need to start with the latter to better comprehend the process.

Injecting a dependency in Angular comes down to defining a token of something and telling the framework we want it somewhere. As shown in listing 2.10, we define what we want by adding a constructor parameter: private authService: AuthService. Upon seeing this, Angular will (somehow) fetch us an instance of that service.

But how will it know where to find the actual instance? Listing 2.9 shows that `Auth-Service` is essentially just a class and can easily have multiple instances. It also receives an instance of Angular's `HttpClient`, so how will that class now know where to get that instance? Well, here is where the second part of the equation comes into play: providers. Providers allow us to define the values for entities that can be injected. Essentially, they are places where we say, "Dear Angular, if you see this token (for instance, `Auth-Service` as in our example), please inject this value (that particular instance)."

When working with Angular v13 or prior, we know of two ways to provide those values: by adding to some `NgModules`' or components' `providers` array or by marking a service as `providedIn: 'root'`. In listing 2.10, we added the `AuthService` directly to the `Login-Component`'s providers, and we're done with it. It is truly the simplest approach here, but it is meant to work only for now, not when the app grows. It also raises several questions with not very favorable answers in the case of modular apps, as outlined in table 2.1.

Table 2.1   Different scenarios of providing dependencies

Question	Answer without standalone APIs	Answer with standalone APIs
Do I need to provide every dependency in every component?	Either this or mark the service as `providedIn: 'root'`.	We can use a standalone API if one is provided.
How do I import services that are provided in other modules (without special standalone APIs)?	Import the module directly into the component.	Use the `importProviders-From` function in the application main.ts file.
How do I import built-in Angular dependencies?	Import the whole module.	Use existing standalone APIs.

In the Answer with Standalone APIs column, we defined the concept of "existing standalone APIs" and a function named `importProvidersFrom`. Let's find out what that means by trying to provide the `HttpClient` for our app. We can remember that those dependencies resided in the `@angular/common/http` package under the name `Http-ClientModule`. Also, in the previous chapter, we encountered a configuration object in the src/app/app.config.ts file with a `providers` property. This is where dependencies are provided in standalone Angular apps. Let's add the `HttpClientModule`'s providers to this array. To do so, we will employ the `importProvidersFrom` function. Let's open the src/app/app.config.ts file, and we willl see the routes provided. Next to them, we will add the new import.

Listing 2.11   Adding providers from other modules

```
export const appConfig: ApplicationConfig = {
  providers: [
    provideRouter(routes),
    importProvidersFrom(HttpClientModule),
  ]
};
```

The `importProvidersFrom` function takes a module (or several modules; we can provide more than one), extracts their providers, and transports them to wherever we want to use them. This function is very simple in the sense that it only exists to provide interoperability between standalone and NgModules.

It is important to understand this method only works in the application injection context, either in the `bootstrapApplication` function or some route providers (we will talk more about route providers in the next section). Next, we should realize this works with any NgModule; so, if we are using some third-party Angular library that has not itself migrated to standalone, we can still use `importProvidersFrom` to continue using that library in full capacity. Lastly, we can actually ditch the `importProviders-From` when dealing with some built-in Angular modules. We should emphasize the word *some* as not all Angular built-in APIs have moved away from NgModules. But, as we saw with the routing (the `provideRouter` function), a bunch of Angular modules have already migrated to standalone APIs, including `HttpClient`. Here is how we really want to provide `HttpClient` in our applications, inside the app.config.ts file:

Listing 2.12 Adding providers from other modules

```
import { ApplicationConfig } from '@angular/core';
import { provideHttpClient } from '@angular/common/http';
import { provideRouter } from '@angular/router';

import { routes } from './app.routes';

export const appConfig: ApplicationConfig = {
  providers: [
    provideRouter(routes),
    provideHttpClient(),
  ]
};
```

We can note the naming convention of `provideSomething`. This pattern is now widely adopted by many library authors, so we want to be prepared and recognize such functions when encountering them in various codebases. Also, if we author a library, it is considered a good practice to export providers in a similar fashion.

So, how do we provide the `AuthService`? Well, we could just add it to this root-level providers array, but instead, we are going to simply mark it as `providedIn: root`, so that the app.config.ts file remains intact.

Finally, we need to create a route for our login component so that it has the first functioning feature of our application. We will quickly discover that essentially nothing has changed regarding this.

Listing 2.13 Using `HttpClient` standalone API

```
import { Routes } from '@angular/router';
import { LoginComponent } from './pages/login.component';
```

```
export const routes: Routes = [
    { path: '/login', component: LoginComponent },
];
```

Of course, this simple registration of a routed standalone component only works when we have a straightforward, eagerly loaded component. What happens if we want to lazy-load a route? We don't have modules now, so we can't use the old approach. Let's now discuss lazy loading components directly.

2.4 Lazy-loading components

Before we begin, let's briefly remember how lazy loading used to be implemented in Angular apps before standalone. As all components and other building blocks were packaged inside of `NgModules`, we could not lazy-load components directly (actually, we kind of could but not via routing, and we are strictly discussing routing here), and instead, we lazy-loaded `NgModules`, which then, in their turn, loaded their own routing module. It then finally loaded the components we want (or maybe even another lazy-loaded module with the same process).

2.4.1 Lazy-loading with NgModules

In this section, we will add lazy-loaded components to our application; namely, we want to begin implementing the `Employees` feature of our application and also add a registration page. Let's first examine how we could do the former with `NgModules`. Figure 2.2 illustrates how Angular lazy-loads a component via `NgModules`.

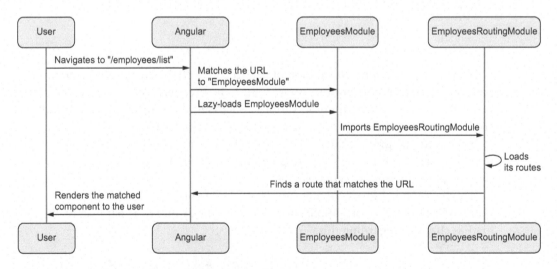

Figure 2.2   Steps to lazy-load a component with `NgModules`

As we can see, this is a fairly complicated process, which can be made even more difficult if, for instance, `EmployeesRoutingModule` actually lazy-loaded yet another `NgModule`, and so on. In addition, even if we have one component we want to lazy-load, we would need to create a module for it (if it does not logically belong in one of our existing feature modules). Using the SCAM approach would alleviate this problem, but we would be pretty much constrained in other scenarios. And, of course, either way, we end up with a bunch of boilerplate code we would like to avoid.

2.4.2 *Lazy-loading a single standalone component*

Now, we will explore how the same process works for standalone components. Let's create a registration component and make it routed. In the src/app/pages directory, let's create a file named registration.component.ts and add an empty `RegistrationComponent`. We want to show the login page when the user first navigates to our application and also have a separate /register route that will load the `RegistrationComponent` lazily. The following listing provides the code we need to accomplish this.

Listing 2.14 **Lazy-loading a component directly**

```
export const routes: Routes = [
    { path: 'login', component: LoginComponent },
    { path: 'registration', loadComponent: () => {
        return import('./pages/registration.component').then(
          (m) => m.RegistrationComponent
        );
    } },
];
```

Note the addition of a specific `loadComponent` option on the route object. This option will take a function that will import the module (in this case, by *module*, I mean the file that contains the code, not `NgModule`) and load that particular component. In this scenario, the process is much simpler than what figure 2.3 describes, mainly by entirely skipping loading any `NgModules`.

There are two important points to note:

- *No changes have been made to the components themselves*—The new routing approach does not in any way affect how we author components. Essentially, when we migrate a routed component to standalone, we only need to change its code to mark it as `standalone: true`.
- *The routing object is not changed either*—Other than using the new `loadComponent` option, nothing is different from how we defined a route previously; we can add guards, resolvers, route or query parameters, and so on

So far, we have lazy-loaded a single component. Although it's a valid use case, in real life, we might want to lazy-load a block of components, which was previously accomplished

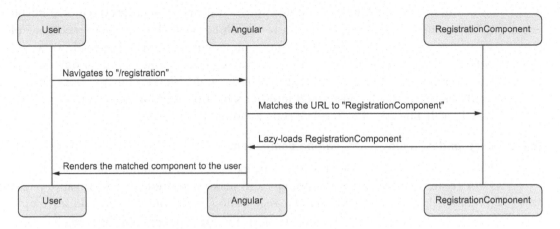

Figure 2.3   Steps to lazy load a standalone component

by lazy-loading an entire `NgModule` with all of its routed components. Let us see how we can accomplish the same thing without `NgModules`.

2.4.3   *Lazy-loading several standalone components*

Before we start, let us understand why we would want the ability to lazy-load several routes at the same time. This scenario becomes important for three reasons:

- If we just keep adding more lazy-loaded components, our app.routes.ts file might eventually get out of hand and potentially contain a thousand or more lines of code—not very easy to navigate and reason about.
- Next, we might believe that several components that logically belong together (e.g., `EmployeeList`, `EmployeeDetails`, `CreateEmployee`, and `EditEmployee`) can be easily lazy-loaded together without taking a significant performance hit. This was previously readily accomplished because those components most likely already belonged to one feature `NgModule` and were lazy-loaded together. With standalone, they can be anywhere and loaded in different ways.
- And last but not least, we also might want our folder structure to better reflect the hierarchies within both our routing and the application in general and thus require several routes.ts files that exist in subfolders that contain some specific feature-related code. Yet again, standalone provides answers to all those concerns without the need to resort to `NgModules`.

Let's now create our first feature module and cover the `Employees` section of our application. As mentioned, it will contain components that allow the user to view the list of employees and a detailed overview of a specific employee, as well as create and edit employees.

In the src/app/pages folder, we are going to create a directory named employees, and this directory will contain all the code related to employees. In this folder, we'll create all the components we mentioned. Those components are not yet routable, as we do not want to put them inside app.routes.ts and, instead, want to have a separate routing configuration file for them. Let's create a file named employees.routes.ts file in the same directory and put the code in the following listing inside it.

> **Listing 2.15 Adding feature level routing**

```
export const routes: Routes = [
    { path: 'list', component: EmployeeListComponent },
    { path: 'details/:id', component: EmployeeDetailsComponent },
    { path: 'create', component: CreateEmployeeComponent },
    { path: 'edit', component: EditEmployeeComponent },
];
```

As we can see, there is absolutely no difference between adding such feature or child routes and just having them in app.routes.ts. However, these routes are not yet connected to our root routing. We can accomplish this by adding a route with load-Children in the root routing file but importing the routes directly without any intermediary NgModule.

> **Listing 2.16 Lazy-loading both single and multiple standalone components**

```
export const routes: Routes = [
    { path: 'login', component: LoginComponent },
    { path: 'registration', loadComponent: () => {
        return import('./pages/registration.component').then(
            (m) => m.RegistrationComponent
        );
    } },
    { path: 'employees', loadChildren: () => {
        return import('./pages/employees/employees.routes').then(
            (m) => m.routes,
        );
    } },
];
```

Again, the only key difference compared to NgModule setup is that the loadChildren function imports the route instead of importing a module that imports a routing module. The loadChildren function works in the same fashion as previously discussed and accomplishes the same result, just in a more direct way. The mental model of this process is also simpler than using NgModules.

Finally, the last thing we want to tackle is being able to provide some dependencies only to certain routes. So, for example, EmployeeService is only available in components related to the employees feature of our application.

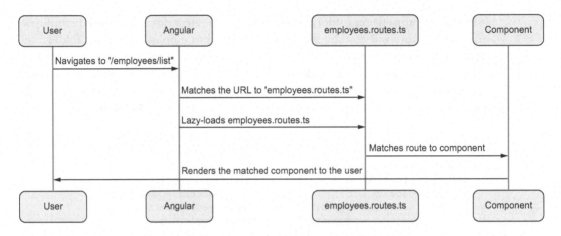

Figure 2.4   Loading a standalone component from a set of multiple lazy-loaded routes

2.4.4   *Providing dependencies only to certain routes*

With `NgModules`, we can provide certain services and other DI tokens in specific lazy-loaded modules by adding them to the `providers` array of that particular `NgModule`. This method provided us with two benefits: being able to also lazy-load services, making the app even more granular, and having different instances of some service for different modules (routes). The last point was especially useful for developers who use some state management libraries like NgRx and NgXS, allowing them to provide certain pieces of application state only to specific routes and making them more isolated from the surrounding codebase. This would both simplify the application state (instead of one huge object, we would have several smaller ones that get picked up when the user visits those parts of the application) and help avoid scenarios when the state is loaded too soon. For instance, some HTTP requests might be made even if they are not needed, resulting in stale data or unnecessary server load.

In our standalone scenario, we do not have any `NgModules` to provide our new dependencies, so we need to look for standalone-based solutions. We might have noticed a pattern: route definitions often act as `NgModules` did (but in the lazy-loading aspect of it). Turns out, it is no different this time: it is now possible to add a `providers` array to a route definition.

To achieve this, let's create an `EmployeeService` in the src/app/services directory and put some code in it responsible for HTTP calls. The actual code does not matter, so we will omit it for the time being; it just has to be not marked as `providedIn: 'root'`):

```
@Injectable()
export class EmployeeService {}
```

Next, we want to go to the app.routes.ts file, where we connected the lazily loaded employee routes. We can modify that particular route definition as in the following listing.

> **Listing 2.17 Adding providers to a lazy-loaded route**

```
{
    path: 'employees',
    providers: [EmployeeService],
    loadChildren: () => {
        return import('./pages/employees/employees.routes').then(
            (m) => m.routes,
        );
    },
},
```

This code will make the `EmployeeService` only available in the routes inside employees.routes.ts, meaning only components routed in that configuration file will have access to this particular instance of `EmployeeService`. We can easily check it by navigating to `LoginComponent`, for instance, and injecting the `EmployeeService` into it via the constructor. If we check the application in the browser, we will surely see the following error "`NullInjectorError: No provider for EmployeeService!`" with some more explanatory details. We have now accomplished isolating this service into a subset of our routing.

2.4.5 *Lazy-loading a component into another component*

So far, we have discussed lazy-loading components via routing (e.g., having a route that would load its component only when the user navigates to it). But what if we want to go even more granular? Let's imagine the following scenario: we are building the `EmployeeListComponent` and put a table of employees there, which will contain data about each employee like full name, age, position, and so on, and an Actions column that would allow us to edit the employee or delete them. When the user clicks the Delete button, we want to present them with a confirmation dialog that asks them if they are sure they want to delete that employee. But here's the catch: the confirmation dialog is going to be a separate, reusable component (we might want to have such confirmation logic on multiple pages), and we do not want the application to download that component's code until the user clicks Delete. After all, the component is invisible anyway, and there is no point in having that code until the very moment it should be used.

In this case, we cannot rely on lazy loading through routing. We can in a sense, accomplish this with named router outlets (https://mng.bz/yowp) and secondary routes (https://mng.bz/M1nQ). Here, however, we do not want a separate routed component; we just want another component that can be loaded and displayed purely on demand. This task can be accomplished fairly easily, especially with standalone components. Let's first create the `EmployeeListComponent`. Add the code in listing 2.18 to the src/app/pages/employees/employee-list.component.ts file.

Listing 2.18 `EmployeeListComponent`

```
@Component({
  selector: 'app-employee-list',
  template: `
    <h2>Employee List</h2>
    <table>
      <thead>
        <tr>
          <th>Full Name</th>
          <th>Position</th>
          <th>Actions</th>
        </tr>
      </thead>
      <tbody>
        <tr *ngFor="let employee of employees$ | async">
          <td>{{ employee.firstName }} {{ employee.lastName }}</td>
          <td>{{ employee.position }}</td>
          <td>
            <button (click)="showConfirmationDialog()">Delete</button>
          </td>
        </tr>
      </tbody>
    </table>
  `,
  standalone: true,
  imports: [AsyncPipe, NgFor, NgIf, NgComponentOutlet],
})
export class EmployeeListComponent {
  employees$ = this.employeeService.getEmployees();
  isConfirmationOpen = false;

  constructor(private readonly employeeService: EmployeeService) {}

  showConfirmationDialog() {
    this.isConfirmationOpen = true;
  }
}
```

As we can see, we have our table but not our dialog yet. We can add a dynamically loaded component into it with three steps:

1 Create the `ConfirmationDialogComponent` in a new file, src/app/shared/components/confirmation-dialog.component.ts.
2 Add a dynamic import function call that asynchronously imports that component.
3 Pass the resulting promise to the `ngComponentOutlet` directive via the `async` pipe.

Let's do it in code and then examine how it works. We are going to create a new folder called shared in the src/app directory and a components folder under it, where we are going to put the reusable component of our application, including the `Confirmation-DialogComponent`. The following listing provides the necessary code.

Listing 2.19 `ConfirmationDialogComponent`

```
@Component({
  selector: 'app-confirmation-dialog',
  template: `
    <dialog [open]="isConfirmationOpen">
      Are you sure you want to perform this action?

      <button (click)="isConfirmationOpen = false">Cancel</button>
      <button (click)="isConfirmationOpen = false">Confirm</button>
    </dialog>
  `,
  standalone: true,
})
export class ConfirmationDialogComponent {
    @Input() isConfirmationOpen = true;
}
```

As we can see, this component is very simple and does not have many capabilities, but it will suffice for now. Next, we need to dynamically import this component when the user clicks the Delete button. We do this by making the `showConfirmationDialog` method an `async` function and loading and storing the component in a property to use further in the template.

Listing 2.20 Importing the component on demand

```
export class EmployeeListComponent {
  employees$ = this.employeeService.getEmployees();
  isConfirmationOpen = false;
  confirmDialog: any = null;

  constructor(private readonly employeeService: EmployeeService) {}

  async showConfirmationDialog() {
    this.confirmDialog = await import(
      '../../shared/components/confirmation-dialog.component'
    ).then((m) => m.ConfirmationDialogComponent);
    this.isConfirmationOpen = true;
  }
}
```

The `confirmDialog` property will hold the reference to the `ConfirmationDialog-Component` class (importantly, the class itself, and not its instance—that one is not yet created). As we can see, whenever the Delete button is clicked, the component we want will be loaded dynamically at that time and not sooner. Finally, the last step will be to render this component in the view. We can accomplish that using the `ngComponentOutlet` directive. So, we add just one line of code to the bottom of our template in the `EmployeeListComponent`:

```
<ng-container *ngComponentOutlet="confirmDialog"></ng-container>
```

As this is a dialog component, we can probably put it anywhere in the template without much difference. If we want to load the component in a specific place in our template, we can put it in that exact place. But what is going on here? See, the ngComponentOutlet directive receives a reference to a component class and renders it into the ng-container on which we have put the directive. In this case, initially, the confirmDialog property is null, so no rendering takes place, and the Confirmation-DialogComponent has not been loaded yet. When the user clicks Delete, we load the component class and put it into a property, triggering a rerender and showing our confirmation dialog both dynamically and lazily. Lazy-loading a standalone component as opposed to one declared in a NgModule gives us the advantage of not having to import a whole module or pass it down as an input to ngComponentOutlet.

Ideally, we would want to have a way to communicate with the component instance that we have dynamically created. We can do so in one of several ways, including passing inputs to the child components or taking the reference of that component and working with it. We will study examples of such manipulations in chapter 4, where we will explore new capabilities of components (not necessarily standalone).

2.5 *Migrations and common pitfalls*

So far, we have examined creating and working with standalone components from scratch in an empty application. We also learned that we can easily create and use standalone components in NgModule-based applications. But what if we want to migrate entire existing applications to fully use standalones? What problems might we encounter after the migration is done? Let's examine several approaches we can take and see those issues first-hand.

2.5.1 *Migrating by hand*

Large projects can have multiple interwoven NgModules that can be hard to easily dismantle in one go (or even automatically). If the codebase is active with multiple developers committing new code, it might be tempting to adopt an incremental approach: as we remember, standalone components, directives, and pipes are fully interoperable with NgModules, meaning we can pick and choose which components to convert first. This determination can be accomplished in four steps:

1 Adopt the rule of authoring all new components, directives, and pipes as standalones.
2 Choose components we want to convert one by one and mark them as standalone: true. Move the NgModule in which this component is declared from the declarations array to the imports array (standalone components are declared in place and cannot be redeclared in a NgModule). If the component is also used in another NgModule, add it to the exports array (it was probably already there). Continue doing so in iterations of a size that is manageable for your project.

3 Remove `NgModules` one by one until only `AppModule` remains. This will mean that we will have to manually import our freshly standalone components manually to wherever we need them until all build errors go away.

4 When only `AppModule` is left, remove it and move the providers to main.ts, also switching to the new standalone providers (`provideRouter`, `provideHttp-Client`, etc)

This method can work more or less smoothly on small projects and maybe on medium-sized projects that do not have too many `NgModules`. However, for larger projects, this approach would take way too long, which is why we can simplify it by adopting the SCAM approach.

2.5.2 Using SCAMs

We already discussed the SCAM approach; let's now see how it can help us transition to standalone. We are going to make most of the steps from the previous section, manual migration, but with some modifications:

1 Again, adopt making all new building blocks standalone.

2 Choose components that we would like to transition first, but instead of making them standalone, create a SCAM module for them and put that component in it. Remove the component from any other `NgModule`. Do this whenever it is most comfortable for the team working on the project.

3 When all components, directives, and pipes have been converted into SCAMs, outside of those SCAM `NgModules`, we will be left with only feature `NgModules` (like `EmployeeModule`, `WorkModule`, and so on, from our HRMS app example). As soon as we've accomplished this, we can start marking all components, directives, and pipes as standalone and remove their SCAM module. This process should be easy, as the module will be in the same file. We would then need to find references to the SCAM module and drop the component directly in its place. We can do so with a simple Find and Replace. While this process looks a bit intimidating, it can essentially be done in one go using basic IDE functionality.

4 After completing step 3, we can start removing feature modules and making their own declarable components/directives/pipes standalone and importing the already standalone (previously SCAM blocks) into them.

5 Now, remove `AppModule` and use standalone provider APIs.

This approach, while containing more steps, can be more intuitive, and the main part can be completed in one go. It also simplifies the structure to a point where the standalone migration schematic can safely do the job itself. Let's discuss this topic next.

2.5.3 Migrating with a schematic command

In v16, the Angular team introduced a special schematic that helps automatically transition legacy `NgModule`-based apps to fully standalone. This task can be accomplished in several ways. Let's start with the most basic: running the command right away, using the following steps:

1 Make sure the app we want to upgrade is on version 16.

2 Open a terminal window in the root folder of this application and run `ng g @angular/core:standalone`.

3 Three options will be suggested: "Convert all components, directives, and pipes to standalone," "Remove unnecessary `NgModule` classes," and "Bootstrap the application using standalone APIs." As per the Angular documentation (https://mng.bz/aV8j), we should run them in this exact order, so let's choose the first option.

4 The first option will make all components/directives/pipes standalone, add whatever they need to import (e.g., directives used in their template), and make them imported rather than declared in their `NgModule`. Run the application to ensure nothing was broken during this step.

5 Next, run the same command and choose Remove Unnecessary `NgModule` Classes. This step will remove all modules that are not part of the application structure (e.g., SCAM modules), leaving us with a mostly standalone project. Again, let's run the app and check everything works.

6 Finally, run the command again and choose Bootstrap the Application Using Standalone APIs. This step will remove `AppModule` and use the `bootstrap-Application` function in main.ts instead.

Now, this migration is not bulletproof, and in most cases, we will be left with some additional work to do:

1 First, we should search for any remaining `NgModules` and remove them manually (usually, there are not very many of them).

2 Next, we should visit the main.ts file and use the standalone routing (we most likely already removed the routing modules left after the automatic migration).

3 Then, we should look into our third-party dependencies, usually provided here via the `importProvidersFrom` function. If you know that more recent versions of those dependencies have standalone APIs, consider upgrading those packages and replacing the `NgModule` definitions with the new standalone APIs. Ideally, we want no usage of the `importProvidersFrom` function at all.

4 Next, you might notice that the HTTP client is provided via the following line:

```
provideHttpClient(withInterceptorsFromDi()).
```

We already met this API, but have not talked about `withInterceptors-FromDi()`. We will talk about it in the next chapter.

5 Finally, if we have code-maintenance tools like linters, prettier setup, or others, we should run those to ensure the codebase is kept pure and fix any arising problems.

2.5.4   *Handling circular dependencies*

With the schematic migration, we might run into a problem that could be hard to anticipate: it may turn out some of our components have a circular dependency. This situation can arise when components recursively render each other. For instance, in the case of our HRMS application, we might have an EmployeeCardComponent, which displays brief info about an employee; a ProjectCardComponent, which displays brief info about a project that has several employees; and in ProjectCard-Component, we might render a list of EmployeeCardComponents, each of which expands to show projects the employee is working on using the ProjectCardComponent, meaning we get a recursion. With NgModules, this won't be a problem, as both might be declared in the same module or get references of each other from a shared module; however, in standalone, they must import each other, which will result in the following error:

```
ReferenceError: Cannot access 'ProjectCardComponent' before initialization
```

While this problem is frustrating, it can be fixed fairly easily: we simply need to use the forwardRef function when importing the components into each other. For instance, the metadata for the ProjectCardComponent might look like the following listing.

> Listing 2.21   Using forwardRef to avoid circular dependency problems

```
@Component({
  standalone: true,
  imports: [
    forwardRef(() => EmployeeCardComponent)
  ],
})
export class ProjectCardComponent {
}
```

The forwardRef function, as per the Angular documentation, is a function designed to allow developers to access references that are not yet defined; in other words, when the ProjectCardComponent is registered, it takes note that this one is going to use some reference when it is actually initialized. The other component, EmployeeCard-Component, will be defined as usual; no forwardRef is necessary there, and thus, circular dependency is avoided.

As we can see, standalone building blocks provide us with new capabilities to simplify our code and reduce boilerplate. This new feature has become very popular with Angular developers everywhere, with more and more teams starting their new projects with standalone outright. Next, we will go a level deeper and see how we can simplify sharing functionality between components with the new way of using DI.

2.6   *Exercises for the reader*

As mentioned in the previous chapter, I encourage you to follow the steps in building this HRMS project with the examples and steps from this book. While following along is very beneficial, I also encourage you to write some code for yourself to test the knowledge you gain in a particular chapter in a practical environment. Here are several things that can be done within the existing example application:

- Implement the other components from the feature we created (`EmployeeList`, `EmployeeDetails`, `CreateEmployee`, and `EditEmployee`) and add some business logic to them.
- Create the other features (work and recruitment, with empty components for now, as we will gradually add more functionality to them in the next chapters) and use lazy-loading practices with standalone components.
- Apply the migration schematic to an existing project with the steps described in section 2.5.3. Migration can be used to completely move an existing app to standalone or experimentally to see how the schematic works and what problems may arise; in the latter case, feel free to discard any changes the automation applies.

Summary

- `NgModules` have outstanding problems like boilerplate, increased complexity, and a steep learning curve.
- Single Component Angular Modules (SCAMs) can mitigate those problems in `NgModule`-based applications
- From v14, standalone Angular components, directives, and pipes are available, marked as `standalone: true` in their metadata.
- Applications can now be built completely without `NgModules` using the special `bootstrapApplication` function in the main.ts file.
- Standalone components, pipes, and directives can import other standalone building blocks via an `imports` array in their metadata.
- Standalone building blocks can fully interop with `NgModules` by either importing the module directly into components or via the `importProvidersFrom` function.
- Lazy-loading routes directly is now possible for standalone components instead of whole modules.
- Existing applications can migrate to standalone either by hand or using the schematic provided by the Angular team; the SCAM approach greatly simplifies this process.

Revitalized
dependency injection

3

This chapter covers

- How the dependency injection mechanism works under the hood
- Injection contexts
- Using the `inject` function instead of constructor-based dependency injection and the benefits of this approach
- Using the `inject` function to convert class-based guards/resolvers/interceptors to functional ones

Dependency injection (DI) is famously the most loved and stable feature that Angular provides as a framework. DI is used extensively in every single Angular project, and it is hard to imagine a flexible and maintainable codebase without its advantages. So what changed, and importantly, why, if it was already so stable? This question will be our subject of exploration in this chapter, which, funny enough, actually revolves around one single function, `inject` (actually not even a new function!), which, almost accidentally, made a minor revolution in Angular projects all over the community.

3.1 How does dependency injection work?

Let's start our exploration by diving into the DI mechanism to understand how it works and how we can utilize it to build more flexible codebases. But first, let's briefly discuss what, in general, DI is and what it is not.

3.1.1 Why do we need DI?

When writing software, we often use other software in the process. For instance, we use built-in objects in a browser to access and manipulate the DOM tree, or in the case of Angular, we use existing directives to render content conditionally. Usually, we do it by importing some token, most probably an object or instance of a class, and then using its methods. In this case, that token becomes a dependency of the code we are authoring. For instance, a class (component, directive, pipe, service, etc.) we write may want to use Angular's `HttpClient` to make HTTP calls, and `HttpClient` is a whole separate class, so we want to import that one into our file. But then there is another level: we do not just want the `HttpClient` class but an *instance* of it. Sure enough, we can write `new HttpClient()` and create a new instance, but we face two problems in this scenario.

First, `HttpClient` has some dependencies it receives via its own constructor, and if we try to provide them, too, it will become apparent they also have their own dependencies, and so on. Of course, we could go on writing that sort of thing, but that would result in more boilerplate code (writing all those constructor arguments every time we need the `HttpClient` is very tedious) and reduced maintainability. If some of the dependencies down the line are changed to depend on one more thing, we would face a nightmare of refactoring.

Second, just making a new instance will mean that we will have a dedicated instance of a service we use in every building block where it is used, meaning if five components make HTTP calls, we have five instances of `HttpClient`. This setup is redundant memory-wise and limiting from the perspective of shared state; if there is any data inside our service, we cannot change it and reflect it somewhere else because each service consumer will have a copy of the data. This limitation can be a serious concern when building software meant to share state between components of an application, like state management libraries, which are an important part of modern frontend applications.

A functioning DI system can efficiently solve this problem. Such a system would take tokens we want to receive references to and return the actual references without duplicating instances and without the need to specify the entire dependency tree manually. It can also add two more benefits: the ability to load dependencies conditionally (like using different services depending on the runtime environment) and the ability to mock dependencies, which can be very useful for unit testing purposes.

As we have seen, such a system solves all problems we have with dependencies and also provides an array of benefits. Now, let us discuss how such a system can work.

3.1.2   *Let's build a primitive DI mechanism*

We are going to build (a very primitive) DI mechanism, which will allow the users to accomplish the following two things:

- *Register dependencies*—Declaring some tokens (constant identifiers) and mapping them to concrete values, also known as "providing" the dependencies. In this part, the "injector" will "learn" about what DI tokens exist and what to return when someone requests that token.
- *Get the dependencies*—Requesting a token from the DI injector and receiving its corresponding value.

We will accomplish this by creating a special `InjectionToken` class (something we might be familiar with from Angular!) and an `Injector` class that handles the DI mechanism using those `InjectionToken`-s (again, something that might already sound familiar to us from Angular).

Listing 3.1   Injector class for a naive implementation of a DI mechanism

```
class InjectionToken<T> {
  constructor(public value: T) {}
}
```
The InjectionToken class, which is just a wrapper around a value, will be used to map tokens to their values.

```
class Injector {
  private readonly dependencies = new Map<
    InjectionToken<any>, any
  >();
```
The map of dependencies; each token has its value.

```
  provide<T>(dependency: T): InjectionToken<T> {
    const token = new InjectionToken(dependency);
    this.dependencies.set(token, dependency);
    return token;
  }
```
Provides a method that allows for registering dependencies, essentially just adding a token to the map with the provided value; returns the token so we can then retrieve the value when needed

```
  inject<T>(token: InjectionToken<T>): T {
    const dependency = this.dependencies.get(token) as T;
    return dependency;
  }
}
```
Inject method that allows for retrieving the value; receives the token and returns the corresponding value from the map of dependencies

---

We can use this code anywhere to create a working DI mechanism. To use it, we would need to define some dependency, maybe a service class, and inject other dependencies into it. Let's see it in action.

Listing 3.2   Using the `injector` class to provide an `inject` to a dependency

```
const injector = new Injector();
```
Creates an injector

```
class HttpClient {
  get(url: string) {
```

```
    return fetch(url);
  }
}

const httpToken = injector.provide(new HttpClient());
```

Provides a dependency and gets a token for later retrieval

```
class UserService {
  http = injector.inject(httpToken)
```

Injects the dependency via the token in another class

```
  getUsers() {
    return this.http.get('https://example.com/api/users');
  }
}
const userServiceToken = injector.provide(new UserService());

const userService = injector.inject(userServiceToken);

userService.getUsers();
```

Uses a method from an injected class instance

As we can see, this code does not look in any way like what we are used to in Angular, but the mechanism is the same: in some places, we provide a dependency (either in an NgModule providers array or by tagging it as providedIn: 'root'), then in another place, we inject it and get the value. Notice that while we called new HttpClient() and new UserService() in our example, we did not need to provide them any dependencies via the constructor because they injected their own dependencies using our DI mechanism. But now, a question will surely come to mind: "Wait, doesn't Angular require us to put dependencies in the constructor?" The answer is, "kind of." Let's dive deep and see how this mechanism we just implemented works in Angular.

3.1.3   *Dependency injection the Angular way*

Angular uses a special abstraction called Injector (the same we named our own DI class) to handle dependency injection. This injector keeps the registry of dependencies (the map we created) and allows the retrieval of values via tokens. In our previous example, notice this line:

```
const injector = new Injector();
```

This line implies we can have multiple injectors. Each would have its own registry of dependencies and its own inject function. So does Angular! Angular creates special injectors when our application runs, provides dependencies, and then injects them into components (directives, pipes, etc.) implicitly. When I say *implicitly*, I mean there is no special code that does this: we just list our dependencies as constructor parameters, and Angular then deduces when to inject what. It's pretty simple and nice, but it can feel like magic, and it limits us to using it only in classes, as we need constructor functions to trigger DI. Later in this chapter, we will discuss how to overcome this limitation, but for now, it is sufficient to know it is caused by having the injector.

Any Angular application has at least one injector, known as the *root injector*, which is globally created for our application at the very beginning. The services marked with providedIn: 'root' are provided here.

Of course, when the application gets more complex, Angular spawns more injectors. Prior to standalone, ElementInjector and ModuleInjector were used to find dependencies. ElementInjectors are injectors created for each DOM node; for example, when we render a component somewhere in a template, it gets an ElementInjector, which is empty by default unless something is added to that component's providers array. ModuleInjectors, on the other hand, were created for NgModule-level DI and were used when ElementInjectors failed to find a dependency in their registry.

This lookup for a dependency works hierarchically. In standalone, which we explored in the previous chapters, we do not have ModuleInjectors, unless our standalone components import some NgModules. In the case of a fully standalone app, DI probably only uses ElementInjectors until it reaches a provider registered on a route or the main.ts file configurations.

In the previous chapter, we created an EmployeeListComponent, which injected EmployeeService (see figure 2.16). Let's consider figure 3.1 and go step by step to see how the component will receive the reference of the EmployeeService.

This process will repeat every time an EmployeeListComponent is created; for example, if we run an *ngFor loop and render five EmployeeListComponents, five ElementInjectors will be created for those component instances, and this process will run five times. We use the example of components, but it is similarly true for directives, with each directive instance having a dedicated ElementInjector and running through these steps.

We can notice that this process looks like a property lookup on a JavaScript Object's prototype chain. When we access a property of an object, we first look at the object itself, and if we don't see the property there, we run to its prototype and look it up there, and then its prototype, and on and on, until we reach the root Object. After that, there is one more step because Object's prototype is null; because it does not have any properties, it will throw an error. The same is true for Angular's DI lookup: when we reach the root injector, there is one more level called the NullInjector, which is the parent of the root injector. NullInjector is special, as it always throws an error when we attempt a dependency lookup on it. This is what we see when we get the NullInjectorError: No provider for Something! message. It means that Angular attempted to look up a dependency, reached the root level, didn't find it there, then went one level up to the NullInjector, and, as always, threw an error.

All of this sounds nice; however, one question remains: Why do we need this complex process? Why can't this work as our primitive implementation from the previous section? The answer lies in understanding that dependency. While, colloquially, it often means just "some service," it isn't always an instance of a service class—very often. A popular example is that we are able to inject references to DOM elements or other directives or components into our components and directives. For instance, if

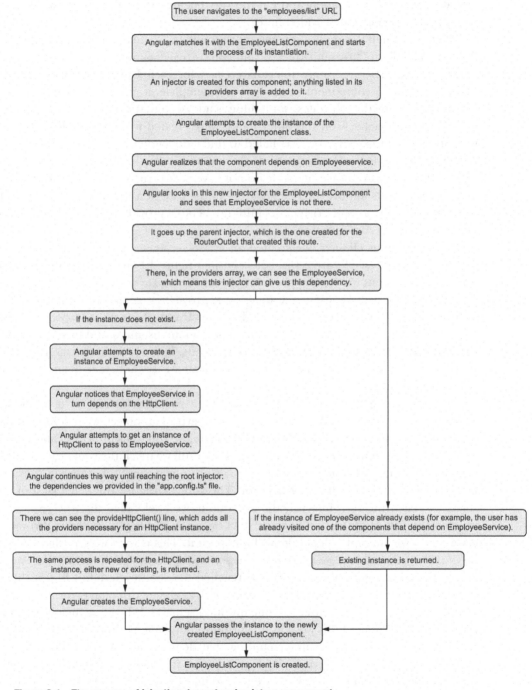

The user navigates to the "employees/list" URL

Angular matches it with the EmployeeListComponent and starts
the process of its instantiation.

An injector is created for this component; anything listed in its
providers array is added to it.

Angular attempts to create the instance of the
EmployeeListComponent class.

Angular realizes that the component depends on Employeeservice.

Angular looks in this new injector for the EmployeeListComponent
and sees that EmployeeService is not there.

It goes up the parent injector, which is the one created for the
RouterOutlet that created this route.

There, in the providers array, we can see the EmployeeService,
which means this injector can give us this dependency.

If the instance does not exist.

Angular attempts to create an
instance of EmployeeService.

Angular notices that EmployeeService in
turn depends on the HttpClient.

Angular attempts to get an instance of
HttpClient to pass to EmployeeService.

Angular continues this way until reaching the root injector:
the dependencies we provided in the "app.config.ts" file.

There we can see the provideHttpClient() line, which adds all
the providers necessary for an HttpClient instance.

If the instance of EmployeeService already exists (for example, the user has
already visited one of the components that depend on EmployeeService).

The same process is repeated for the HttpClient, and an
instance, either new or existing, is returned.

Existing instance is returned.

Angular creates the EmployeeService.

Angular passes the instance to the newly
created EmployeeListComponent.

EmployeeListComponent is created.

Figure 3.1   The process of injecting dependencies into a component

we write a directive, we will very likely need the reference to the element on which the directive is called. We do this by injecting the `ElementRef`, which, in turn, is provided on the `ElementInjector` of this particular directive instance. The same directive can be applied in many different parts of the application, so the `ElementRef` instance will be different each time and determined by its own injector. Essentially, we have a tree of dependencies/injectors in which the instances of the same token can be different. Let us see this concept in a diagram, as shown in figure 3.2.

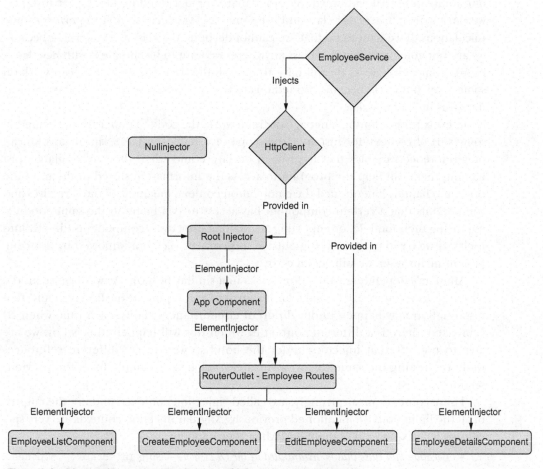

Figure 3.2   Diagram illustrating the hierarchy of injectors and dependencies

Here, we can clearly see both the relations of injectors and the path that Angular will traverse to retrieve the reference to `EmployeeService` for the `EmployeeListComponent`. This tree is incomplete: each component here has a template that renders its own injector. For instance, we used an `*ngFor` directive in `EmployeeListComponent`, meaning an injector was created specifically for that instance of the directive, and so on.

Later in this chapter, we will learn how we can manipulate this lookup process to latch onto specific instances of some services or values. We need to understand one final concept before learning about the inject function.

3.1.4 *Injection contexts*

We already mentioned in passing that we rely on class constructors to inject dependencies in Angular; another necessary parameter is a class decorated by one of Angular's decorators, like `Component`, `Directive`, `Pipe`, or `Injectable`. This further limits our ability to use DI with anything other than Angular building blocks; for instance, we can't write a `UserModel` class and use some `UtilityService` in it to perform some calculations. If we want to do that, we cannot decorate the class as `Injectable` because we are not going to inject that class anywhere; we want to instantiate it with `new User-Model()`, meaning we again will have to pass all the dependencies. This can work on some level, but it will become too tedious to type whenever we need the class. So why does this limitation exist?

In every programming language or framework, the code that we run is executed in some sort of context; for instance, the scope of variables in JavaScript means we can only reference variables that have been declared, and when they are available, just naming them will help the program to access the information stored in them. In the previous chapter, I mentioned the compilation context, meaning all the directives and components that a certain component has access to (via being in the same module, importing their module, or importing standalone directives/components directly into itself). If we try to use something outside this context (i.e., not imported by this component in any way), we will get an error.

Angular's dependency injection works in a similar fashion. As we have seen, the DI happens when we try to make an instance of a component or directive, and that instantiation may happen under different circumstances. Thus, each time when DI is invoked, there is a different context in which this will happen: this is how we are able to use different injectors under the hood so we can get different references while requesting the same token (as in the `ElementRef` example from the previous section).

These contexts, unsurprisingly, are called "injection contexts" and are the culprits of all the limitations we mentioned previously. Angular injection contexts are very specific, so let's explore all of them and when they happen:

- *Creation of a class that is instantiated by the DI system*—Using `Injectable`, `Component`, etc. (as opposed to just using the `new` keyword). We have already encountered this scenario—it's how all explicit DI worked before v14, via writing parameters in the constructor.
- *Initializer fields of such a class*—Because the TypeScript gets compiled to JavaScript in the end, all such property initializations end up in the constructor anyway.
- *Factory function for the* `useFactory` *option when providing a dependency*—Helps inject all dependencies listed in the `deps` option into the function's parameters.

- *Factory function for an* `InjectionToken`—We will explore this in depth later in this chapter (section 3.2.3).
- *Within a stack frame of an injection context*—If we call a function in a `Component`'s constructor, this function will also be in that injection context, and any other function it calls in its turn, and so on.

I have already mentioned that in this chapter, we will discuss the possibility of using DI outside of classes. Before we do that, we need to understand and keep in mind that the limitations imposed by injection contexts will still be applicable to all those scenarios. We will cover those a bit deeper in later sections of this chapter. Now, let us learn about the so-much-advertised `inject` function.

3.2 *The inject function*

I mentioned that the problem with not being able to inject dependencies in places other than classes is primarily the absence of a constructor where we can name the dependencies. Let's first understand how it can be possible to avoid it.

3.2.1 *Another way of injecting dependencies*

If we want to circumvent this problem, we need a function that takes a token, like the name of the service we want to inject, as a parameter and returns the value. This function works like the `Injector.inject` method in listing 3.1. The `inject` function works exactly in this way.

It's time we see it in action. Let us open the `EmployeeListComponent` we created in the previous chapter and change its DI mechanism to use the `inject` function instead of the constructor.

Listing 3.3 `EmployeeListComponent` using the `inject` function

```
import { Component, inject } from '@angular/core';
import { EmployeeService } from 'src/app/services/employee.service';

@Component({
  selector: 'app-employee-list',
  template: `...`,
  standalone: true,
})
export class EmployeeListComponent {              Uses the inject
  employeeService = inject(EmployeeService);   ◁──  function
  employees$ = this.employeeService.getEmployees();
  isConfirmationOpen = false;
  confirmDialog: any = null;
                                              No need for a constructor;
  async showConfirmationDialog() {      ◁──   we can write other methods.
    this.confirmDialog = await import(
      '../../shared/components/confirmation-dialog.component'
    ).then((m) => m.ConfirmationDialogComponent);
    this.isConfirmationOpen = true;
  }
}
```

This listing looks mildly different from constructor injection. We want to focus our attention on a few things:

- This approach could save us one or two lines if we have multiple dependencies listed in a constructor.
- There is no need to write an empty constructor method only for the purpose of injecting a dependency.
- We can also drop access modifiers with the `inject` function. With the constructor, we need to add `public`, `private`, or `protected` to the name of the property in the constructor so that it is stored as a class property rather than just a constructor argument. In this scenario, we can drop it, and it will be inferred as `public` (although it is a good practice to still mark services and dependencies as `private readonly` to prevent them from being accidentally overwritten or accessed in the wrong place).

The `inject` function gives us some minor nice things, but I wouldn't have dedicated an entire chapter to it if that was it. Further, let's discuss how we can use this function to escape our dependence on classes for DI.

3.2.2 *Injecting dependencies outside classes*

In our very first encounter with the `inject` function, we used it to inject `Employee-Service` and get a list of employees. You might think that this scenario is common, but in real life, it would not make sense to start wrapping all method calls in functions just to skip one line of code in components. However, it can be useful in some scenarios. For instance, imagine we want to have a way of checking whether the user is authenticated and getting notified if they log in/out of our application. We could create a `BehaviorSubject` in our `AuthService` and flip it when this happens. Now, it would make sense to be able to expose that `BehaviorSubject` to components that might want to consume it, but those components probably won't need the entire package of the `AuthService`. We can mitigate this problem by wrapping `BehaviorSubject` into a function. First, let's add that `BehaviorSubject` to our `AuthService`.

Listing 3.4 Showing user's authentication status

```
import { Injectable, inject } from '@angular/core';
import { HttpClient } from '@angular/common/http';
import { BehaviorSubject } from 'rxjs';
import { tap } from 'rxjs/operators';

@Injectable()
export class AuthService {
    private readonly http = inject(HttpClient);
    isAuth$ = new BehaviorSubject(false);          ◁─── The authentication BehaviorSubject

    login(credentials: { email: string, password: string }) {
        return this.http.post('/api/auth/login', credentials).pipe(
```

```
            tap(() => this.isAuth$.next(true)),
    );
}

logout() {
    return this.http.post('/api/auth/logout', {}).pipe(
        tap(() => this.isAuth$.next(false)) ,
    );
}
}
```

← **Flips the value to true when the user logs in**

← **Reverses when the user logs out**

Now, as we have the `BehaviorSubject` in place, we can inject the service anywhere and use it. To simplify it a bit, let's write a function that returns `BehaviorSubject`, so that components can consume it directly. We will create a functions folder under the shared directory and, in there, an auth.ts file.

Listing 3.5 Function that returns a value from an injected service

```
import { inject } from '@angular/core';
import { AuthService } from '../../services/auth.service';

export function isAuth() {
    const authService = inject(AuthService);
    return authService.isAuth$.asObservable();
}
```

As we can see, we injected the `AuthService` into the function without a constructor. We also encapsulated the `isAuth$` `BehaviorSubject` by exposing it as an `Observable` so that everyone can read it, but only `AuthService` can modify it. Now, we can just as easily use it in any component.

To illustrate, let's create a `FooterComponent`, which will show some links related to the HRMS product and legal info. However, we want to show the legal information only to users who are not logged in and might be seeking to use the product, as logged-in users are members of companies who are already customers of the HRMS application. In the src/app/shared/components directory, create a new file named footer.component.ts and put a component that uses our new function to perform conditional logic in its template inside.

Listing 3.6 Component using a function to inject a value from another service

```
@Component({
  selector: 'app-footer',
  template: `
    <div>
      <h2>HRMS</h2>
      <p>Welcome to HRMS platform!</p>
      <div class="links">
        Follow us on social media:
        <a href="https://linkedin.com" target="_blank">Linkedin</a>
        <a href="https://x.com" target="_blank">X (former Twitter)</a>
      </div>
```

```
      <div *ngIf="isAuth$ | async" class="legal">
        <a routerLink="/terms">Terms of Service</a>
        <a routerLink="/privacy">Privacy Policy</a>
        <a routerLink="/cookies">Cookies Policy</a>
      </div>
    </div>
  `,
  standalone: true,
  imports: [AsyncPipe, RouterLink, NgIf],
})
export class FooterComponent {
  isAuth$ = isAuth();
}
```

We can then use this component in the `AppComponent` to render the footer content on all pages. As we can see, we no longer need to import and inject `AuthService` and extract the conditional property from it; we can retrieve it directly via a function. This can become very handy in situations where some complex logic related to a service is duplicated in multiple places in an Angular application.

We can use it almost anywhere. In section 3.1.4, where we discussed injection contexts, I mentioned that even without classes, the DI must happen in such a context. The same is true for the `inject` function: we can use it to initialize fields, we can use it in the body of a constructor, and we can use it in functions that are going to be called in class constructors. We cannot call those functions in arbitrary places. For instance, doing the following would result in an error:

```
export class FooterComponent implements OnInit {
    isAuth$: Observable<boolean>;

    ngOnInit() {
        this.isAuth$ = isAuth();
    }
}
```

The error occurs because `ngOnInit` (and all class methods but the constructor) is not being run in an injection context, so injecting dependencies there is impossible. Essentially, when those methods run, the class instance is already created, and DI has already happened. Despite this limitation, `inject` provides us with a variety of new capabilities outside classes and some benefits even if we ditch the constructor in components in its favor. Later in this chapter, we will discuss those new capabilities; for now, let us focus on the immediate benefits when we switch to `inject`.

3.2.3   *Why we should always use inject*

This function is new, and as we have seen, it does not look very different from the constructor DI. However, it provides a multitude of less obvious improvements. Let's investigate them one by one.

IMPROVED REUSABILITY

We have already encountered the topic of improved reusability. We have seen that we can now use DI inside functions, meaning we can extend service functionality to places where it would not have been possible previously. Functions are known to be better for composability (we can, for instance, return new functions from existing ones), and adding DI to them can be a huge win for large, interconnected applications. Also, some Angular building blocks that previously needed to be classes to have DI are now free to be written as functions. We will discuss this in detail in the next section of this chapter.

TYPE INFERENCE OF INJECTIONTOKENS

Not all dependencies are services; sometimes, we need to be able to inject some constant values or even functions directly. A good example is when large applications have some shared constants used in various parts of the application. For instance, we might want a specific way of formatting dates in our application. We want it to be the same everywhere, but we also want to be able to change it easily and mock it in unit tests to test for different scenarios. We can't just decorate a constant with `Injectable`, as it is not a class, so we will need to create an injection token. To demonstrate, let us go into the shared project of our example application and create a constants.ts file, in which we will create our `InjectionToken` and put the application-wide date format.

Listing 3.7   Injection token for application-wide constants

```
import { InjectionToken } from '@angular/core';

const CONSTANTS = {                    ⟵── The actual constants
    dateFormat: 'dd/MM/yyyy',
};

export const Constants = new InjectionToken('Constants', {
    factory() {
        return CONSTANTS;          ⟵─┤ Injection token factory
    },                               │ that returns the value
    providedIn: 'root',    ⟵─┐
});                          │ Provides the InjectionToken in the
                             │ root (i.e., the entire application)
```

We cannot use the conventional constructor DI To inject this token as it is not a service class. Previously we had to resort to using the `Inject` decorator (with a capital letter *I*, not to be confused with the new `inject` function) in the following way:

```
import { Inject } from '@angular/core';
import { Constants, CONSTANTS } from 'app/shared/constants.ts';

export class MyComponent {
    constructor(@Inject(Constants) constants: typeof CONSTANTS);
}
```

This approach is both a bit wordy (we type a lot and import three different things) and somewhat insecure: even if we mistype the constants property, the `Inject` decorator will still correctly inject the `Constants InjectionToken`, resulting in an incorrect typing of the property and possibly bugs down the line. This problem, however, is nonexistent with the `inject` function:

```
export class MyComponent {
    constants = inject(Constants);
}
```

`constants` will now correctly infer the type of the property without any need to type it out manually.

EASIER COMPONENT INHERITANCE

In general, inheriting components is not considered a best practice; however, there are scenarios where it can be useful, or we might be dealing with some legacy code that already has such component inheritance. With constructor DI, we have to redeclare all the dependencies in the child class and pass it back to the parent constructor. This task can be quite tedious, as, for example, in the following:

```
export class ParentClass {
    constructor(
        private router: Router,          ◄───  The parent class has some
    ) {}                                        dependency injected.
}

@Component({
    ...
})
export class ChildComponent extends ParentClass {   The child class needs to
    constructor(                                     inject it in its constructor.
        private router: Router,          ◄─────
        private http: HttpClient,        ◄───┐  The child class then adds
    ) {                                      └  its own dependency.
        super(router);      ◄─┐
    }                         └  The dependency of the parent class
}                                needs to be passed to its constructor.
```

Passing dependencies to a parent component class will grow even worse if we have a component that extends from another one that is already a child class, making this code even more complicated. This scenario is even more popular in the case of services, where inheritance has more accepted usage than in components. With the `inject` function, however, none of these problems occur:

```
export class ParentClass {
    private router = inject(Router);   ◄───  The parent class injects
}                                            something without a constructor.

@Component({
    ...
})                                           The child class injects
                                             something else, again with
export class ChildComponent extends ParentClass {   no constructor; the parent
    private http = inject(HttpClient);   ◄──  dependency (router) is also
}                                            available in the child.
```

We already discussed some of the benefits related to DI usage in classes. Another benefit is outside of the realm of OOP.

CUSTOM RxJS OPERATORS

More complex Angular applications tend to rely heavily on RxJS, and in some advanced scenarios, developers also create their own custom RxJS operators. Those operators often need a dependency from the DI tree—for instance, a utility service to help perform a mapping on some emitted value. In this case, before the introduction of the `inject` function, the only option was to pass the reference as a parameter to the custom operator. Now, we can just inject the dependency directly in the operator and use it (but carefully—always run it in an injection context). We will talk about such custom operators in detail in chapter 5.

DITCHING THE CONSTRUCTOR ALTOGETHER

Almost every component we write has some initialization logic. For instance, the `EmployeeListComponent` we created previously loaded the list of employees as soon as it was created. In our example, we wrote it as a field initializer. Sometimes, developers write that sort of code in the `ngOnInit` method based on when exactly they want to load that data. What *does not* happen often is developers putting that sort of code in the constructor method itself. In the vast majority of the scenarios, the constructor function is empty and exists only to inject dependencies. It is so widespread that lots of automatic tools (even the Angular CLI) generate component classes with empty constructors by default. With the `inject` function, as we have seen, it became possible to get by without the constructor method entirely.

3.2.4 What about the drawbacks?

So far, I have only sung praise for the `inject` function, but in real life, all solutions come with some tradeoffs, and our new favorite function is no exception. Let's see when we might encounter problems with it.

CONFUSING USAGE

As I repeatedly mentioned, the function does not change the way the DI mechanism functions, meaning that it still needs to be called in an injection context. For less experienced developers, this can be a source of confusion when it is not entirely clear why something is not working as expected. More senior developers need to pay attention to such situations to avoid bugs and blockers.

PROBLEMS WITH UNIT TESTING

The `inject` function generally works well with unit testing in Angular if we use default tools like `TestBed`. However, especially in the case of services, developers often forgo using `TestBed` when creating instances of the building blocks they want to test. Doing so creates a problem, as just calling `new MyService()` is not running in an injection context. This problem, however, can be mitigated with other tools, which we will discuss at length in chapter 8, where we will dive deep into unit testing.

IN SUM

So far, we have discussed the local benefits of the `inject` function, like reduction in boilerplate and other code-level improvements. Of course, I would not dedicate an entire chapter to this function if the changes were only cosmetic. Further, let us discuss how the inject function revolutionized the way we author three of the Angular building blocks.

3.3 *Functional guards, resolvers, and interceptors*

In enterprise applications, it is very common to have some sort of restrictions on what pages some categories of users can and cannot access. Historically, Angular has always provided an official way of creating restrictions via some of its building blocks like `Guards`. Let's see how the `inject` function changed the way we write them.

3.3.1 *Building an AuthGuard*

Probably the most popular use case for this functionality is restricting access based on the user's authentication status. For instance, the business logic pages of the HRMS application we build should be available to authenticated users only. We can build a guard that handles the functionality to achieve this restriction. First, we will do this the "old way" to see the difference between class-based guards and the new approach.

Let's start by creating a guards folder in the shared directory of our project and putting an auth.guard.ts file in it. The guard itself will look something like the following listing.

Listing 3.8   Angular route guard as a class

```
import { Injectable, inject } from '@angular/core';
import { CanActivate, Router, UrlTree } from '@angular/router';
import { Observable } from 'rxjs';
import { map } from 'rxjs/operators';
import { AuthService } from '../../services/auth.service';

@Injectable()
export class AuthGuard implements CanActivate {
    authService = inject(AuthService);
    router = inject(Router);

    canActivate(): Observable<boolean | UrlTree> {
        return this.authService.isAuth$.pipe(
            map((isAuth) => isAuth || this.router.createUrlTree(['/login'])),
        );
    }
}
```

As we see, we create a class that implements a specific interface, which forces it to have a method named `canActivate`, which returns a `boolean` or an `UrlTree` for redirects depending on the user's auth status.

Let's examine this class a bit further. The main thing immediately noticeable is that it has one singular purpose (which is not bad in and of itself), accomplished by the `canActivate` method. Unlike a component, which might need several methods to perform different tasks (e.g., handle multiple user events like clicks on different buttons), this class does not need any other methods than `canActivate`. Of course, we could write some other methods to simplify `canActivate` itself, but doing so is not a requirement and does not happen in the vast majority of scenarios. This class also does not have any state of its own (data properties) because it does not keep the state from one usage to another: each time a route requires this guard, it reuses the instance but does not touch the state. Essentially, in most cases, the only properties such a class has are the dependencies it injects.

Given this discussion, we can safely arrive at the conclusion that guards in Angular are only written as classes for the sole purpose of being able to utilize DI. But we have already shown that with the `inject` function, we do not need classes to use DI! We have already used this function to inject dependencies into this class. Let us now go one level deeper and discard the class altogether with the help of the `CanActivateFn` type that Angular now provides.

Listing 3.9   Functional route guard

> **The guard is now just a function that must implement the CanActivateFn interface, which acts like the CanActivate interface we implemented in the previous example.**

```
import { inject } from '@angular/core';
import { CanActivateFn, Router, } from '@angular/router';
import { map } from 'rxjs/operators';
import { AuthService } from 'src/app/services/auth.service';

export const authGuard: CanActivateFn = () => {
    const router = inject(Router);
    const authService = inject(AuthService);

    return authService.isAuth$.pipe(
        map((isAuth) => isAuth || router.createUrlTree(['/login'])),
    );
}
```

Inject dependencies with the inject function

The actual business logic is unchanged.

CanActivateFn forces our function to return a Boolean, an observable of Boolean, or UrlTree for redirects, same as the CanActivate interface.

As we see, we reduced the number of imports and lines of code and simplified the process itself. It is now easier to explain to a newcomer. In the previous example I described guards as a class that implements a specific interface with a method that returns a Boolean or an observable of a Boolean. Now, we can just say that guard is a function that returns a Boolean or an observable of a Boolean. This will also (albeit mildly) reduce the boilerplate in unit tests.

So far, we have only created the guard but have not added it to any routes. Let's go to app.routes.ts and make the `'employees'` path only accessible when the user is logged in. This method works in exactly the same way as it used to with class-based guards.

> **Listing 3.10   Registering a functional route guard**

```
{
    path: 'employees',
    providers: [EmployeeService],                    We put the function in
    canActivate: [authGuard] ,      ⊲─┘              the canActivate array.
    loadChildren: () => {
        return import('./pages/employees/employees.routes').then(
            (m) => m.routes,
        );
    },
},
```

Now, let us move forward and tackle the next routing-related building block, which was also revolutionized by the `inject` function.

3.3.2   *Building an EmployeeResolver*

Another common task when developing complex web apps is ensuring some data is loaded via an HTTP request before rendering the component that requires that data. In the case of our HRMS application, we already have a list of employees. We now want to build an `EmployeeDetailsComponent`; the user will be able to navigate it from the list of employees. When the user navigates, we want to first load the employee details via HTTP and only then the component itself to avoid a flickering UI or a situation where the call results in an error and we end up with a blank page. We can accomplish this task using Angular's `Resolvers`, which, just like guards, have also been implemented with classes. We will skip the class implementation and write the resolver as a function outright, utilizing the `inject` function.

First, let us create a new file at src/app/infrastructure/types/employee.ts and put the employee type definition there:

```
export type Employee = {
    id: number;
    firstName: string;
    lastName: string;
    email: string;
    position: 'Developer' | 'Designer' | 'QA' | 'Manager';
    level: 'Junior' | 'Middle' | 'Senior' | 'Lead';
    isAvailable: boolean;
    profilePicture: string;
}
```

Next, we will create a resolvers folder next to the guards folder in the shared directory and add an employee-details.resolver.ts file there. The implementation is going to be very straightforward and, in some ways, mimic what we did with `AuthGuard`.

Listing 3.11   Functional resolver

> The function has to implement a generic ResolveFn interface, which
> receives a type argument. Via this type argument, we explain what
> type of data we will return from the resolver.

```
import { inject } from '@angular/core';
import { ActivatedRouteSnapshot, ResolveFn } from '@angular/router';
import { Employee } from 'src/app/infrastructure/types/employee';
import { EmployeeService } from 'src/app/services/employee.service';

export const employeeDetailsResolver: ResolveFn<Employee> = (      <—

    route: ActivatedRouteSnapshot,      <—|   The current route information is
) => {                                        already available via an argument.
    const employeeService = inject(EmployeeService);
    const id = +(route.paramMap.get('id') ?? 0);      <—

    return employeeService.getEmployee(id);      <—
}
```

The current route information is already available via an argument.

We take the id param from the route and convert it to a number. In this case, we do not handle null, but in real life, it would need separate logic.

In the end, we return the result of our service's HTTP call.

Next, we want to register the resolver on the appropriate route. Again, we use the same method as we used with class-based resolvers.

Listing 3.12   Registering a functional resolver

```
{
    path: 'details/:id',
    component: EmployeeDetailsComponent,
    resolve: { employee: employeeDetailsResolver },
},
```

Finally, we can inject the route data into our component and get access to the resolved data.

Listing 3.13   Using resolved data in a component

```
@Component({
  selector: 'app-employee-details',
  template: `
  <h2>Employee Details</h2>
  <div>
    <label>First Name: </label>{{ employee.firstName }}
    <label>Last Name: </label>{{ employee.lastName }}
    <label>Position: </label>{{ employee.position }}
  </div>
  `,
  standalone: true,
})
export class EmployeeDetailsComponent {
  employee = inject(ActivatedRoute).snapshot.data['employee'] as Employee;
}
```

Again, it all comes down to injecting the relevant data where it is needed. The process is simplified, boilerplate code is reduced, and getting the data inside the component is achieved via just one line of code. Now, as we covered tasks related to routing, let's move to another Angular building block that turned functional in the wake of the introduction of the `inject` function.

3.3.3 Adding tokens to HTTP requests

Another common need is the ability to modify HTTP requests or responses on the fly. Almost all enterprise applications introduce this sort of logic somewhere in their codebase. The most common scenario is adding authentication tokens to HTTP request headers so that the API can verify the user's identity and permissions. Of course, we could write out the HTTP headers every time we make an HTTP call, but large applications can potentially have up to thousands of different HTTP requests, and copy-pasting that code everywhere we need results in unmaintainable code. To avoid this, Angular has previously introduced the concept of an interceptor, which acts as a middleware for HTTP calls. As with resolvers and guards, inceptors were also previously a class-based solution, but now they have become functional, too.

Let's go on and create our authentication interceptor, which will add the user's token to all HTTP requests. We will assume that the token is stored in `localStorage` (for the sake of simplicity; in real life, it would probably involve some more complex steps) and can be retrieved via a `getToken` method on our `AuthService`. To build our interceptor, let's create an interceptors folder in the shared directory and add a file named auth.interceptor.ts.

Listing 3.14 Authentication interceptor

```
import { HttpHandlerFn, HttpRequest, HttpInterceptorFn } from
    '@angular/common/http';
import { inject } from '@angular/core';
import { AuthService } from 'src/app/services/auth.service';

export const authInterceptor: HttpInterceptorFn = (
    req: HttpRequest<any>,
    next: HttpHandlerFn,
) => {
  const authService = inject(AuthService);
  const token = authService.getToken();
  const newReq = req.clone({setHeaders: {
    'Authorization': `Bearer ${token}`,
  }});
  return next(newReq);
}
```

The function implements the HttpInterceptorFn interface to enforce its return type and parameters.

The function receives the current request as a parameter, which we can use to modify.

The next interceptor or handler will deal with this request on its own line; in the end, we must invoke it to pass the request further until it gets executed. This is what makes interceptors essentially middleware.

Passes the new, modified request to the next handler

Adds the token to the cloned request

With this step out of our way, the last thing we need to do is register this interceptor so that Angular knows to invoke it when an HTTP call is made. In a standalone setup like ours, we can use the `provideHttpClient` function and a special helper called `withInterceptors` in the app.config.ts file.

Listing 3.15 Registering an interceptor

```
export const appConfig: ApplicationConfig = {
  providers: [
    provideRouter(routes),
    provideHttpClient(
      withInterceptors([authInterceptor]),
    ),
  ],
};
```

As we can see, we are able to add multiple interceptors, all of which will work when any HTTP call is made in our application.

So far, we have discussed these changes in the context of standalone applications, where we just created those functions from scratch. However, a similarly important scenario is where developers want to migrate their existing, class-based building blocks to functional ones. Let's discuss what steps can be taken to accomplish that.

3.3.4 *Migrating to functional guards/resolvers/interceptors*

In real life, lots of developers are still dealing with projects that have all these building blocks as classes. If we consider a project that uses, let's say, Angular v12, upgrading to v15 or v16 will involve some refactoring. Class-based guards/resolvers/interceptors are deprecated as per v15 in favor of functional ones. So, we need to think about ditching the previous versions of those building blocks and switching to functions. Of course, as with anything, we can manually change the codebase to reflect this change; migrating a single resolver, let's say, would probably not take too much time. However, refactoring dozens of them in one go will probably result in problems, especially if we have unit tests that also have to be refactored. Thankfully, Angular provides some utilities we can use to provide backward compatibility until we change all the guards/resolvers/interceptors.

MIGRATING GUARDS AND RESOLVERS

Class-based building blocks related to routing can be converted to functions with a special set of utility functions named in a convention of `mapTo<name of guard/resolver type>`. For instance, if we already had our `AuthGuard` as a class and wanted to use it as a function on a route's `canActivate` option, we could use the `mapToCanActivate` function to achieve this. The following listing shows how it looks in the code.

Listing 3.16 Registering a class-based guard in a functional setup

```
{
    path: 'employees',
    providers: [EmployeeService],
    canActivate: mapToCanActivate([AuthGuard]),
    loadChildren: () => {
```

```
        return import('./pages/employees/employees.routes').then(
            (m) => m.routes,
        );
    },
},
```

The `mapToCanActivate` function will convert the array of class-based guards to an array of `CanActivateFn` functions, which keeps them compatible with the new API. We can then manually change those class-based guards to functional ones one by one at our convenience. This function, as mentioned, is also available in other flavors to support guards for other scenarios and resolvers:

- `mapToResolve()`
- `mapToCanDeactivate()`
- `mapToCanMatch()`
- `mapToCanActivateChild()`

Each of these functions does the same thing for a different type of routing task.

MIGRATING INTERCEPTORS

In the case of interceptors, previously, registering them worked a bit differently, with Angular exposing a special `HTTP_INTERCEPTORS InjectionToken`, which we could then use to add multiple interceptors. As we saw in listing 3.14, the process is now simpler with the `withInterceptors` functions in the standalone setup. However, older registration of class-based interceptors using the `HTTP_INTERCEPTORS` may still be included.

I briefly mentioned in the previous chapter (section 2.5.3 on the migration to standalone) that the automatic migration using Angular's standalone schematic will switch to the standalone API for importing the `HttpClient`, and add a special function called `withInterceptorsFromDi`. This function, again, exists only for backward compatibility and will basically add all of those legacy class-based interceptors to the overall pipeline, allowing us, for a while, to use both functional and class-based interceptors. We then can remove class-based ones until we are done and finally remove the `withInterceptorsFromDi` call.

So far, we have covered everything that changed in Angular with the introduction of the `inject` function. Now, let's dive deeper and see the most profound features of Angular's dependency injection and explore how the `inject` function can help us simplify those complex use cases.

3.4   *DI deep dive*

In this section, we will discuss more complex scenarios. We already covered the basic and most common use cases for DI in Angular; now it is time we learn about manipulating DI in specific ways to simplify our code further. To do so, we first need to gain a bit of a deeper understanding of how DI functions and what can be done to alter its behavior.

3.4.1   *DI lookup and how to modify it*

We already talked about how dependency injection works in section 3.1: we provide a token and then request it somewhere; Angular searches the DI tree starting from the current component up to the `NullInjector`, finds the value (or fails to find one), and returns it. However, it is possible to alter this process to some extent. For instance, we can specify where the lookup should start (maybe we do not want to include the current context providers and want to start from the parent immediately). We can also specify where we want the lookup to end—maybe we only look for dependencies in this current context. All of those tasks previously used special decorators like `Self`, `Optional`, `SkipSelf`, and `Host`.

Let us now discuss use cases where those can be applicable and see how the `inject` function makes working with those use cases easier and our code shorter and simpler. The decorators we mentioned do different things, so let's first see what each of them is used for, and then we'll discuss how they work when we discard constructor DI and use the `inject` function:

- `@Optional`—This decorator marks a dependency as optional, which means if Angular does not find it, it will not go up to the `NullInjector` and throw an error; instead, it will return `null`. This may sound useless at first glance, but it can become handy when the developer can provide a global value for some dependency, but a component wants to use a default one if the global one is not provided.
- `@Self`—This decorator limits the search for a given dependency to the component's own `ElementInjector` or, in other words, to whatever is provided in that component. This can be useful if the component wants to have its own separate instance of some service, to encapsulate its data, or for any other purposes. A good example is components that recursively render themselves and want different instances of the same service for child components.
- `@SkipSelf`—This decorator is the opposite of `@Self` and starts the search for a given dependency from its parent injector. `@SkipSelf` can be used in some scenarios to enforce using a global provider instead of a local one.
- `@Host`—This decorator will limit the search for a dependency to the component and its direct parent. This can be useful for components that are usually used in pairs—for instance, `ListComponent` and `ListItemComponent`, where we want to use the same provider as the parent list in the child item.

Before the `inject` function became publicly available, these modifiers were used to add one or more of those decorators to the property declared in the constructor. It looked something like this:

```
export class MyComponent {
  constructor(
    @SkipSelf() @Optional() private readonly someDependency: SomeDependency,
  ) {}
}
```

Now, as we are moving toward ditching the constructor DI altogether, we can't use this approach. Instead, the inject function can accept a second parameter, a configuration object, where we can put our modifiers:

```
export class MyComponent {
    someDependency = inject(SomeDependency, {optional: true, skipSelf:
      true});
}
```

While this code is still kind of a mouthful, this approach actually allows more flexibility when trying to combine injected properties with other Angular concepts like inputs or outputs. Let's build a reusable directive and see this process in action.

3.4.2 *Truncating text with DI*

In a large web application like the one we are building now, it is commonplace to have lots of text data on different pages. Usually, this text is user-generated, so it can be quite long, meaning that sometimes we might want to limit the number of characters displayed on the page, also known as truncating the text. For instance, we have built an `EmployeeList` component, and we show several columns with text in the table. For some columns, we want to truncate this text to avoid making the table go over the user's viewport. We are going to build a directive that accomplishes this functionality, but before we do, let's set some requirements for this directive:

- This directive is going to be used in multiple places, so it has to be flexible and reusable.
- By default, it will limit text to 80 characters.
- An optional Input can be provided to change the limit on some given element.
- If we want a different character limit globally, we can provide it and not have to type the input every time we use the directive.
- If a global value is provided but we want a different limit in some component (based on its relation to the viewport), we should be able to provide that limit to that component only.

With all this in mind, let's first build the basic version of this directive that only satisfies the first two conditions. In the shared directory, let us add a new folder named directives and create a truncate.directive.ts file with the content in the following listing.

Listing 3.17   Basic implementation of `TruncateDirective`

```
import { Directive, inject, ElementRef,
  Input, AfterViewInit } from '@angular/core';

@Directive({
    selector: '[appTruncate]',
    standalone: true,
})
export class TruncateDirective implements AfterViewInit {
```

```
    @Input() limit = 80;
    private readonly elRef = inject(ElementRef);

    ngAfterViewInit() {
        this.elRef.nativeElement.textContent =
      this.elRef.nativeElement.textContent.slice(
            0,
            this.limit,
        );
    }
}
```

Flexibility is provided only via an Input, providing reusability on an element level.

After the view is initialized, the directive will change the text content of the target element.

Now, this code is enough to have very basic reusability, but if we wanted to make another global character limit, we would not be able to. To achieve that, we will employ DI and create a special `InjectionToken` that will hold the value for the character limit. We'll then provide it wherever necessary. Let's add it directly to the trunctate.directive.ts file.

Listing 3.18 Injecting a configuration into `TruncateDirective`

```
export const TruncateLimit = new InjectionToken<number>('TruncateLimit');

@Directive({
    selector: '[appTruncate]',
    standalone: true,
})
export class TruncateDirective implements AfterViewInit {
    @Input() limit = inject(TruncateLimit);
}
```

Defines the token

Injecting it back into the directive

As we can see, we effortlessly combined the `Input` decorator with our `InjectionToken`, something previously impossible with constructor DI. Now, we can define a global value via the `providers` array in app.config.ts:

```
{ provide: TruncateLimit, useValue: 70 }
```

All the directive instances will have this configurable limit. If we want a particular instance to have a different option, we can provide it as an `Input`:

```
<td appTruncate [limit]="10">{{ employee.position }}</td>
```

Finally, what's left to do is allow the developers not to provide global value at all if they would like to use a default. We will use our knowledge of DI lookup modifiers to achieve this.

Listing 3.19 Final implementation of the `TruncateDirective`

```
export class TruncateDirective implements AfterViewInit {
    @Input() limit = inject(TruncateLimit, {optional: true}) ?? 80;
    private readonly elRef = inject(ElementRef);
```

```
ngAfterViewInit() {
    this.elRef.nativeElement.textContent =
     this.elRef.nativeElement.textContent.slice(
        0,
        this.limit,
     );
  }
}
```

As we can see, we used the `optional` flag and the `??` operator combined with an `Input` to achieve all the requirements we set. If an input value is not provided, we try to inject the globally provided limit value; if that is not provided either, we use a default value. This also makes it possible to use components for which the value of the character limit is entirely different from the rest of the application by manually providing that value in the `providers` array of that component.

Now that we have deeply familiarized ourselves with Angular's modern dependency injection mechanism, we can test it out on practical examples.

3.5 *Exercises for the reader*

After this chapter, you should create services, components, and directives utilizing the `inject` function:

- Create an `InterviewService` for the Recruitment feature of the HRMS application and use it in relevant components.
- Write a higher-order permission guard—a function that will return another function that is a guard (complies with `CanActivateFn`). The parent function receives the name of the user permission as a string and uses the closure to create a guard that is specific to that permission and will not allow the user without that permission to access certain pages. It will be used with route definition, securing multiple permissions in different places: `canActivate: [hasPermission('CreateEmployee')` and `hasPermission('DeleteEmployee')]`. This way, we won't be compelled to create multiple guard functions for each permission.
- Try switching DI in some of your existing Angular codebases to use the `inject` function.

Summary

- The `inject` function has been publicly available since Angular v14.
- The `inject` function will take any dependency token and return its provided value.
- The `inject` function can be used to inject dependencies and services into functions, as opposed to only classes.
- The `inject` function is now commonly preferred over the constructor DI.
- Guards/resolvers/interceptors have now switched to being fully functional.

- Legacy class-based guards/resolvers can still be used with helper functions.
- Legacy interceptors can still be used with the `withInterceptorsFromDi` function.
- Legacy class-based guards, etc. can be migrated to functional incrementally.
- The `inject` function supports dependency lookup modifiers like `host`, `optional`, `self`, and `skipSelf`.

New capabilities of
Angular building blocks

This chapter covers

- Supercharging input properties to make them required, transform their values, or bind them to routing parameters

- Using host directives to compose new directives from existing ones

- Switching to type-safe reactive forms to ensure the best interaction with TypeScript and improved developer experience, coupled with other improvements to forms

- Improving image load time by using the new `NgOptimizedImage` directive

- Using fetch-based backend instead of XHR in HTTP requests

Previously we covered some changes in Angular that could be deemed quite revolutionary—changes that affected entire applications and their structure and even changed the nature of some building blocks (like functional route guards, which we covered in the previous chapter). Now it is time we go a level deeper and familiarize

74

ourselves with some improvements that aim at reducing boilerplate and improving performance, as well as bettering our code quality on a more local magnitude.

For the purpose of learning, we will continue building our HRMS application. This time, we will cover the "Work" feature of this application and build several components and directives in it. This feature is related to the projects that a given organization using the app will want to add and view. The user will be able to view the list of projects, and their details, and see employees on days-off. In chapter 2, you were encouraged to create those pages and the respective routes as an exercise; if you have not done so, and still want to code along with the book, you can create only the pages mentioned in this chapter.

Now, as everything is set, let's embark on a new journey and see how we can improve reusable components that receive data through inputs.

4.1 Powerful inputs

When learning Angular, one of the very first lessons is about component interactions, mainly how a parent component can manipulate the behavior of its child. This plays well with the concept of having reusable components, where a component can receive data from parents and render its UI based on that data. This is, as is commonly known, achieved through inputs, special properties marked with the `@Input` decorator, which allow us to pass data from the parent component to a child in the template similar to HTML attributes. Such input properties have been used widely in the Angular developer community, resulting in the discovery of several approaches and some pitfalls that we might encounter. Starting from v15 and v16, the Angular framework acquired several new capabilities for input properties, and this is what we are going to discuss in this section.

4.1.1 Required inputs

To understand our use case, let us start with building pages related to the "Work" feature of our application. Namely, we want a page in which the user can browse all the projects that their company is working on. This "project list" page will contain small snippets of data about projects but without in-depth detail. As there are not *that* many projects running at any given time in a given company, it would be better from the user experience perspective to have them displayed as a list of cards or tiles, with the project logo and some superficial information about it.

However, before we start implementing this component, we can analyze our application at large and realize that such project tiles can possibly be used in multiple places and not only in the project list page. For instance, an employee might be enrolled in multiple projects, and on the employee details page we might want to display the tiles for the projects they are working on; alternatively, we might also want to show such tiles of subprojects of a given project on its own details page. This has the potential to become a reusable component, so let us start building it.

Such a component will display a basic UI and receive data about the project via an `@Input` property. We will go one step forward and make it only receive the "id" of the project it needs and then load its own data. In our case, this can result in many HTTP calls, but projects that use some state management solutions (either custom or existing ones like NgRx) can mitigate this problem, so we will leave it as is, as the way the component pulls this data from the server is not our concern in this chapter. Let us go on and build this component.

In the src/shared/components directory let us add a new file named project-card.component.ts and put the code in the following listing inside of it.

Listing 4.1   `ProjectCardComponent` **initial implementation**

```
@Component({
    selector: 'app-project-card',
    template: `
        <div *ngIf="project$ | async as project" class="card">
            <img [src]="project.image"/>
            <div class="card-body">
                <h3>{{ project.name }}</h3>
            </div>
        </div>
    `,
    imports: [NgIf, AsyncPipe],
    standalone: true,
})
export class ProjectCardComponent implements OnChanges {
    private readonly projectService = inject(ProjectService);

    @Input() projectId: number;
    project$: Observable<Project> | null = null;

    ngOnChanges(changes: SimpleChanges): void {
        if (changes['projectId']) {
            this.project$ = this.projectService.getProject(this.projectId);
        }
    }
}
```

As we can see, this is a fairly simple implementation. However, we can notice that Type-Script is complaining a bit. Notably, we get this warning/error: `Property 'projectId' has no initializer and is not definitely assigned in the construc tor.ts(2564)`. This is related to the fact that we do not have any default value for this `projectId` property (what would a default value for an `id` property even be?). If we continue our analysis, we will quickly understand that this *is* a problem—not a major one, but still one that can cause problems down the line. For instance, a future developer on this project may want to use this component but accidentally forget to set the value of the `projectId`, and run into problems at runtime. A former approach to handling such things was adding an `ngOnInit` method and checking if the input's value has been provided from the get-go:

```
ngOnInit() {
    if (!this.projectId) {
```

```
        throw new ReferenceError('Project ID is required!');
    }
}
```

This solves our problem to an extent; however, it is a bit "boilerplate-y" and may become harder to read if we have multiple such required properties. Also, it does not cover another concern that we might have: readability. We want future developers to open the component code and immediately see what inputs are required for the component to function in a way that does not require them to read lots of error-throwing code; also, we want them to see the missing input immediately in the editor, as soon as they make the mistake, not when they open the browser and see the custom runtime error. The error does add clarity as to what went wrong, but it still requires more steps and a bit more complex mental model.

To address this, Angular v16 added required input properties. From now on, we can make any inputs required, and the *compiler* will ensure those values are provided wherever necessary. As mentioned, it will be done in compile-time and will immediately show errors in the template where we use the component but omit a required input. The process of marking an input property as required is very straightforward. The following listing shows what our component code will look like.

Listing 4.2 Input marked as required in the `ProjectCardComponent`

```
export class ProjectCardComponent implements OnChanges {
    private readonly projectService = inject(ProjectService);

    @Input({required: true}) projectId!: number;          ◄─┐  Input marked with
                                                             │  {required: true}, so we
    project$: Observable<Project> | null = null;            │  can safely put ! in front of
                                                             │  the property name as we
    ngOnChanges(changes: SimpleChanges): void {             │  know it is guaranteed not
        if (changes['projectId']) {                         │  to be null or undefined
            this.project$ = this.projectService.getProject(this.projectId);
        }
    }
}
```

Now if we try to use this without providing the input's value, we will receive an error.

Listing 4.3 Input marked as required in the `ProjectListComponent`

```
@Component({
    selector: 'app-project-list',
    template: `
        <div class="row">
            <app-project-card *ngFor="let project of projects$ |
    async"></app-project-card>
        </div>
    `,
    standalone: true,
```

```
        imports: [NgFor, ProjectCardComponent, AsyncPipe]
})
export class ProjectListComponent {
    private readonly projectService = inject(ProjectService);
    projects$ = this.projectService.getProjects();
}
```

Immediately in our code editor, we will see an error with the following text: `Required input 'projectId' from component ProjectCardComponent must be specified.ngtsc`. The error message is quite clear: the `ProjectCardComponent` has way less code and focuses more on the business logic rather than implementation details and is more readable. Next, let us discuss another scenario related to the boilerplate caused by input properties.

4.1.2 Transforming input values

To get a grasp of what we want to achieve here, let us build another reusable component. Our HRMS application is an enterprise, business-heavy application. So it is not hard to imagine it has features related to document exchange. For instance, the recruitment section will need the capability of uploading a candidate's CV file, and the user will probably want to be able to upload their profile picture to be recognizable on the platform. For this purpose, we want a component that handles various things related to uploading a file so that we can reuse it in multiple places. This component will render a button that will allow the user to select a file, validate the selected file, and emit an event when files are selected so the parent component can handle the files as it sees fit. Let's make a quick implementation; again, in the src/shared/components folder, we will add a new file, file-upload.component.ts, with the functionality shown in the following listing.

Listing 4.4 `FileUploadComponent` with an "accept" input

```
@Component({
    selector: 'app-file-upload',
    template: `
        <div class="file-upload">
            <label for="upload">{{ label }}</label>
            <input type="file" id="upload" (change)="onFileSelected($event)"
    />
            <span class="error" *ngIf="errorMessage">        ⟵   Shows an error
                {{ errorMessage }}                                message using
                Only the following file types are permitted:     the "accept"
                <ul>                                             input property
                    <li *ngFor="let type of acceptArray">
                        {{ type }}
                    </li>        ⟵    Uses a property that
                </ul>                is different from
            </span>                  "accept" to get its
        </div>                       values as an array
    `,
    standalone: true,
```

```
    imports: [NgIf, NgFor],
})
export class FileUploadComponent {
    @Input({required: true}) label!: string;
    @Input() accept = '';
    @Output() selected = new EventEmitter<FileList>();
    errorMessage = '';

    get acceptArray() {
        return this.accept.split(',');
    }

    onFileSelected(event: any) {
        const files: FileList = event.target.files;
        this.errorMessage = Array.from(files)
            .every(f => this.acceptArray.includes(f.type))
            ? '' : 'Invalid file type';

        if (this.errorMessage === '') {
            this.selected.emit(files);
        }
    }
}
}
```

Getter to transform the "accept" string to an array to use for validation and displaying

Uses the array of accepted file types to validate files selected by the user

As we can see, we are doing quite an operation here to ensure we both receive the input value as a string *and* use it as an array, like the following example:

```
<app-file-upload label="Upload profile picture"
    accept="image/jpeg,image/png"></app-file-upload>
```

Of course, we could argue that we can just accept an array straightaway, but that would place an unnecessary strain on the parent component, which now will need to declare an array binding, and also restrict our component from being dynamic. For instance, we could receive a list of acceptable file types from the backend in some scenario, and it probably can come just as a string list, so the approach we adopted could work better in this case. However, it has some downsides: for instance, the readability will suffer, as the getter and the actual property that it transforms can be located far from each other in the code, and also this will trigger change detection multiple times as we are using the getter, which is essentially a function, in the template. We will talk more about such side effects in chapter 10; for now, it suffices to say this is not the most optimal approach. So how can we remedy this?

Thankfully, starting from Angular v16.1 we have the ability to define a transformer function on a component/directive input. This will apply a function of our choice to the received value and set that calculated value, which this function returns as the actual value of our input property. Let us refactor our component.

Listing 4.5 `FileUploadComponent` **with a transformed "accept" input**

```
export class FileUploadComponent {
    @Input({required: true}) label!: string;
```

```
@Input({
  transform: (value: string) => value.split(','),
})
accept: string[] = [];                                    ◄───── Applies a transforming
@Output() selected = new EventEmitter<FileList>();               function on an input
errorMessage = '';

onFileSelected(event: any) {
    const files: FileList = event.target.files;
    this.errorMessage = Array.from(files)
        .every(f => this.accept.includes(f.type))   ◄───── Uses the
        ? '' : 'Invalid file type';                        transformed
                                                           input directly
    if (this.errorMessage === '') {
        this.selected.emit(files);
    }
  }
}
```

This approach allows us to be way more flexible and to reap multiple benefits:

- There is no more getter function with a separate name; we use the property as declared.
- Reading the property definition itself gives us all the information necessary to understand its behavior.
- The transformation logic is applied every time the input property is changed, instead of the getter being triggered on each change detection cycle, resulting in better performance.
- Refactoring inputs gets easier: there is no need to redefine how they are passed from the parent components.

A lot of scenarios with transforming input properties involve casting a string to a number, or a string to a Boolean. For instance, when we define a numerical input but put it as a conventional attribute instead of an Angular binding (like `<some-component numberProperty="10"></some-component>`), we will see that Angular will read and pass on the number provided as a string (no matter what type we specified in the component's TypeScript file). Of course, we can use the transform option when defining an input and provide a function that does this type-casting properly. However, the Angular team predicted the popularity of these scenarios and added two built-in transformer functions specifically for those: `numberAttribute` and `booleanAttribute`. Now we can just import them and add to any inputs and the transformation will happen automatically:

```
@Input({transform: booleanAttribute}) booleanProperty = false;
@Input({transform: numberAttribute}) numberProperty = 0;
```

Next, we can freely use them in any template without binding unnecessarily:

```
<some-component numberProperty="12" booleanProperty="true"></some-component>
```

Let us now discuss how we can use inputs as means of getting data into the component other than what was passed from the templates. Let's see if we can simplify the logic of dealing with routing parameters and data using Angular inputs.

4.1.3 Binding routing parameters to input properties

When building user interfaces for showing data, we usually have a page that shows a list of items, like our `ProjectListComponent`, and we have a specific "details" page for each item, where we can comfortably show more data. This usually involves having a route parameter, like an id, which we can use to make the specific HTTP call. Let us build the `ProjectDetailsComponent` and see what challenges may arise and how we can use component inputs to overcome them.

We want our component to take the id of a particular project and make an HTTP call to retrieve the relevant data. Additionally, we want to display the list of subprojects, but there is a catch: the user can navigate to the subprojects, meaning they will navigate "back" to the same component but with a different id and, thus, different data. Of course, we do not want to reload the entire page: we want to just react to the id change and simply make the same HTTP call with the new id and then display the new data. Let us build this component using conventional tools Angular provides and then see how new input capabilities can help us simplify this component. Under the src/pages/work directory let's add a new file named project-details.component.ts, create a `Project DetailsComponent` inside it, and add it to the work.routes.ts file with a parameter:

```
{ path: 'projects/:id', component: ProjectDetailsComponent }
```

Next, let's write the actual implementation of the component.

Listing 4.6   Component using a routing parameter to load data

```
@Component({
  selector: 'app-project-details',
  template: `
    <div class="project-details">
      <h3>Project Details</h3>
      <div *ngIf="project$ | async as project">
        <span>Project Name: {{ project.name }}</span>
        <span>Project Description: {{ project.description }}</span>
        <span>Logo: {{ project.image }}</span>
        <div class="subprojects">
          <span>Subprojects:</span>
          <app-project-card                                       ⟵┐ Renders
            *ngFor="let subProjectId of project.subProjectIds"    ⟵┘ a list of
            [projectId]="subProjectId"                               subprojects
          >
          </app-project-card>
        </div>
      </div>
    </div>
  `,
  standalone: true,
```

```
    imports: [NgIf, NgFor, AsyncPipe, ProjectCardComponent],
})
export class ProjectDetailsComponent implements OnInit, OnDestroy {
    private readonly route = inject(ActivatedRoute);
    private readonly projectService = inject(ProjectService);
    project$: Observable<Project> | null = null;
    destroy$ = new Subject<void>();

    ngOnInit(): void {
        this.route.paramMap.pipe(
            takeUntil(this.destroy$),
        ).subscribe((params) => {
            this.project$ = this.projectService.getProject(
                +params.get('id')!,
            );
        });
    }

    ngOnDestroy(): void {
        this.destroy$.next();
    }
}
```

Subscribes to the id parameter change so we can load the new project's data

Actually loads the data

Unsubscribes from the router parameter stream when the component is removed from the UI

As we can see, this implementation is quite wordy and contains many implementation details that are not exactly related to the business logic (e.g., unsubscribing from the Observable). Another downside is that we just subscribed to the router parameter Observables but did not store the value; we would need another property for this if we want to use the id elsewhere in the TypeScript code. Additionally, we need to cast the parameter from a string (all route parameters are strings by default) to a number so we can pass it to the ProjectService for the HTTP call. Let's now see how Angular proposes to mitigate all these problems. To do this, let's visit the app.config.ts file once more and change how we register our routing:

```
provideRouter(routes, withComponentInputBinding()),
```

The withComponentInputBinding option became available in Angular v16, and it automatically passes the value of route parameters to the respective component if that component has an input property that has the same name as the parameter—for instance, when we previously added the ProjectDetailsComponent to our routing with a parameter :id. With this option, if we have an input property on ProjectDetailsComponent named id, Angular will automatically pass the value of the parameter to this property! This means we can cut a lot of boilerplate from our component code. The following listing shows how.

Listing 4.7   Component using inputs bound to routing parameters to load data

```
export class ProjectDetailsComponent implements OnChanges {
    @Input({transform: numberAttribute}) id!: number;
```

The input with the name "id" automatically receives the route path parameter and is transformed into a number in place

```
private readonly projectService = inject(ProjectService);
project$: Observable<Project> | null = null;

ngOnChanges(changes: SimpleChanges): void {
  if (changes['id']) {
    this.project$ = this.projectService.getProject(this.id);
  }
}
}
}
```

If the id has changed, just repeats the HTTP call with the new id

The advantages of this approach are pretty clear: we inject one fewer class and we have direct access to the `id` property if we need it somewhere else, no `Observables` and unsubscription logic, and less boilerplate code; the component is now only focused on the business logic. The following are several important things we need to know about component-routing input binding:

- The binding also works with resolved data and optional query parameters.
- If there is a naming clash (e.g., if a query parameter and a path parameter have the same name), Angular will resolve it by using the following precedence: first, it will match the *resolved data*, then the *path parameter*, and finally, if the first two did not match, the *query parameter*.
- The binding only works for routed components. If a component is rendered via the template of another one, rather than routing, the automatic binding will not work, and we will have to instead rely on other means of passing that information down (most commonly, just a "usual" input that gets the data from the template of the parent).
- It is now quickly becoming the suggested way to use this approach instead of `ActivatedRoute`.

Next, let us see how input properties can work with components created programmatically, rather than from the template.

4.1.4 Inputs for dynamic components

Sometimes we want to create components dynamically, rather than just spelling them out in the template. We already encountered such a scenario in section 2.4.5, when we lazy-loaded and then dynamically opened a confirmation popup. There are many other scenarios—for example, rendering child components from directives when dealing with structural directives. We haven't discussed how we can pass inputs to those dynamic components, as we do not invoke that component in a template to spell out a binding.

Let us examine the following scenario: we are building a loader component, which receives some content and, if an input property indicates so, displays a custom spinning loader over it to signal to users that they should wait. Let's first implement this component in a new src/app/shared/components/loader.component.ts file.

Listing 4.8 Loader component with an input and projected content

```
@Component({
  selector: 'app-loader',
```

```
template: `
  <div class="loading-container">
    <ng-content></ng-content>                    ◁──┐ Where the child's
    <div *ngIf="loading" class="blocker">           └ content will be projected
      spinner          ◁──┐ Some spinner to
    </div>                └ display when necessary
  </div>`,
standalone: true,
styles: [
  `                      ◁──┐ css to display this content over
  .loading-container {      └ everything else in the template
    position: relative;
  }
  .blocker {
    background-color: black;
    position: absolute;
    top: 0;
    z-index: 9999;
    width: 100%;
    height: 100%;
    opacity: 0.4;
  }
  `,
],
imports: [NgIf],
})
export class LoaderComponent {        ┐ The actual
  @Input() loading = false;     ◁────┘ input
}
```

This is not a very complicated component, but using it many times in the same template is quite tedious, especially if loaders are nested. For instance, in the `Project DetailComponent` we could have a loader for the entire page, then one on the list of subprojects, one in parallel to it on a list of employees, and so on, resulting in lots of nested code:

```
<app-loader [loading]="loading">
  <div class="p-grid">
    <div class="p-col-12">
      <p>Some content</p>
    </div>
    <app-loader [loading]="otherLoading">
      <div class="p-col-12">
        <p>Some other content</p>
        <app-loader [loading]="evenMoreLoading">
          <div class="p-col-12">
            <p>Even more content</p>
          </div>
        </app-loader>
      </div>
    </app-loader>
  </div>
</app-loader>
```

This is not very beautiful. However, we can remedy this by writing a structural directive that will dynamically create the `LoaderComponent` and pass the input value to it, wrapping its template inside it. Let's create a new file named loader.directive.ts in the src/app/shared/directives folder and implement this directive, so we can see it in action and familiarize ourselves with the way we can pass the component's input dynamically.

Listing 4.9   Directive that dynamically renders projected content

```
@Directive({                                           Reference to the
  selector: '[loading]',                       template the structural
  standalone: true,                              directive is applied to
})
export class LoaderDirective implements OnInit, OnChanges {
  private readonly templateRef = inject(TemplateRef);         ViewContainerRef
  private readonly vcRef = inject(ViewContainerRef);          that will create and
  @Input() loading = false;                                   render the dynamic
  templateView: EmbeddedViewRef<any>;                         component
  loaderRef: ComponentRef<LoaderComponent>;        Reference to our dynamically
                                                   created LoaderComponent
  ngOnInit() {
    this.templateView = this.templateRef.createEmbeddedView({});
    this.loaderRef = this.vcRef.createComponent(
      LoaderComponent,                     Creates the component
      {
        injector: this.vcRef.injector,              Passes the template
        projectableNodes: [this.templateView.rootNodes],  as content to the
      },                                                  dynamically created
    );                                                    LoaderComponent

    this.loaderRef.setInput('loading', this.loading);   The most important
  }                                                     part: passing the input
                                                        property "loading" to
  ngOnChanges() {                                       the LoaderComponent
    this.loaderRef?.setInput('loading', this.loading);
  }
}
```

Now we can use this directive if we want to apply dynamic loading anywhere instead of nesting the original component:

```
<p *loading="isSomeContentLoading">
    Some content
    <span *loading="isOtherLoading">
        Some other content
    </span>
    <p *loading="isEvenMoreLoading">
        Even more content
    </p>
</p>
```

This reduces the complexity of the template significantly and improves readability. Now one might ask: why don't we just write `this.loaderRef.instance.loading = this.isContentLoading;`? Well, in this manner, we would set the property of the instance class, but it won't immediately trigger a change detection run and also will work outside of the component life cycle, meaning if, for instance, the `LoaderComponent` implemented the `ngOnChanges` method, it would not have been called. The `setInput` method mitigates this problem and is a powerful tool when dealing with dynamic components.

Finally, let us talk about passing inputs to dynamic components in the template. Let's review a scenario in the "recruitment" feature: we have a list of candidates for hiring that the user can see and then navigate to the details page of a given candidate. On that page, they can see the general information about the candidate, their CV, and so on. The candidate has a status, which can be "Pending CV review," "Pending interview," "Pending evaluation," "Rejected," or "Waiting for onboarding." For each of these scenarios, under the candidate's general information, we can see a different section; for instance, for "Pending CV review," we will see an `EvaluateCVComponent` where we can write a description and approve or reject for an interview, for "Pending Interview" we can see an `InterviewPreparationComponent` where we can add questions we want to ask during the interview, for "Rejected" we can see a `RejectionLetter` component where we can detail reasons for rejection, and so on.

Also, in some cases, we might not only depend on the status of the candidate but some other information; for example, in the case of an "Approved" status we might also want to check if the candidate also accepted the company's offer and only then show the `OnboardingPreparationComponent` and so on. This logic might be a bit too complicated for a simple `*ngSwitch` in the template, so we prefer to use the `*ngComponentOutlet` directive and dynamically choose the component we want in the TypeScript code of the `CandidateDetailsComponent`. Let's see how that works in action.

Listing 4.10   **Dynamic component via** `NgComponentOutlet`

```
@Component({
  selector: 'app-candidate-details',
  template: `
    <div class="candidate-details">
      <div>
        <h2>{{ candidate.firstName }} {{ candidate.lastName }}</h2>
        <p>Email: {{ candidate.email }}</p>
        <p>{{ candidate.position }}</p>
      </div>
      <ng-container *ngComponentOutlet="actionsSection">
      </ng-container>          ◄──
    </div>                          Dynamically loads a component
  `,                               using NgComponentOutlet
  standalone: true,
  imports: [NgComponentOutlet],
})                                           Candidate data
export class CandidateDetailsComponent implements OnChanges {   is received
  @Input() candidate!: Candidate;      ◄──   from a resolver
  actionsSection: Type<any> | null = null;   ◄──┐ via an input.

  ngOnChanges(changes: SimpleChanges): void {       The reference to the component
                                                    we will choose to render
```

```
    if (changes['candidate']) {
      this.actionsSection =
        this.selectActionsComponent();      ◁──┤ When the candidate
    }                                             data arrives, chooses the
  }                                               component to render

  private selectActionsComponent(): Type<any> {  ◁──┤ Actual logic of
    switch (this.candidate.status) {                  determining which
      case 'CV evaluation':                           component to render
        return CvEvaluationComponent;
      case 'Interview preparation':
        return InterviewPreparationComponent;
      case 'Interview Feedback':
        return InterviewFeedbackComponent;
      case 'Rejected':
        return RejectionLetterComponent;
      case 'Approved':
        return this.candidate.offerAccepted
          ? OnboardingPreparationComponent
          : CandidateFinalizationComponent;
      default:
        throw new Error(`Unknown candidate status:
      ${this.candidate.status}`);
    }
  }
}
```

As we can see, this is something we already did in chapter 2. However, there is a new concern: how will this component know which candidate they are working with? We need a way to send the reference to it to the child component, but as we rendered it dynamically, without explicitly calling them in the template, it seems like this is impossible! However, from Angular v16.2, there is a new way of passing inputs to components dynamically rendered using *ngComponentOutlet. Let's see how we can amend this; in our case, all of the components that can be rendered receive an input called candidateId. We can do this by passing a record as a second parameter for the *ngComponentOutlet directive named inputs:

```
<ng-container *ngComponentOutlet="actionsSection; inputs: {candidateId:
    candidate.id}"></ng-container>
```

Using this, we can easily pass any data we need from parent to child, even if the component is rendered dynamically. Note that right now the implementation is *not* type-safe, so it fully relies on spelling the inputs out correctly, but other than that, we see no downsides and a new, improved way of intercomponent communication.

We have seen component inputs grow to become more robust and cover many more cases and components become simpler and more powerful than ever because of this. Now it is time to address the second most important building block in Angular, the directives, and see how they improved and what new capabilities they have acquired.

4.2   Host directives

New adopters of Angular often hear a phrase like this: "A component is a directive that has a template." If we take this as a given (which it is, to an extent), we can say the converse is also true to an extent: "A directive is a component without a template." This makes perfect sense, as directives are intended to work with individual DOM nodes and do not require a template, so the absence of the template does not exactly sound like a problem. However, if we analyze how we write components and try to apply the same to directives, we will see that the absence of the template in the case of directives poses a certain limitation.

With components, we can use the template to invoke other components, meaning we can compose simpler components into larger ones. With directives, we can add a piece of template wherever the directive was called or manipulate the DOM in the case of structural directives, but if we want to add some other directives when our directive is called, we run out of options. Sometimes several directives are often used together, and it makes perfect sense to us to be able to create a parent directive that will call the other ones, instead of constantly spelling them out, or if we have a directive that uses the functionality of another directive while adding some of its own; but again, there was no real and official way of doing this.

The good news is, starting from Angular v15, a new concept of host directives has been added to the framework that allows us to add directives to another directive when the latter is applied. Let us see it in action.

4.2.1   Extending existing directives

Let us consider the following scenario: on many pages, we show links to individual employees' details page. We want to provide lots of information in a meaningful way. So we think it would be nice if the user knows beforehand if the employee is currently available or is, say, on vacation. Maybe links to employees that are not available are grayed out, indicating we probably should not bother them. Of course, we can write a global CSS class, say, `.not-available`, which will gray out the text, and use the `ngClass` directive to switch it on and off depending on the employee's availability status.

This sounds good, but this solution is not very scalable. First, we would need to find all links (`<a>` tags with a `[routerLink]`) in our applications that point to the employee details page, then pull the employee data in the parent component, and finally apply the `ngClass` directive to it with the relevant class. This means lots of manual work, but even worse, we would need to keep doing this any time we put a link to an employee's page somewhere. This has the potential for lots of problems down the line. To avoid this, we will use the host directives feature to automatically add the `ngClass` directive and pass the inputs to it. Let us author this new directive in the src/app/shared/directives/employee-not-available.directive.ts file and see how it works.

Listing 4.11 Using a host directive to add an `NgClass` directive on some RouterLinks

```
@Directive({
    selector: 'a[routerLink]',          ←──  Applies the directive to all the <a>
    hostDirectives: [NgClass],               elements that have a routerLink
    standalone: true,                   ←──  Adds NgClass as a host directive to
})                                           the EmployeeNotAvailableDirective
export class EmployeeNotAvailableDirective implements AfterViewInit {
    private readonly ngClassRef = inject(NgClass);
    private readonly routerLinkRef = inject(RouterLink);      ←─┐
    private readonly employeeService = inject(EmployeeService);│
                                                               │
    ngAfterViewInit() {                       Obtains references to the NgClass
        if (                                      and RouterLink directives
          this.routerLinkRef
            .href!.startsWith('/employees/details')
        ) {                                  ←──┐  Checks if the link points to
            const employeeId = this.routerLinkRef  the employee details page
              .urlTree?.root.children['primary']
                ?.segments.at(-1)?.path;     ←──┐  Gets the id of the employee
                                                 │  from the route path
            if (employeeId) {

    this.employeeService.getEmployee(+employeeId).subscribe(employee => {
                    this.ngClassRef.ngClass = {
                      'not-available': !employee.isAvailable
                    };                ←──┐
                });                       │  Adds or removes the class based
            }                             │  on the employee's status
        }
    }
}
```

As seen here, it becomes very simple to combine directives and use them in other directives. Next, let's see how we can combine multiple and automatically pass inputs to it.

4.2.2 Using multiple directives and adding inputs

Let's say we have a tooltip directive that adds a specific message to an element that will be shown on hover. Let's improve our directive by adding this directive and showing a default message saying "Employee is not available." This should not be a problem with the knowledge we already have:

```
hostDirectives: [NgClass, TooltipDirective],
```

Then what is left is to assign the tooltip value:

```
this.tooltipRef.tooltip = employee.isAvailable ? '' : 'Employee is not
    available';
```

This solves our problem, but what if we want to be able to provide a way for the user to show a custom tooltip in certain scenarios, instead of "Employee is not available"?

Of course, we could declare an optional tooltip input on our `EmployeeNotAvailable Directive` and then implement an `ngOnChanges` method on it and pass the input down the line using the `tooltipRef`. This approach, however, is very tedious and in the case of multiple inputs will quickly become unmanageable. But what if we could just tell Angular to pass the input from the `EmployeeNotAvailableDirective` directly to the `TooltipDirective`? It turns out there is a special syntax to achieve precisely that:

```
hostDirectives: [NgClass, {directive: TooltipDirective, inputs:
    ['tooltip']}],
```

Instead of manually doing all the work of passing the data through, we can just declare that we are using the input from the `TooltipDirective`, and Angular will act as if `EmployeeNotAvailableDirective` itself has that input and will pass the value to `TooltipDirective` automatically. Also, notice that, despite the "magic strings," this is safe and Angular will not allow using properties that do not exist on the `Tooltip- Directive` or are not marked as inputs. The same approach can be used to automatically pass directive outputs the opposite way. Now let us go a level deeper and learn what caveats to expect when dealing with host directives.

4.2.3 *Things to know when using host directives*

As we have seen, host directives are pretty simple, but there are several things we need to consider when using them. Let's examine those next.

USAGE SPECIFICS

Host directives can be used only when the hosted directives in question are standalone. The child directives themselves need to be declared as standalone and cannot be a part of a `NgModule`. The directive that hosts, however, does not have the same constraint and can be either standalone or not. This is a big limitation if we work with applications that have not yet transitioned to standalone. Currently, there is no way to mitigate this other than to convert the directives to standalone.

Another thing to keep in mind is that we can host directives not only on other directives but also on components (which also need to be standalone). Any component will be able to have a `hostDirectives` option in its metadata. In case of adding host directives to a component, the directives will be automatically applied to the host element of the components, as follows:

```
<my-component hostDirective1 hostDirective2></my-component>
```

Note that this is just a visualization; in reality, Angular does not explicitly put the directive name and just executes the functionality of it, ignoring the selectors of the host directives. Everything else will work in the same fashion as with applying host directives to another directive.

HIERARCHY AND EXECUTION ORDER

To understand how this whole thing functions, we first need to keep in mind that host directives are applied during *compile-time*, not run-time, meaning they are static and cannot be applied dynamically later on, posing another limitation. In our example, when the `EmployeeNotAvailableDirective` uses `NgClass`, Angular first creates the instance of the host directives like `NgClass`, then the `EmployeeNotAvailableDirective`; then it passes the inputs to hosted directives and the `EmployeeNotAvailableDirective` receives its inputs and host bindings. This order ensures that parent components and directives can override the host directive's inputs and host bindings.

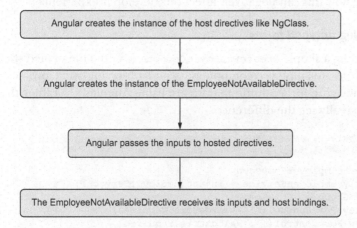

Figure 4.1 Steps Angular undertakes when applying a host directive

As we have seen, we are able to inject references to the host directives. In another dependency injection-related concern, if both the component/directive that has host directives and the host directives themselves provide the same token, the *former* will take precedence, meaning parent providers are where the children will look for their dependencies initially.

PERFORMANCE CONCERNS

We should be careful with host directives, especially when using them in directives that can match a lot of elements in our DOM tree. As we saw, every time the directive is matched, instances for all host directives are created, which can cause memory leaks in specific scenarios. For instance, if we apply the `EmployeeNotAvailableDirective` to a large table of employees, we could potentially see hundreds of `Tooltip` and `NgClass` directives, which can affect performance. Extra care should be applied when dealing with directives that have multiple host directives and those that have many RxJS subscriptions. Remember to unsubscribe properly and to not subscribe to sources that emit lots of values frequently. Use the memory profiler tool in the developer console to make sure there are no memory problems.

Host directives are a powerful tool, and now we are equipped to use them in our applications. Let's pivot back to components for now and see what improvement Angular has in store for those who use reactive forms.

4.3   *Type-safe reactive forms*

Reactive forms have always been one of the most popular features of Angular. Because they are easy to set up, have built-in validations, and are extensible and composable, they have been a choice for multitudes of Angular developers worldwide. They, however, are not without their own problems, including the fact that they are not type-safe. Let's first see how this can negatively affect our developer experience.

4.3.1   *Downsides of using untyped forms*

Let's start by building a simple `CreateEmployeeComponent` in the file named src/app/ pages/employees/create-employee.component.ts and observing what problems will arise. Let us also imagine for a minute that we are using Angular v13 rather than the current version to really see the difference.

Listing 4.12   Using an untyped reactive form

```
export class CreateEmployeeComponent {
  private readonly employeeService = inject(EmployeeService);
  form = new FormGroup({
    firstName: new FormControl('', Validators.required),
    lastName: new FormControl('', Validators.required),
    emali: new FormControl('', [Validators.required, Validators.email]),    ◁────
    position: new FormControl('', Validators.required),
    level: new FormControl('', Validators.required),            Notice we intentionally
  });                                                                 made a typo.

  submit() {
    if (this.form.valid) {
      const employee = this.form.value;
      this.employeeService.createEmployee(employee);
    }
  }

}
```

With Angular prior to version 14, when typed forms were introduced, the `this.form` `.value` would be typed as `any`, meaning even with the typo we could pass the value and the service method will accept it, make the call, and get a (possibly quite cryptic) error from the backend, resulting in time spent trying to debug this. Furthermore, accessing form control properties in the template is also both boilerplate-ish and time-consuming as we get no IDE autocomplete:

```
form.controls['email']
```

This becomes more tedious if we have nested forms. For example, if we create the `AddProjectComponent`, in it our form will have a `FormArray` of subprojects, which in turn are `FormGroups`, meaning accessing them will become something like the following:

```
form.controls['subprojects'].at(i).controls['name']
To amend this, Angular introduced the get method, which allows us to express
    these forms of control access in the following way:
form.get('subprojects.' + i + '.name')
```

This solves the problem, but it still looks a bit ugly and relies on magic strings again. Moreover, as `this.form.value` returns `any`, it also overlooks the fact that, even with validations, we cannot guarantee that all fields are filled in—a fact that developers often overlook, resulting in more hard-to-find bugs. So what's the solution?

4.3.2   Introducing type-safe forms

If we actually wrote the component in listing 4.12 in our HRMS application, we would immediately notice many errors. This is because, from Angular v14, reactive forms infer the type of the value they have, meaning the form controls we declared when creating our forms get represented as an actual TypeScript type, rather than any, with all the fields like name, position, and so on in place. For instance, in this very example, if we get back to the reality of Angular v16+, we will immediately get an error:

```
Argument of type 'Partial<{ firstName: string | null; lastName: string |
null; emali: string | null; position: string | null; level: string | null;
}>' is not assignable to parameter of type 'Employee'.
  Type 'Partial<{ firstName: string | null; lastName: string | null; emali:
string | null; position: string | null; level: string | null; }>' is
missing the following properties from type 'Employee': id, email,
isAvailable
```

While this seems somewhat confusing, in reality this error just notifies us that the reactive form's value is only `Partial`, meaning TypeScript thinks that any of the fields could possibly be absent. This makes sense because, even with validations, there is no clear guarantee that the values will be there (we could theoretically access the form's value *before* the user fills in the necessary data). However, because we already checked the form's validity in the `if` statement and all the fields have "required" validators, we can safely assume that all fields are present and just do the following:

```
submit() {
    if (this.form.valid) {
        const employee = this.form.value as Employee;
        this.employeeService.createEmployee(employee);
    }
}
```

We can type-cast the form's value because we are sure it complies with the "Employee" type.

Now we have a nice working thing, but what about the typo? We can type-cast to Employee, and TypeScript will just go with it, but the problem is still there! It turns out that when we try to use the fields in the template, we will get a nice error message:

```
<input type="text" placeholder="Email" [formControl]="form.controls.email" />
```

This code, where we correctly used the "email" name without a typo, will immediately throw an error:

```
Property 'email' does not exist on type '{ firstName: FormControl<string |
null>; lastName: FormControl<string | null>; emali: FormControl<string |
null>; position: FormControl<string | null>; level: FormControl<...>; }'. Did
you mean 'emali'?
```

This allows us to quickly discover the typo and fix it. Another benefit is we do not have to use index notation (`form.controls['email']`) to access controls but rather the dot notation, which is arguably somewhat more readable. Also, if we had nested form controls, like the subprojects we mentioned, we can now just access them directly, without using the `form.get` method: `form.controls.subprojects.at(i).controls.name`. These are all very important developer experience improvements, but let's also consider that adding TypeScript into the equation usually means more work down the line. Let's see how it affects us here.

4.3.3 Common pitfalls when working with type-safe forms

If we pay closer attention, we will notice that we have already encountered one of the complications—mainly that FormGroup by default returns a partial of the type that our form has. In general, we will see that all the problems that arise here are in some way or other connected to having null-ish values. For example, if we use the FormBuilder utility to create our FormGroups, it will also have forms with values that are nullable. If we refactor our code to use FormBuilder, we will have the option to create a nonnullable form:

```
private readonly formBuilder = inject(FormBuilder);
form = this.formBuilder.nonNullable.group({
  firstName: new FormControl('', Validators.required),
  lastName: new FormControl('', Validators.required),
  email: new FormControl('', [Validators.required, Validators.email]),
  position: new FormControl('', Validators.required),
  level: new FormControl('', Validators.required),
});
```

However, the name nonNullable is a bit misleading. The problem is that the nonnullable FormBuilder only deals with null-ish values—for instance, when calling `form.reset()`, all values can become null. The nonnullable does not in any way affect the possibility of having undefined as a value, which should also be checked. However, using the nonNullable FormBuilder is a good practice for all forms that we definitely know cannot contain null values.

Another kind of trap can be the ability to provide a generic type for the form. We can do this as follows, instead of relying on type inference:

```
type EmployeeForm = {
  firstName: FormControl<string>,
  lastName: FormControl<string>,
  email: FormControl<string>,
  position: FormControl<string>,
  level: FormControl<string>,
}

form = new FormGroup<EmployeeForm>({
  firstName: new FormControl('', {nonNullable: true, validators:
    [Validators.required]}),
  lastName: new FormControl('', {nonNullable: true, validators:
    [Validators.required]}),
  email: new FormControl('', {nonNullable: true, validators:
    [Validators.required, Validators.email]}),
  position: new FormControl('', {nonNullable: true, validators:
    [Validators.required]}),
  level: new FormControl('', {nonNullable: true, validators:
    [Validators.required]}),
});
```

This is probably the best way to approach type-safe forms, but it introduces the possibility of forgetting to set the {nonNullable: true} option and possibly then still sending a null-ish value to the server, for instance.

However, despite the mentioned pitfalls, type-safe forms represent a superior way of dealing with forms in general, and if we are using reactive forms (rather than template-driven ones), we should consider switching to the type-safe alternative. Let's see how it can be done.

4.3.4 Migrating to type-safe forms

If we use Angular v13 or prior and use the CLI upgrade command, it will automatically switch our FormGroups to UntypedFormGroups and UntypedFormControls. Those are special classes that work the same way the usual FormGroup and FormControl classes did before switching to type-safety. Using those classes will produce no type-related errors, meaning our codebase will continue functioning the same way it did previously. From this point, we should manually update our forms one by one to become type-safe. This is mostly mechanical work but will produce no breaking problems in our code itself. Rather, every time we switch a form, we can run the build and fix type errors (if they arise, which is quite possible).

While we are on the topic of reactive forms, let's also address one small but effective addition to forms in Angular.

4.3.5 Form events

If you have worked with forms in the past, you know that any reactive FormControl provides several observables that emit notifications about the changing state of the form. For instance, `valueChanges` emits when the value of the form changes (either by user input or programmatically), and `statusChanges` emits when the validity of the form control changes (for instance, it becomes valid as the user types in a required field). However, there was no way of running some general side effects on *any* event. For example, we might want to notify a parent component about the change of the form (this is especially useful if we are implementing the `ControlValueAccessor` interface to build a custom form control component), and to do this, we might be forced to do some magic with RxJS:

```
merge(this.form.valueChanges, this.form.statusChanges).subscribe(() => {
  // perform some logic here
});
```

However, in v18, a new property called `events` has been added to all `FormControls` (including `FormGroup` and `FormArray`). Essentially, `events` is an combined observable that emits every time the control changes its value, validity, or dirty status. We can subscribe to it in the same way we did with distinct event observables:

```
this.form.events.subscribe(() => {
  // perform some logic here
});
```

If we want to, we can also differentiate between different events using the `instanceof` operator:

```
this.form.events.subscribe((event) => {
  if (event instanceof StatusChangeEvent) {
    // perform logic here
  }
});
```

While the change itself is small, it can be very impactful for highly dynamic applications, where multiple events are used to propagate data through the app. It is also worth noting that previously available observables are still available and will continue working in the same way as always, so this change is nonbreaking.

Now that we've covered a lot of developer experience improvements, let's take a slight detour and discuss what runtime performance improvements Angular has in store for us.

4.4   NgOptimizedImage

Putting images on web pages is one of the first exciting things we developers learn to do. In Angular, so far, it always came down to just putting an `<img/>` tag somewhere in our template. However, with large applications that serve thousands of people with huge pages, it becomes very important to improve loading time. One useful metric here is the Largest Contentful Paint (LCP), which is the render time of the largest image or text block visible within the viewport (visible part of the user's screen), starting from when the page began loading.

This metric allows us to understand when the user first sees a meaningful visual representation on the page and is a better metric than, say, checking for the DOM tree to be loaded, because the DOM tree might contain lots of images, which will need to be loaded next for the user to see the actual contents. Another concern is the responsiveness and the correct representation of images; for instance, we do not want them to appear distorted, which usually happens when the width and height of images we set do not correspond to the actual image's aspect ratio. Let's see how Angular helps us address those things.

4.4.1 Adding lazy loading and remembering to set width/height

We will go back to the `EmployeeListComponent` we created in chapter 2 and add user profile pictures to the table next to users' full names. We will do so using the new `NgOptimizedImage` directive Angular provides from v15, which will help us answer all the questions we raised in this section. It is worth mentioning that this new directive has also been backported to some earlier versions and is available even if we use Angular v13. The directive is standalone, so we pretty much just need to add it to the `imports` array of the components and use it as shown in the following listing.

Listing 4.13 Using the `NgOptimizedDirective`

```
<tr *ngFor="let employee of employees$ | async">
  <td>
    <img
    [ngSrc]="employee.profilePicture"          Uses ngSrc instead of src to
                                               utilize the NgOptimizedDirective
    width="20" height="20"/>
    <a [routerLink]="['/employees/details', employee.id]">   This directive
      {{ employee.firstName }} {{ employee.lastName }}       requires us to
    </a>                                                      provide width and
  </td>                                                       height for the image.
</tr>
```

If we now open the component in the browser and look at the resulting HTML in the developer console, we will see the following:

```
<img width="20" height="20" loading="lazy" fetchpriority="auto" src="path-to-
    profile-picture">
```

Note that now all the images are marked with `loading="lazy"` and `fetchpriority="auto"`. Lazy loading essentially means what we might think it means: the image won't be loaded unless the user navigates (using scrolling or in some cases opening a closed element) in a way that brings it to the viewport. `fetchpriority` indicates how "fast" the image should load when compared to the other images on the page. We can set this priority to be high or low, while auto, the default setting, means the browser itself will decide which images to load first. These two attributes are very important for improving the performance of the page, especially the LCP metric.

4.4.2 Prioritizing image loading

Now let's examine the next use case: as the user now has a profile picture, it will make sense to also put it in the user's details page, to which we can navigate from the `EmployeeListComponent`. Again, we are going to use the `NgOptimizedImage` directive, but this time, we have an important concern: there will be multiple images on the page (for instance, all the logos of all the projects the user is enrolled in) and the one main profile picture. We want the profile picture to load first, to show the users exactly what the page is about. Thankfully, now we can achieve this in a very simple fashion:

```
<img [ngSrc]="employee.profilePicture" width="50" height="50"
    [alt]="employee.firstName" priority />
```

The priority input property will tell the `NgOptimizedImage` to put a high `fetchpriority` on this particular image, resulting in fast loading time and an improved LCP metric. While we can possibly put the priority property on multiple images on one page, doing so is discouraged, as it would result in performance tanking again. Instead, we should try to determine which image(s) constitute our LCP and focus on improving that specifically. For better dynamics, we do not even need to set the priority on "low" for the `ProjectCardComponent`, so that those images definitely do not interfere with LCP, because having one prioritized image will already tell the browser how to determine which to load first. If we want those images to be loaded immediately (even when not in the viewport), we can just set the loading input:

```
<img [ngSrc]="project.image" width="100" height="100" loading="eager"/>
```

This way, the default lazy setting will be overridden. Now let's see how we can further optimize and customize the way our images are loaded.

4.4.3 Srcsets and image loaders

Sometimes we want the websites we build to be better accessible on mobile devices. For instance, with the HRMS tool, we want employees to be able to see the application in a responsive way when they open it on mobile phones, without the need for downloading an additional dedicated app. While CSS helps us accomplish most of this, images often stand in our way. On large pages, some images may look fine, but when switching to mobile, they might distort, or only a (wrong) part of it may become visible.

A common practice to combat this problem is having multiple versions of the same image, each fitting a specific viewport size, and letting the browser choose a version that best fits the current viewport size. For instance, in the `ProjectDetailsComponent`, we might want to display a large cover photo of the project with the logo and additional information and for smaller screens, only the logo. This can be done via the `srcset` and `sizes` attributes, but with `NgOptimizedDirective` we can just put the sizes we prefer and it will generate the `srcset` automatically for us:

```
<img [ngSrc]="project.image" width="100" height="100" loading="eager"
    sizes="100vw, 50vw"/>
```

Content delivery networks (CDNs) have also become very popular; they both provide faster loading times and offer various improvements for better page responsiveness, in addition to other advantages. Such CDNs can accept some parameters to determine what transformations to apply to an image; for instance, an image URL might look like "some-cdn.com/https://other-site.com/image.jpg/quality=low," where the CDN takes a picture from elsewhere, makes it low quality for a slower connection, and returns it to our application that requested it.

Several other image parameters can be sent via the query params, and because most popular CDNs have specific API contracts for these parameters, Angular now provides built-in loaders for four of them. To use a custom CDN, we first need to add a preconnect link into our application HTML's head. We can do this with just one line of code:

```
<link rel="preconnect" href="https://my.cdn.origin" />
```

This will ensure that the LCP image will load as fast as possible, due to the connection being established in the early stages of loading the page. If we do not set this, the NgOptimizedImage directive will show a warning pushing us to provide the preconnect link. Next, we need to provide the loader in our application's app.config.ts file; for example, we can add the built-in Imgix loader with the base URL of our own:

```
providers: [
    provideImgixLoader('https://my.base.url/'),
],
```

By default, Angular provides built-in CDN loaders:

- Cloudflare Image Resizing
- Cloudinary
- ImageKit
- Imgix

All of these loaders will transform attributes of our images (like width, height, and so on) into a URL that has the previously mentioned query params to then load the image from the respective CDN. However, if we use none of the built-in CDNs, and instead rely on another one, we can provide a custom loader manually:

```
providers: [
    {
    provide: IMAGE_LOADER,
    useValue: (config: ImageLoaderConfig) => {
      return `https://another-
    cdn.com/images?src=${config.src}&width=${config.width}`;
    },
  },
],
```

The `ImageConfig` interface will contain the width and src of the image and also an additional `loaderParams` property that can have any keys from the `img` tag that uses this loader, which might be specific for our CDN.

Finally, let us talk about several other, relatively minor but still very useful improvements in the latest versions of Angular.

4.5   Other improvements

Apart from the major, revolutionary changes (some of which we have already discussed), the Angular team also added a couple of smaller tweaks that might help simplify our development life. Let's now briefly discuss those minor changes.

4.5.1   Self-closing component tags

As opposed to other popular frameworks like React, in Angular templates to invoke other components we needed to provide both opening *and* closing tags, even if the component did not have any projected content, resulting in lots of unnecessary code. A typical template could look like the following:

```
<some-component></some-component>
<another-component></another-component>
<yet-another-component></yet-another-component>
```

With multiple components in the same template, this could quickly get out of hand. However, from Angular v15, the framework allows us to have self-closing component tags (if the component has no projected content). The same template will look simpler now:

```
<some-component/>
<another-component/>
<yet-another-component/>
```

The method of adding content to be projected into a component remains the same.

4.5.2   Fetch-based HttpClient

One of the most well-known tools Angular provides, the `HttpClient` service, has previously utilized the old `XMLHttpRequest` API to make HTTP calls. This caused problems when running Angular in NodeJS environments (like server-side rendering in an Express app with Angular Universal), as NodeJS does not have an implementation of `XMLHttpRequest` and instead uses `fetch` starting from Node v18. Angular used a special polyfill for it, but the polyfill had some undesirable side effects, and also it would be way better to use the latest native implementation. Now we can opt-in to use fetch under the hood by a single line of code in app.config.ts:

```
provideHttpClient(withFetch())
```

Note that this does *not* in any way change how we use the `HttpClient`; all the methods continue to work in the same fashion as previously. However, if we ran into problems with server-side rendering due to the polyfill, we can now forget about those problems using this approach.

4.5.3 *Support for default export components in routing*

When lazy loading components, we usually import the component's file dynamically and use a callback to extract the component itself and provide it to `loadComponent`, as we have done in chapter 2. Nowadays it can be simplified by making the component's class its files default export and then just dynamically importing only the file itself. For instance, here we have some component that is a default export in a file named some.component.ts:

```
@Component({
  selector: 'app-some',
  standalone: true,
  templateUrl: 'some.component.html',
})
export default class SomeComponent {}
```

We can now simplify its lazy loading:

```
const routes = [
  {path: 'some', loadComponent: () => import('some.component')},
];
```

While this is a small change, and it is sometimes debated whether default exports are preferable in general, the ability to do this is a minor improvement.

4.5.4 *Improved error messages*

Error messages have long been a pain point for Angular developers. Because Angular runs in the context of zone.js, error messages have very messy stack traces, showing different callbacks from the Zone context and making it hard to understand which function called the other. A typical error message in older versions of Angular looked something like the following:

```
ERROR Error: Uncaught (in promise): Error Error

at app.component.ts:18:11 at Generator.next (<anonymous>)
at asyncGeneratorStep (asyncToGenerator.js:3:1)
at next (asyncToGenerator.js:25:1)
at _ZoneDelegate.invoke (zone.js:372:26)
at Object.onInvoke (core.mjs:26378:33)
at ZoneDelegate.invoke (zone.js:371:52)
at Zone.run (zone.js:134:43) at zone.js:1275:36
at _ZoneDelegate.invokeTask (zone.js:406:31)
at resolvePromise (zone.js:1211:31)
at zone.js:1118:17
at zone.js:1134:33
```

As we can see, these stack traces are not very informative, and they are shrouded by multiple zone-related callbacks. However, from Angular v15, these stack traces have been improved and filtered, to deliver the best developer experience, and now look like the following:

```
ERROR Error: Uncaught (in promise): Error

Error
at app.component.ts:18:11 at fetch (async) at (anonymous)
    (app.component.ts:4)
at request (app.component.ts:4)
at (anonymous) (app.component.ts:17) at submit (app.component.ts:15)
at AppComponent_click_3_listener (app.component.html:4)
```

Now we can clearly see the sequence of steps that lead to the error, the event that started it, the callback that handled the event, and the HTTP call that caused it in the end. This is arguably one of the best "silent" improvements in Angular's developer experience and will save lots of time and energy when dealing with bugs.

4.6   Exercises for the reader

- Build a `UserBadgeComponent` that displays a specific icon (admin, employee, HR team) next to the user's profile picture. It receives the user's data as input and transforms it into the CSS class of the corresponding icon.
- Build an `UnlessDirective` that hosts `NgIf` but uses a negated condition.
- Build a custom image loader that adds a specific "quality" query parameter depending on the user's preference (stored in `localStorage`). Quality can be low, normal, high, or ultra.
- In an existing project (you can use our HRMS application if you have been coding along with the book), refactor the templates to use the self-closing component tags.

Summary

- We can now mark inputs as required, transform their values before setting on component properties, and bind routing data (query parameters, path parameters, resolved data) to them.
- It is now possible to compose directives using the new `hostDirectives` metadata option, adding existing directives to new ones, and pass inputs/outputs to them.
- Angular reactive forms are now type-safe, where types could both be inferred from the form definition or provided explicitly.
- A new `NgOptimizedImage` directive is available to boost image loading performance, mark its priority, or seamlessly integrate with CDN providers.
- Angular now provides the ability to use the `fetch` function as basis for HTTP calls rather than `XMLHttpRequest`.
- In templates, we can now use self-closing tags instead of writing out the closing tag in its entirety.

RxJS in modern Angular

This chapter covers

- Reactive programming principles
- Using RxJS to build functionality that uses reactive programming
- Unsubscribing from observables in a new way
- Using dependency injection in custom RxJS operators

So far in this book, we have built many features using the different tools that Angular provides. We have already interacted with RxJS several times, mainly when making HTTP calls and handling them in interceptors. However, we can safely say that this is only a tiny part of all the capabilities that RxJS can give us when we are developing frontend applications. In this chapter, we are going to learn about reactive programming and explore RxJS, the first-choice tool for working in this paradigm, its complex (and sometimes sadly overengineered) relationship with Angular, and learn how new modern tools provided by the Angular team help us integrate RxJS seamlessly into our Angular applications. First, let's understand what RxJS is used for, and what is this "reactive programming" we keep hearing about all the time.

5.1   What is reactive programming?

To understand reactive programming, let us first understand how frontend in general works. With Angular, we know that an app is basically a collection of interconnected components. Each of these components takes some data, renders some UI, and then reacts to events from that UI (let's emphasize the word "react" here). Take this most basic of examples, a component that shows a counter, where we can increment or decrement a number, shown in the following listing.

Listing 5.1   Counter component example

```
@Component({
  selector: 'app-counter',
  template: `
    <button (click)="decrement()">-</button>
    <span>{{ count }}</span>
    <button (click)="increment()">+</button>
  `,
})
export class CounterComponent {
  count: number = 0;

  increment() {
    this.count++;
  }

  decrement() {
    this.count--;
  }
}
```

Here, the "data" is the count property, which can be changed in the future. From now on, we refer to this data as "state," as this is the most popular naming convention when dealing with this particular terminology. So the state is essentially all the data we use to show the UI. The UI is the template we created. Notice we used our state to display a part of this UI: {{ count }}. Finally, we have event handlers like increment() and decrement(), which we bound to "click" events. Thus the life cycle of our component can be described with a very simple diagram, shown in figure 5.1.

The dotted line in the figure indicates that events are what change the state (which further triggers changes in the UI). Notice that the state is the single source of truth here (to change UI we need to change the state), and the state itself can only be changed via (asynchronous) events. These designations are not very consequential for us right now but will become very important in the future when we discuss change detection in Angular. What *is* actually important is

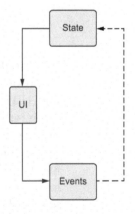

Figure 5.1   Life cycle of a component

that we have a system where we *react* to changes in a "chaotic" manner, as we do not call the methods we defined ourselves but rather pass them to event handlers so that they can be called later, meaning we "react" to events. Let's further explore this distinction and introduce two new (rather simple) terms. Take the following code, for example:

```
const data = getData();
alert(data)
```

Now this isn't very meaningful, but it does not have to be. We call a function, get a result, and then `alert` it. This is what we would call a "pull" system; we need some data that is "stored" elsewhere, so we call a function and pull this data. We, as developers, get the data on demand, whenever we need it in the code, and then work with it. Now let's look at this piece of code:

```
document.addEventListener('click', event => alert(event))
```

Here, however, we can see something that is called a push system: we wrote some code, but it will not execute until the event listener *pushes* an event in our direction and calls the callback function we provided. In this scenario, we do not make any demands for the data we (might) work with and rather wait for another actor (the "click" events in this case) to send the data to us.

We might be tempted to equate pull-based systems to synchronous code and push-based systems with asynchronous code, and in a vast number of scenarios this will be the case, but practically, there is nothing that requires a system to be asynchronous to be push-based or vice versa (we can write asynchronous code with the `async` keyword and from the code perspective it will be a pull-based system). Again, right now this distinction might not seem very important to us, but in the next chapter, when we learn about signals, we will see how large of a difference this makes.

So what does it have to do with reactive programming? Well, to keep everything simple, reactive programming is essentially the parts of a codebase that work with push-based systems, and instead of providing on-demand access to data, they handle the data whenever it arrives. Essentially, if we go back to figure 5.1, for us reactive programming represents the "events" part of the flow and how it affects the state and, consequently, the UI.

Let us now dive deeper and see why Angular uses RxJS for this, what the problems are, and what the team offers as solutions to those problems.

5.2 Why we (still) need RxJS

As mentioned earlier (and as we probably already knew anyway), for Angular applications, the go-to solution for reactive programming problems is RxJS, the Reactive Extensions library for JavaScript. This immensely popular library offers framework-agnostic building blocks like observables, subjects, operators, and so on to work with streams of events, which comes in handy when working on frontend applications. Angular uses RxJS both internally (tools like the `EventEmitter`, for instance, are built using Observables) and externally (for example, the `HttpClient` returns an Observable for developers to use, or an async pipe is available for us to put Observables in the template).

RxJS also provides a robust set of operators (over 100!), which allow us to manipulate, transform, and combine observables. In addition to the existing ones, we can also define our own custom operators specific to our applications' business logic, making the library super flexible. All of these things make RxJS very appealing for frontend developers, especially those working with Angular.

So in what situations do we use RxJS? Of course, we use it when dealing with asynchronous programming. As mentioned, Angular's `HttpClient` already utilizes observables as its return values for HTTP call methods. Another important use case is reacting to events originating from the framework; for example, when working with reactive forms, we sometimes have to react to certain changes in form values—for instance, disabling a certain input when the user selects a specific value on another one. To do this, we use the `valueChanges` observable that reactive form controls have and that signals changes to the value of the corresponding input.

Finally, there is the most popular use case, which is quite surprising. While RxJS is designed to work with streams of events, we often use it to represent state (that changes over time). In fact, we have already encountered such a scenario. In chapter 3, listing 3.4, we have created an `isAuth$` subject, which represents both the state of the user being authorized or not *and* the event of the change of that status. This is an example of how state is shared between components, with a subject (or BehaviorSubject) stored in some service while its value is read (and subscribed to) in multiple other components. This is essentially how many popular state management libraries (NgRx, NGXS, and others) work, building an ecosystem of data exchange on top of RxJS.

All of this theoretical information will become very important to us in the next two chapters when we discuss the new alternative way of dealing with state that changes over time and Angular's change detection. For now, we contextualized RxJS in Angular and discussed problems it solves and why we need it; now we can move on to explore problems that arise when we write RxJS code. Let's begin with the most popular one.

5.3 *Unsubscribing from observables*

As we discussed, the main characteristic of observables is the ability to subscribe to the notifications they send. Subscribing involves providing a callback function or, often, several callbacks, that will be executed on new notifications, on errors, and upon the stream's completion. However, the subscription itself involves storing references to those functions in places of the memory that we do not have access to; in simple terms, we can imagine that the observable stores the callbacks in a big array, and then goes through it, invoking them when a new item arrives.

5.3.1   Why unsubscribe?

The problem is that we do not "see" the array, so there is no direct way to remove some of the subscriber callbacks (or all of them). This can become a problem when we no longer need the observable but subscriptions remain in place. We might even remove the observable itself (for instance, assign a null to the only variable that holds a reference to the observable, forcing it to be garbage-collected), but the subscription will continue to work. Take a look at the following very simple example:

```
let obs$ = interval(1_000);
obs$.subscribe(console.log);
obs$ = null;
```

Even though we immediately removed the obs$ observable, the subscription will continue to work and execute a console.log call each second. Such subscriptions that continue to work after losing the reference to the observable are colloquially known as "zombie" subscriptions, and they can potentially cause some serious problems. If we accumulate enough zombie subscriptions, we might overextend the RAM memory and end up with a memory leak. Also, from the UX perspective, we probably want to stop some subscriptions when the user, for instance, leaves a certain page, so that we can begin fresh the next time they visit that page.

In Angular, we often subscribe to observables in pages that are routed (i.e., the ones that have a route path pointed to them). Subscribing to some router-related observables like queryParams, for example, can potentially cause problems. If we forget to unsubscribe from those observables, a user coming and going to that page's component several times can result in a memory leak.

5.3.2   Problems with unsubscribing

So how do we unsubscribe from observables? From the RxJS perspective, there are two ways to accomplish this. The first one is done from the side of the subscription. The subscribe method, which we use to subscribe to observables, returns a special subscription object, which holds information about the subscription and has a method named unsubscribe, which terminates that particular subscription. The following is a short code example:

```
let obs$ = interval(1_000);
const subscription = obs$.subscribe(console.log);
subscription.unsubscribe();
```

This achieves our stated goal but is not very good in terms of code quality. In a given Angular component, we can have multiple subscriptions, so we will have to create as many unsubscriptions, resulting in code clutter. We can create one "master" subscription, add all the others to it, and unsubscribe from the main one, but that still involves quite a lot of code.

The other approach is to come from the observable and make the stream itself stop emitting values. This can be done with a family of operators named `take`, `takeWhile`, and `takeUntil`. Of particular interest to us is the `takeUntil` operator, which takes another observable and terminates the source one when the other one emits. In an Angular component, developers often create a special `destroy$` subject, then use `take-Until` on all subscriptions, and finally trigger `unsubscription` in the `ngOnDestroy` method. The following listing shows a short example.

Listing 5.2   Unsubscribing from an observable using the `takeUntil` operator

```
export class AppComponent implements OnInit, OnDestroy {
  destroy$ = new Subject<void>();

  ngOnInit() {                          Tells RxJS to stop the emissions
    interval(1_000).pipe(               from this observable when
      takeUntil(this.destroy$),         destroy$ fires an event
    ).subscribe(console.log);
  }
                                        Sends a notification to all
  ngOnDestroy() {                       observables to complete when
    this.destroy$.next();               the component is removed
  }

}
```

Now this is a very clean and concise approach, so it is not surprising that it became the most widely used solution to the "unsubscribe" problem. However, it still has some (albeit minor problems). First, this code will be copy-pasted in multiple places and is never related to business logic; it is only an implementation detail. Next, different authors might give this observable different names (`destroy$`, `destroyed$`, `onDestroy$`, and so on), resulting in confusion among developers reading the code. Finally, this is just one approach; it isn't official in any way and it can still be mixed with other approaches, resulting in further confusion.

Deciding when to unsubscribe is important. From the component perspective, we usually resort to using `ngOnDestroy`, which does the job pretty well. But what if we subscribe to observables in, say, some reusable functions and do not have access to a component's life cycle method to dispose of the subscription?

Let us now see what solutions Angular provides to these problems and start with accessing the component life cycle from a function.

5.3.3   *Introducing DestroyRef*

In the previous chapter, we created a `CandidateDetailsComponent` but have not implemented the `CandidateListComponent` yet. To see this new feature, let us go back and actually create it so that it has a table that displays a list of candidates and an input field that would allow the user to search for a specific candidate by full name.

Note one caveat: we want to limit the number of requests that we send to the server because the user might be typing a lot of characters, and there is no need to send a request each time the user hits a key on their keyboard; instead it makes more sense to send one request when the user is done typing. We will achieve this by creating a form control and then subscribing to its `valueChanges` observable while utilizing the `debounceTime` operator, which is an operator that ignores emissions until there are no more notifications in a given time period (in our case, say, if the user stops typing for 500 milliseconds). The following listing shows an implementation with the unsubscription logic.

Listing 5.3   Building candidate search with time delay

Destroys subject for unsubscribing

Creates a form control to attach to the search input

```
export class CandidatesListComponent implements OnInit, OnDestroy {
  private readonly candidateService = inject(CandidateService);
  candidates$ = this.candidateService.getCandidates();
  searchControl = new FormControl('');                         ←
  destroy$ = new Subject<void>();                              ←
  search$ = this.searchControl.valueChanges.pipe(
    debounceTime(500),                                         ←
    takeUntil(this.destroy$)                                   ←
  );

  ngOnInit(): void {
    this.search$.subscribe((value) => {                        ←
      if (value) {
        this.candidates$ = this.candidateService.getCandidatesByName(value);
      } else {
        this.candidates$ = this.candidateService.getCandidates();
      }
    });
  }

  ngOnDestroy(): void {
    this.destroy$.next();                  ←
  }
}
```

Delays time before any search can be made for 500 milliseconds

Completes the observable when the destroy subject fires

Actually subscribes to the search term changes to make the HTTP call

Fires the destroy subject to complete all subscriptions

At this point, this is quite a clean implementation that does not really need much improvement. However, soon we might realize that such search functionality (with debouncing time and a form control) might be necessary in other places too—for example, in the `EmployeeListComponent`.

We can, of course, copy-paste this solution to that place, and any other component, but that will reduce the ability to refactor our code in the future. What if we decide the debounce time in every component needs to be 700 milliseconds and not 500? So, thinking of a solution, we might want to implement a function that takes a `FormControl` and returns the search observable coupled with the debounce and unsubscription logic.

Immediately we can see a problem: how can we unsubscribe upon a component's destruction if we are writing code in a function not a component? It turns out, in Angular 16, we can do this using a special token called `DestroyRef`. Let's see it in action when we implement our function. In the src/app/shared/functions folder let's create a file named create-search.ts and put our implementation there.

Listing 5.4   Reusable function for performing searches with time delay

```
import { DestroyRef, inject } from '@angular/core';
import { FormControl } from '@angular/forms';
import { Subject } from 'rxjs';
import { debounceTime, takeUntil } from 'rxjs/operators';

export function createSearch<T>(control: FormControl<T>) {
    const destroyRef = inject(DestroyRef);
    const destroy$ = new Subject<void>();
    destroyRef.onDestroy(() => destroy$.next());
    return control.valueChanges.pipe(
        debounceTime(500),
        takeUntil(destroy$),
    );
}
```

So what is this `DestroyRef`? Essentially, it is a reference to the destruction of the context in which the function is invoked. For example, if we invoke the function in a component, the `DestroyRef` will reference us that specific component's destruction life cycle, meaning the callback we provided to the `onDestroy` method will be invoked when the component is destroyed as if we have written that callback inside that component's `ngOnDestroy` method. Now we can use this function anywhere; for instance, the following listing shows how it will simplify the `CandidateListComponent`.

Listing 5.5   Candidate list component with the reusable search logic

```
export class CandidatesListComponent implements OnInit {
  private readonly candidateService = inject(CandidateService);
  candidates$ = this.candidateService.getCandidates();
  searchControl = new FormControl('');
  search$ = createSearch(this.searchControl);

  ngOnInit(): void {
    this.search$.subscribe((value) => {
      if (value) {
        this.candidates$ = this.candidateService.getCandidatesByName(value);
      } else {
        this.candidates$ = this.candidateService.getCandidates();
      }
    });
  }

}
```

As we can see, there is no further need for an `ngOnDestroy` method here. Of course, this is a specific (albeit very useful) scenario. But what about unsubscribing in general from other observables in components or directives? It turns out we have an official way of doing that now.

5.3.4   *The takeUntilDestroyed operator*

We already covered in the previous two sections how using a subject that signals the destruction of a component to unsubscribe from observables is the most popular and clean way of dealing with the problem, and we also mentioned some downsides of this approach. Starting from Angular v16, the core team has begun implementing a new package, called rxjs-interop, which, as evidenced by its name, is intended to enhance the interoperability between Angular and RxJS. The package can be found under the core package:

```
import * from '@angular/core/rxjs-interop';
```

The package contains many useful tools, most of which we will discuss in the next chapter when we talk about interoperability between signals and RxJS. However, one of the tools provided is of great interest to us here and now. Previously, we briefly mentioned that RxJS is flexible in terms that we can add custom operators to work with observable streams. Here the Angular team did the same thing, adding a custom RxJS operator that binds to the Angular context (for instance, the component in which the source observable was created) and automatically unsubscribes when that context is destroyed. To better visualize this, let us add a new feature to our HRMS application— one that handles user permissions. Under the src/app/services directory, let's create a `PermissionsService` that will handle permissions using observable streams.

Listing 5.6   Permissions service

```
type Permissions = 'ViewEmployees' | 'EditEmployeeGeneralDetails' |
    'EditEmployeePrivateDetails' |
'DeleteEmployee' | 'CreateEmployee';          ◁── List of all possible permissions; only
                                                   employee-related permissions are
                                                   included for the sake of brevity.
@Injectable({providedIn: 'root'})
export class PermissionsService {
    private readonly permissions$ = new BehaviorSubject<
      Partial<Record<Permissions, boolean>>
    >({                                       ◁── BehaviorSubject that holds
        ViewEmployees: true,                  ◁──   the value of the permissions
    });
                                              ViewEmployees permissions
    hasPermission(permission: Permissions) {  set to true as an example
        return this.permissions$.pipe(map(permissions => permissions[permission] ??
      false));
    }

    setPermissions(permissions: Partial<Record<Permissions, boolean>>) {
        this.permissions$.next({...this.permissions$.getValue(), ...permissions});
    }
```

```
    revokePermission(permission: Permissions) {
        this.permissions$.next({...this.permissions$.getValue(), [permission]:
    false});
    }
}
```

Now any time we want to work with permissions, all we would have to do is inject this service, use the `hasPermission` method, and subscribe to the observable it returns. We do it via an observable for a couple of reasons, mainly to be able to support real-time (for example, an admin revoked a user's permission while they were browsing the application) and also to reflect changes made by the user themselves (the user edited their information, which resulted in them gaining/losing some permissions).

Let's now examine a scenario where we might need to subscribe to a permission. As we can see, we have two distinct permissions for editing the employee details: one is general editing, which includes, for instance, contact information, which a team lead of the given employee should be able to edit without involving human resources (HR) personnel. However, editing private user data (full name, email address, and so on) is a privilege reserved for the members of the HR department to prevent fraud/malicious attacks. It means in the `EditEmployeeComponent` we would want to subscribe to the permissions and see if the user has that private editing permissions and, if not, disable some of the inputs based on that permission. Naturally, after the component is destroyed, we want to unsubscribe from that particular stream, and we are going to do so using the new `takeUntilDestroyed` operator. Let's take a look at the `EditEmployeeComponent`.

Listing 5.7 Unsubscribing from an observable with `takeUntilDestroyed`

```
import { Component, inject, DestroyRef, OnInit } from '@angular/core';
import { takeUntilDestroyed } from '@angular/core/rxjs-interop';
import { FormControl, FormGroup, Validators } from '@angular/forms';
import { EmployeeForm } from 'src/app/infrastructure/types/employee-form';
import { PermissionsService } from 'src/app/services/permissions.service';

export class EditEmployeeComponent {
  permissionsService = inject(PermissionsService);
  form = new FormGroup<EmployeeForm>({              ◄──┤ The actual employee
    firstName: new FormControl('', {                    editing form
      nonNullable: true,
      validators: [Validators.required],
    }),
    lastName: new FormControl('', { nonNullable: true }),
    email: new FormControl('', { nonNullable: true }),
    position: new FormControl('', { nonNullable: true }),
    level: new FormControl('', { nonNullable: true }),
  });

  constructor() {
    this.permissionsService.hasPermission('EditEmployeePrivateDetails').pipe(
      takeUntilDestroyed(),           ◄──┐ takeUntilDestroyed operator will
    ).subscribe(hasPermission => {          automatically unsubscribe from this
                                            stream when the component is destroyed.
```

```
    if (!hasPermission) {
      this.form.controls.firstName.disable();
      this.form.controls.lastName.disable();
      this.form.controls.email.disable();
    } else {
      this.form.controls.firstName.enable();
      this.form.controls.lastName.enable();
      this.form.controls.email.enable();
    }
  });
  }
}
```

Logic we perform
on subscription

Now this is beautiful: we implemented our subscription and did everything we would do anyway, and just in a single line of code we also took care of unsubscribing from the stream we used! A real cherry on top is the fact we did not create any subjects to signal about the destruction of the component and did not even implement the ngOnDestroy method. This approach, besides being now the official way of unsubscribing, is also cleaner and easier to explain.

We previously mentioned several ways of unsubscribing from observables; one of them is the signaling subject. With this new approach, it would be beneficial if we had that approach implemented in our previous, existing projects: the subject approach makes it way easier to migrate to the new official solution. All we have to do is remove the destroy subjects, remove the ngOnDestroy method (unless it had other, unrelated logic in it, so we have to be careful there), and use the takeUntilDestroyed custom operator instead of RxJS's takeUntil.

However, there is a small caveat that we need to discuss related to the takeUntil Destroyed operator. Here we must dive a bit deeper and understand how it actually works. For this, let's go back to listing 5.4 and remember that we already used the DestroyRef injectable to unsubscribe from an observable. There, the DestroyRef was used to hook onto the event of the destruction of the component in which the function is called and to terminate the subscription. It turns out that takeUntilDestroyed does the same thing; it utilizes the DestroyRef to learn about context destruction and completes the observable on which we use it.

But here is a catch: in chapter 3, section 3.2.2, we learned that the inject function only operates in an injection context; as the takeUntilDestroyed function uses it to inject the DestroyRef, it means that the takeUntilDestroyed function can only be used in similar injection contexts. In our example, we used that operator to subscribe to an observable inside a component's constructor, which works as expected; but what if we wanted to subscribe to an observable inside, say, the ngOnInit method, or any other method for that matter?

Thankfully, Angular has got us covered here. Because takeUntilDestroyed is a function, it can accept an argument, so we can provide the relevant DestroyRef whenever we use the operator outside of an injection context. For instance, if we did the same thing in the `ngOnInit` method, the component code would be mostly the same, with one notable exception, as shown in the following listing.

> **Listing 5.8 Using `takeUntilDestroyed` outside injection context**

```
export class EditEmployeeComponent implements OnInit {
  permissionsService = inject(PermissionsService);
  destroyRef = inject(DestroyRef);                          ⟵─  Injects the DestroyRef into the
  form = new FormGroup<EmployeeForm>({                           component to pass it on to the
    firstName: new FormControl('', {                            takeUntilDestroyed operator later
      nonNullable: true,
      validators: [Validators.required],
    }),
    lastName: new FormControl('', { nonNullable: true }),
    email: new FormControl('', { nonNullable: true }),
    position: new FormControl('', { nonNullable: true }),       Now subscribes
    level: new FormControl('', { nonNullable: true }),          inside the ngOnInit
  });                                                            method instead of
                                                                 the constructor
  ngOnInit() {                                          ⟵─
    this.permissionsService.hasPermission('EditEmployeePrivateDetails').pipe(
      takeUntilDestroyed(this.destroyRef),              ⟵─
    ).subscribe(hasPermission => {                          Passes the component's
      if (!hasPermission) {                                 DestroyRef to the
        this.form.controls.firstName.disable();            takeUntilDestroyed operator
        this.form.controls.lastName.disable();
        this.form.controls.email.disable();
      } else {
        this.form.controls.firstName.enable();
        this.form.controls.lastName.enable();
        this.form.controls.email.enable();
      }
    });
  }
}
```

Now we can easily use the operator in any method we want, as long as we pass the `DestroyRef` to it. One important observation here would be that, back in listing 5.4, we also used the `DestroyRef` (and there other scenarios where we use that injectable in functions) when writing our `createSearch` function, meaning that the function will not work outside injection contexts too. So how can we work around this? Well, we can make it work like `takeUntilDestroyed`—meaning, it can accept an optional reference to the `DestroyRef` as an argument. The following listing shows a slightly revised version of that function.

> **Listing 5.9 Passing the `DestroyRef` into a function as an argument**

```
export function createSearch<T>(
  control: FormControl<T>,                             DestroyRef is now an optional
  destroyRef = inject(DestroyRef),        ⟵─           argument on the function and
) {                                                    can be passed from the code
  const destroy$ = new Subject<void>();                that invokes it.
```

```
    destroyRef.onDestroy(() => destroy$.next());
    return control.valueChanges.pipe(debounceTime(500), takeUntil(destroy$));
}
```

Notice how the `destroyRef` still defaults to `inject(DestroyRef)`, meaning our existing code that uses the function without the parameter will continue working in the same fashion. Also note that we could have used the `takeUntilDestroyed` operator here instead (preferable), but we would still need to have the `DestroyRef` as an optional argument to be able to pass that reference to the `takeUntilDestroyed` operator.

We have explored a new, built-in custom operator in Angular, which greatly relieved our efforts when working with RxJS code and helped us remove lots of boiler-plate from the project. Now let us dive deeper into this topic and see how we can write our own custom RxJS operators and how the `inject` function greatly improves the developer experience when dealing with them.

5.4 Writing our own custom RxJS operators

RxJS operators are a great way of enhancing observables and providing new things that we can do with them. There are more than 100 built-in RxJS operators, and the nature of the library allows us to create our own operators, which can now also incorporate the business logic of our applications inside observables. First, let us see what an RxJS operator is, and how a custom one can be created, and then focus on writing an actually useful custom RxJS operator for our application. Let us start by under-standing the nature of RxJS operators.

5.4.1 What is an RxJS operator?

RxJS is rich with different functions that we can use to enhance our experience with the library and achieve different behaviors. Some of those functions are the creation functions: functions we can use to create observables with different predefined behav-iors. For example, one such function is the `of` function, which takes some values and returns an observable that emits those values in the specified order:

```
of(1, 2, 3);
```

This will emit `1`, `2`, `3`. This function is especially useful for learning examples, as we can directly show what values are going to be emitted, so we will use it often in this sec-tion. Next, there are combining functions, that take several existing observables and return a new observable that somehow combines the behavior of the source observ-ables. For example, the `merge` operator will take several observables and emit when-ever one of them emits something:

```
merge(of(1, 2, 3), of(4, 5));
```

This will emit `1`, `2`, `3`, `4`, `5`. These sorts of functions will become very important in the next two chapters when we learn about signals and how they can replicate functionality similar to what we can achieve with these functions in RxJS. For now, the topic of our discussion is the third, and by far the largest and most popular, category of functions RxJS provides: the operators.

At this point we have used and interacted with a number of RxJS operators—mostly the ones related to unsubscribing from streams. However, let us dive deeper and actually understand what is going on here by examining the probably most popular built-in RxJS operator: `map`. This operator takes every emission from a source observable and transforms it into a new value, according to a function we provided. For instance, this code will emit `10, 20, 30`:

```
of(1, 2, 3).pipe(map(x => x * 10));
```

We provided a function that multiplies a value by 10 and returns the result, and then this function will be applied to each emission of the observable `1, 2, 3` will become `10, 20, 30`.

Often to better visualize how a certain function or operator works, RxJS developers use marble diagrams that show the behavior of a function when applied to an observable. Figure 5.2 shows a marble diagram of the `map` operator.

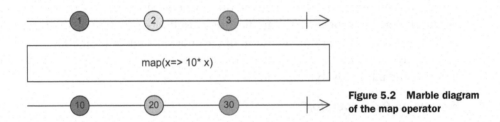

Figure 5.2   Marble diagram of the map operator

In this section, we will utilize these sorts of diagrams to better illustrate our custom RxJS operators (and some built-in ones too).

From what we have seen, we can apply operators to add behaviors to the observable in question. However, if we dive a bit deeper, we will understand that the phrase "add behavior to the observable" is actually *quite wrong*. But how? The operators we saw so far clearly resulted in new behaviors, so why should we not describe it as such? Well, let us explore what an operator actually does.

We see here that `map` is a function that takes a function and returns—well, we are not yet familiar with what it really returns (and then passes to the `pipe` method). What it does return is in fact something known in RxJS as an `OperatorFunction`. Wait, but wasn't the map itself the operator function? It turns out this is actually a bit of a misleading naming convention, and what `map` itself is can be better described as an operator creator (not official nomenclature). So `map` will *create* another function that will be then used to cast the values of the source observables into whatever the function we provide defines. Let us now explore what kind of function this `OperatorFunction` is.

An `OperatorFunction` is a special function that takes an observable as its argument (this one is called the source); creates a new observable (known as destination), which internally subscribes to the source one; performs some operation; and finally returns it. So in simple terms, an `OperatorFunction` is a function that takes a source observable and returns a destination observable based on it. Now, with this information, let's examine how they work and what we can do with this feature to further customize our codebase.

5.4.2 How do operators work?

We have seen multiple times that to utilize RxJS operators, we need to pass them to the pipe method of an observable. But what is this pipe method? Let's talk a bit about functional programming to understand what pipe is exactly.

In the functional programming paradigm, functions are the most important building block of an application. This is in opposition to, for example, object-oriented programming, where objects are the most important, and functions usually are just methods on those objects. In functional programming, we can use functions not only to express some functionality to call it later but also to build more complex functionality from simpler functions. This process is known as *function composition*. Composing two functions that each accept exactly one parameter (also known as *unary functions*) is creating a new function that takes one parameter, calls the first function with the parameter, then passes the result to the other function, and finally returns the result. Essentially, composing is like chaining function calls, taking one argument and passing it through several functions. We can create a small utility function that takes two unary functions and returns a composed function derived from them:

```
const compose = (f, g) => param => f(g(param));
```

Here we just apply the functions in the order provided. We can see it in action in a simple example:

```
const increment = (n: number) => n + 1;
const double = (n: number) => n * 2;
const doubleAndIncrement = compose(increment, double);
console.log(doubleAndIncrement(5));
```

This piece of code here will log 11, as the functions will apply one after another (see figure 5.3).

But if we are attentive enough, we will notice that the functions will execute in the reverse order! This is usually what comprising functions means. If we want the order of functions in the arguments to reflect the order of their execution, we can do the reverse, which in functional programming is known as *piping* (familiar name, right?):

```
const pipe = (f, g) => param => g(f(param));
```

Now if we build a new function from two other ones using this function, we will get the "correct" execution order. The pipe method in RxJS is essentially this, but it accepts an arbitrary number of functions to pipe and works only with `OperatorFunctions`.

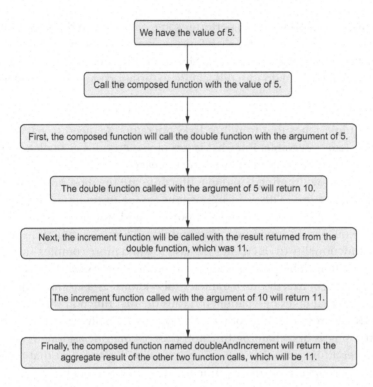

We have the value of 5.

Call the composed function with the value of 5.

First, the composed function will call the double function with the argument of 5.

The double function called with the argument of 5 will return 10.

Next, the increment function will be called with the result returned from the double function, which was 11.

The increment function called with the argument of 10 will return 11.

Finally, the composed function named doubleAndIncrement will return the aggregate result of the other two function calls, which will be 11.

Figure 5.3   Steps a composed function undertakes when called with a parameter

With this knowledge, we can understand operators better. They are functions that can be combined with the pipe operator to create one big function, which will then be applied to the source observable. Notice the wording that we used in the previous section: "OperatorFunction is a function that takes a source observable and returns a destination observable based on it." The destination observable is a *new* observable that is created by combining the OperatorFunctions into one big operator and calling it on the source observable. If we do a small coding example, this can be seen here:

```
const numbers$ = of(1, 2, 3);
const doubledNumbers$ = numbers$.pipe(map(n => n * 2));
doubledNumbers$.subscribe(n => console.log(n));
```

We can see that the doubledNumbers$ is a new observable derived from the first one, and we subscribe to it to read the numbers that are emitted. Figure 5.4 shows what is going on here.

So what happens with the source? The answer is *nothing*. The source observable has its own life—we just derived a new observable from it, but the source one will continue to work in the same way it used to. That is why we say that phrases like "operators add behavior on observables" or "operators modify how observables work" are not really correct. What operators do is only create new observables from existing ones.

While this might seem like a pedantic distinction or a weird limitation, it in fact empowers us to be able to customize our RxJS-related codebases. Let's see this in action.

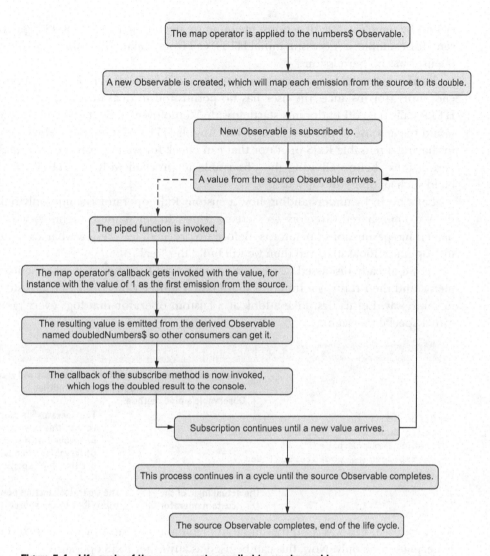

Figure 5.4   Life cycle of the `map` operator applied to an observable

5.4.3   Building custom operators

We already added a permissions system to our HRMS application, meaning different functionalities now might only be possible if the user has the relevant permissions granted to them. We used it to disable or enable inputs depending on whether the user has permission to edit them. But more often, handling permissions boils down to just restricting a particular feature altogether.

   In the vast majority of cases, this involves not allowing certain HTTP calls when the permissions are not granted. Usually, we do this by removing or disabling the part of the UI that is making this HTTP call, but sometimes the HTTP call is "implicit" and is caused by some cascade of actions, meaning we need to write some RxJS logic to prevent, for example, a successful initial HTTP call from making the other one, for which the user has no permissions.

Furthermore, in certain cases, we just want to disable all HTTP calls to particular endpoints (for instance, the user has no permission to deal with employees, so any HTTP calls the API endpoints starting with "/employee" must be discarded), and it would make sense to put that logic in any Angular HTTP interceptor. The case arises for having a reusable RxJS operator that can check for some permission (or multiple permissions) before allowing the observable to proceed with the HTTP call. Let's build such an operator ourselves.

Let's begin by understanding how a custom RxJS operator is commonly built. In the src/app/shared directory let's create a new folder named operators and a file named has-permissions.operator.ts. Before we proceed, let's review what a simple custom operator looks like, and then we will build the "real" one.

As we already discussed, a custom operator is a function that takes some arguments and then returns a function that takes a source observable and transforms it in some way. Let us first take a look at a custom operator that logs every emission with a special message.

Listing 5.10   Custom RxJS operator that logs every new item

This is our custom operator, the function that will return an OperatorFunction and will be used in other Observable's pipe method.

The OperatorFunction we return; this is what will be invoked with source Observables when we use the "log" operator.

```
function log() {
  return function<T>(source: Observable<T>) {
    return source.pipe(
      tap(item => console.log(item)),
    );
  }
}
```

The actual logic of the custom operator

The OperatorFunction now subscribes to the source.

As we can see, this was a pretty simple implementation, most of which involved just boilerplate code only. Now, this can be used as any other RxJS operator:

```
of(1, 2, 3).pipe(log()).subscribe();
```

This will log 1, 2, 3 to the console.

We can further customize this operator by adding a string parameter that we can use to discern between different observables that use this operator.

Listing 5.11   Custom RxJS operator with a configurable parameter

```
function log(message: string = '') {
  return function<T>(source: Observable<T>) {
    return source.pipe(
```

Here we declare an optional parameter that the operator can take.

```
      tap(item => console.log(`${message ? message + ': ' :   ''}${item}`)),
    );
  }
}
```

**Uses the parameter to log a
customized message**

Now we can use the operator with a custom message:

```
of(1, 2, 3).pipe(log('Number')).subscribe();
```

This will log `Number: 1`, `Number: 2`, `Number: 3` to the console. Now we have an operator that is itself custom and can be further customized with a parameter. But can we
do something about the boilerplate code? It would be really nice if we could just write
the business logic directly, instead of all the same code we did here. It turns out RxJS
provides tools for building such custom operators out of the box. Let's learn about the
`MonoTypeOperatorFunction` type and the `pipe` function.

First, let us briefly discuss the `MonoTypeOperatorFunction`. We already talked about
the `OperatorFunction` type, a generic type description of an RxJS operator. There,
`OperatorFunction` is a type that accepts two type parameters: one for the source observable and one for the result. Note those can be different; for instance, the `map` operator
that we touched on in this chapter takes one type of an observable but can possibly
return another type (for instance, convert an observable of strings to numbers). The
`MonoTypeOperatorFunction`, on the contrary, is extended from `OperatorFunction`
but only takes one type parameter, because it represents an operator that does not
change the type of the source observable. For instance, the `filter` operator is an
example of a `MonoTypeOperatorFunction`, because it does not change the type (or the
value, for that matter) of emissions from the source and only restricts them on the
basis of the predicate function that we provided. Our custom `log` operator is also an
example of a `MonoTypeOperatorFunction`, as it only performs a side effect (logging to
the console) but does not interfere with the stream itself in any way.

The other tool we mentioned is the `pipe` function. Note that it is different from
the `pipe` method, as this one is an independent function, *not* a method on the
`Observable` class. Despite being different from the code's perspective, this function
essentially does the same thing: pipes RxJS operators to create a new large operator.
We will now use this to rewrite our log operator without all the boilerplate.

Listing 5.12   Using RxJS built-in tools to create a custom operator

**We specify the return type as a MonoTypeOperator-
Function to avoid any typing problems if we make a
mistake in the actual implementation.**

**We use the pipe function
to invoke other operators.**

```
function log<T>(
  message: string = ''
): MonoTypeOperatorFunction<T> {
  return pipe(
    tap(item => console.log(`${message ? message + ': ' :   ''}${item}`)),
  );
}
```

Note that in this scenario it would have been enough to just write `return tap(item => console.log(`${message ? message + ': ' : ''}${item}`))`, without the pipe function, as we only used a single operator. But in general, we write custom RxJS operators to be able to combine several existing operators with a sprinkle of business logic, so the `pipe` function is naturally used almost always.

Now, having familiarized ourselves with these powerful tools, let us use them to build and test our permissions operator in action.

Listing 5.13 Custom RxJS operator that uses dependency injection

```
export function hasPermissions<T>(
    permissions: Permissions[],
    permissionsService = inject(PermissionsService),
): MonoTypeOperatorFunction<T> {

    return pipe(
        withLatestFrom(permissionsService.hasPermissions(permissions)),

        filter(([, hasPermissions]) => hasPermissions),

        map(([value]) => value)

    );
}
```

List of permissions to check against before proceeding

Yet again we inject the service as a parameter with a default value, so as to be able to use the operator outside of injection context by providing the reference to the **PermissionsService** manually.

We map the value back to whatever the source observable has emitted originally so as to not change anything from the perspective of the developer who uses this operator on some observable of theirs.

Here we can see that the value emitted is a tuple, where the first element is the item that the source observable has emitted, and the second one is a Boolean returned by the hasPermissions method. We do not need the first item, as we do not perform any logic on it, so we ignore it by putting a comma first. We pick the second value and check if the permission is there.

We use the withLatestFrom operator, which takes another stream and adds its latest emission to the value of the current observable, making the next emission a pair of the value of the source observable and the latest value from the other observable.

As we can see, we did quite a lot of heavy lifting by just three to four lines of code. This operator gets the list of permissions, injects the service, and uses it to check the existence of certain permissions, and then either allows the operator to proceed or not, and finally, after proceeding, it returns the original emission. Let's use this in an interceptor to see how it functions and disallow calls to employee-related APIs if the user has no employee-related permissions. In the src/app/shared/interceptors folder, let's create a new file named employee-permissions.interceptor.ts and put the code in the following listing there.

Listing 5.14 Using a custom RxJS operator in an Angular interceptor

```
export const employeePermissionsInterceptor: HttpInterceptorFn = (
  req: HttpRequest<any>,
  next: HttpHandlerFn
) => {
  return next(req).pipe(
    hasPermissions(['CreateEmployee', 'DeleteEmployee',
      'EditEmployeeGeneralDetails', 'ViewEmployees']),
  );
};
```

Here we make sure that no HTTP request made even by accident will pass through unless the user does have the permissions; this also potentially makes the server's life easier, as we do not make calls that would result in, say, a "403 Forbidden" response. Let's visualize this with a marble diagram of our own making (see figure 5.5).

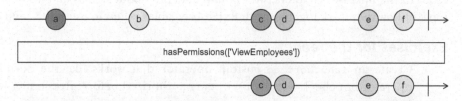

Figure 5.5 Marble diagram of the `hasPermissions` custom operator. Initially, the user has no permissions, but at some point in time before emission `c`, the permission has been granted.

Note that this looks pretty much like the marble diagram for the `filter` operator (see figure 5.6).

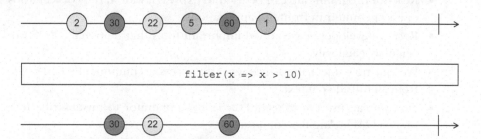

Figure 5.6 Marble diagram of the filter operator

This is because our operator is essentially a multilayered wrapper around that operator, which is the one that performs the actual logic we want.

Furthermore, this can be used in other scenarios; for instance, we can add such preventions on observables that are not related to HTTP calls in any way; our implementation of the operator does not include any assumptions about the source observable that it will be used on. This can become very handy if we use state management libraries like NgRx, which use RxJS observables extensively.

We also encountered a further use case for using the `inject` function as opposed to the constructor DI. With the constructor approach, we would not be able to inject dependencies and would be required to *always* pass them as a parameter to our custom operators. With this added capability, writing custom RxJS operators (which in itself was always possible) becomes more appealing, increasing the reusability of our Angular codebases and reducing code copy-pasting.

So far, we have extensively discussed the state of RxJS in Angular, what new tools we have, and how we can improve our coding experience when using reactive programming in Angular applications. The exciting news is that this journey is far from over: for now, we have only covered RxJS coupled with Angular as it used to be prior to version 16. In version 16, the introduction of signals—the new reactive primitive—happened, bringing with it a host of new problems and solutions when dealing with RxJS. In the next two chapters, we will talk in-depth about signals and also cover the topic of how they work together with RxJS observables, when to use which, and so on.

5.5   *Exercises for the reader*

- Create an `isAuthorized` custom operator that works like the permissions operator but checks for the user being authorized before proceeding with an HTTP request.
- In an existing application, convert different patterns of unsubscription logic to use the `takeUntilDestroyed` operator.

Summary

- RxJS continues to be a vital part of Angular codebases.
- Reactive programming can be used to express a wide variety of scenarios developers encounter in frontend applications.
- Recent developers have added important tools that help make RxJS work with Angular seamlessly.
- We can now inject the `DestroyRef` to access a component's end-of-life event from an outside context.
- Now we can use the `takeUntilDestroyed` operator to unsubscribe from RxJS observables in Angular components.
- We can use the `inject` function to write custom RxJS operators that benefit from dependency injection.

Signals: A new approach to reactive programming

This chapter covers

- Problems developers face when working with RxJS in Angular
- Introducing signals, Angular's new reactive primitive
- Creating new signals and side effects from existing ones
- Signals interoperability with RxJS

In the previous chapter, we talked about reactive programming, how it is useful when working with frontend applications, and how Angular's commonly chosen library to work with reactivity is RxJS. We covered new approaches and tools Angular provides for working with RxJS, but we did not cover the problems that RxJS itself has that cannot be mitigated simply by adding new tools into the arsenal of Angular developers. In this chapter, let's focus on these new changes and discuss signals: a new reactive primitive introduced by the Angular core team into the framework itself, which allows us to read values, subscribe to them, derive new values, and execute side effects without having to deal with RxJS at all. Let us see why this new primitive will be helpful and allow us to mitigate various problems with reactivity.

6.1   Why go beyond RxJS?

Previously, we described RxJS as a powerful, flexible, and very capable library for working with reactivity-related logic. So if this library is so mighty, why do we need to introduce another approach? It turns out the vast capabilities of RxJS might actually be a part of the problem in this case. Let's see what the problems are and then discuss the solutions.

6.1.1   What are the problems with RxJS?

Every Angular developer at some point has to start a phase of learning RxJS. Often, the obstacles they encounter on their way are the same regardless of the application they work on or the level of complexity of the problems they try to solve. So what are those problems? Let us see.

A QUITE STEEP LEARNING CURVE

RxJS is hard, and that is no secret. In the previous chapter, we spent quite a bit of time explaining the simplest, core concepts of RxJS like observables and operators. Lots of stuff goes on under the hood too, like how observables work together and how to combine them. Vertically it gets no better; when we understand how, say, operators function, we then realize there are so many of them: RxJS has more than 120! No one knows all of them by heart, but it makes sense to understand different "families" of operators, which takes time. Often operators differ very, very slightly while offering seemingly the same functionality. Observables have other related concepts like schedulers, subscriptions, and so on. Learning and mastering all of those takes time and effort that, in the case when we are *not* developing an extremely large application, might be considered wasted. The Angular community long yearned for a simpler way to do basic reactivity; hence, signals were introduced in v16.

THE STATELESS NATURE OF OBSERVABLES

To better understand this point, let us explore this simple component that uses RxJS.

Listing 6.1   Subscribing to an observable for its latest value

```
@Component({
  template: `
    <div>
      <h2>Data</h2>
      <ul>
        <li *ngFor="let item of data$ | async">          Displays the
          {{ item.name }}                                 data with the
          <button (click)="deleteItem(item)>Delete item</button>   async pipe
        </li>
      </ul>
    </div>
  `,
  standalone: true,
})
```

```
export class DataComponent implements OnInit {
    private dataService = inject(DataService);
    private permissionsService = inject(PermissionsService);
    private destroyRef = inject(DestroyRef);
    private dialogService = inject(DialogService);
    data$ = this.dataService.getData();
    permissions: Permission[] = [];
```
◄── **Data is an observable.**

◄── **We cannot store permissions as simply an observable, because we need its value somewhere in the component code, not the template.**

```
    ngOnInit() {
        this.permissionsService.hasPermissions(this.permissions).pipe(
            takeUntilDestroyed(this.destroyRef),
        ).subscribe(permissions => {
            this.permissions = permissions;
        });
    }
```
◄── **A subscription that exists purely to extract the value from the permissions observable into a component property to be able to use it later**

```
    deleteItem(item: Item) {
        if (!this.permissions.includes('DeleteItem')) {
            return this.dialogService.open('You do not have permissions to
    delete this item.');
        }
```
◄──

Uses the latest value of the permissions observable

```
this.dataService.deleteItem(item);
    }
}
```

As we can see, the fact that permissions are represented by observables is a problem here. We now need to write a bunch of boilerplate code to be able to access the latest value of the permissions. In the case of the data, this problem is mitigated by the async pipe and the fact that we only use it in the template. In the case of the permissions, its value is not displayed anywhere in the template but rather is used by the component's code to perform a check.

In this case, we either need to somehow extract it in the template (even if it is not really needed there) and pass it as an argument to the deleteItem method (which will introduce even more complexity and confusion) or subscribe to it and extract to a local property (what was done here). Another approach would be to convert the permissions observable to a BehaviorSubject so that we can access the latest valuer any time we want, but that again would introduce some complexity, require unsubscribing under the hood, and make the component generally harder to explain to newly-onboarded team members.

Thus, observables not being representative of a state, but rather events (as we discussed in the previous chapter), poses a significant problem when authoring Angular components. Larger components can have dozens of lines of code filled with such boilerplate subscriptions, which only exist to cover up an implementation detail and have zero relation to the actual business logic of the component. Further in this chapter, we will see how signals help us avoid such scenarios. Now, let us explore the last major problem RxJS brings into the world of Angular applications.

ASYNC VS. SYNC AND GLITCHES

We mainly talked about RxJS observables in the context of asynchronous programming, but we also mentioned that observables can be either synchronous or asynchronous. Thus, when combining several observables into a single stream, we can run into hard-to-debug problems, especially when the observables are of two different "sorts." Again, let us consider an example component to better see the problem.

Listing 6.2   Combining asynchronous and synchronous observables

```
@Component({
  standalone: true,                                          Lets the user decide if
  imports: [AsyncPipe, ReactiveFormsModule, NgIf],           duplication is allowed
  template: `
      <input placeholder="Name" [formControl]="form.controls.name"/>
      <label>Can have duplicates</label>
      <input type="checkbox" [formControl]="form.controls.allowDuplicates"/>  ←──┘
      <button>Save</button>
      <button *ngIf="canSaveAsDuplicate$ | async">
        Save as duplicate
      </button>                    ←──────  Button only visible if a
  `,                                        condition on duplication
})                                          of names is met
export class App {
  private readonly dataService = inject(DataService);
  form = new FormGroup({
    name: new FormControl(''),
    allowDuplicates: new FormControl(false),   ←──     Form control that is
  });                                                  responsible for the user being
                                                       able to allow duplicate names

  hasDuplicates$ = this.form.controls.name.valueChanges.pipe(
    switchMap(
      name => this.dataService.checkForDuplicates(name)     Observable that
    ),                                                       continuously checks if a
  );                                                         duplicate name already
                                        ←─────────────       exists by making an HTTP
                                                             call via a service whenever
  canSaveAsDuplicate$ = combineLatest([   ←──┐               the user changes the name
    this.form.controls.allowDuplicates.valueChanges,
    this.hasDuplicates$,                             Combines the result of the
  ]).pipe(                                           HTTP call with the local
    map(                                             checkbox's value
      ([allowDuplicates, hasDuplicates]) =>
      allowDuplicates || !hasDuplicates),   ←──  The actual condition's logic: either
    );                                           the user allowed duplications via
}                                                the checkbox or duplicate names
                                                 do not exist anyway.
```

Now this is a solid, reactive implementation of a somewhat complex logical condition; it is very concise and easy to read. However, it has one glaring problem: if we actually run this code and click on the checkbox immediately, the "Save as duplicate" button will not appear. So what is the problem here? The combineLatest operator takes several observables and emits whenever one of the source observables emits. However, it *starts* emitting only when *all* of the source observables have emitted a value at least once (otherwise, there would be `null`s all over the place when the first emission occurs). But in our case, the `hasDuplicates$` observable is asynchronous (it is making an HTTP, and that is only after the user actually inputs some characters in the name input), but the `form.allow-Duplicates.valueChanges` observable is synchronous, meaning that its combination might have to wait a while before it actually emits a value. Thus, even if the user has clicked on the checkbox, the button will not appear until they input some characters.

This can be mitigated by using the `startsWith` operator and putting some default value into the streams that we combine, but this introduces more complexity, and in a large component such things can easily get overlooked only to then become bugs that are really hard to trace and fix. This behavior of being able to be either sync or async can also become a source of race conditions, when some data we anticipate earlier arrives later, causing a bug, and further complicating things. Again, this all comes back to the fact that observables represent events, but in Angular applications, developers very often try to describe a state of things with them, rather than just streams of notifications.

Now that we have laid the main foundational problems with RxJS in Angular, let's focus on the solution and find out what we expect from such a potential solution for this problem. Afterward, we will introduce signals and explore how they fix all the problems we mentioned here.

6.1.2 *What must the solution look like?*

Before we go forward and lay out the principles on which a potential solution will be built, let's also state that it is not possible to "fix" RxJS from inside Angular, meaning there is no logic that the Angular core team could put, say, in the rxjs-interop package that we mentioned in the previous chapter so that all these problems go away. The problems are intrinsic either to RxJS itself (observables can be either sync or async, and there's nothing we can do about it) or to the way developers treat RxJS in Angular apps (they are going to represent state as an observable, and we cannot expect to persuade everyone to stop doing this). With this in mind, let's now set up our rules for the new reactive primitive.

VALUE CAN ALWAYS BE READ

This one is simple: we can access the latest value of the reactive primitive whenever we want, without the need to "subscribe" to it. Value is read synchronously, it always has some default value, and so on.

READING THE VALUE DOES NOT AFFECT THE APPLICATION IN ANY WAY

In RxJS, as we saw, reading the value means subscribing to it. Sometimes this entails some other effect in the application. For instance, if we subscribe to an observable created by Angular's `HttpClient`, this will trigger a new HTTP request, which is a behavior that might not be obvious to developers who are not very familiar with the inner workings of observables. Also, subscribing will entail storing the value somewhere, in another variable or class property, to be reused later. With a new reactive primitive, this should not be the case: value must be readily available to read.

VALUE CAN BE CHANGED ON THE FLY

Again, this one is simple: we can always set a new value, unlike observables, which are immutable. The new reactive primitive represents a value (that can change over time and notify about changes), not a stream of events.

EVERYTHING IS SYNCHRONOUS

As we have seen, some problems stemming from observables are a result of them possibly being async. As we said, the new reactive primitive should represent a state, not events, thus it has no need to be async and should only be synchronous.

WE CAN PERFORM SIDE EFFECTS BASED ON CHANGES OF THE VALUE

An important part of having values that can change over time is the ability to perform actions whenever a change happens. This is what is known as a side effect. For instance, we might want to log the latest value in the `localStorage`, and this would be a side effect.

WE CAN CREATE NEW REACTIVE VALUES FROM EXISTING ONES

Another powerful and flexible capability of observables that needs to be transferred to the new reactive primitive is the ability to construct new ones from existing ones. This is often known as "deriving state" or "computed properties." For instance, we might have a list of products with their prices, and we want to display the total price for all items. The total price does not exist in a vacuum by itself and is totally dependent on the list of products and their quantities. Thus, we should be able to compute a new reactive primitive with the total price of products *from* the list of products, and this second computed property will always update whenever the list of products changes. Essentially, what we do with the `map` operator or the `combineLatest` operator should be possible with the new reactive primitive (but only synchronously).

UNSUBSCRIPTION WILL BE AUTOMATIC

This one is more about being developer-friendly. As the new reactive primitive will be part of Angular itself, it should be possible to handle the unsubscription from it internally, without forcing the developer to write some logic in the `ngOnDestroy` method.

IT SHOULD INTEROPERATE WITH RxJS

Finally, as we said, the reactive primitive should be synchronous, meaning the async stuff will still fall (rightfully so) on the mighty shoulders of RxJS, which in its stead means that we should have a way to communicate between this new reactive primitive and RxJS observables. Namely, we should be able to convert an observable to this new reactive primitive and vice versa.

   With all these rules laid out, we can finally dig into signals, the new reactive primitive Angular offers, and see how they fulfill all the checkboxes here and fixes all the problems we had with RxJS. Let's get started!

6.2   *What is a signal?*

Signals are the basic building blocks of the reactivity approach Angular offers. Essentially, a *signal* is an object that is callable (can be invoked like a function) and when called will return its latest value. While this might seem a bit like "magic," in Java-Script, everything is an object, including functions that we define, so a signal is essentially a function that has some added properties to it. This function/object also has several methods to update the value. As the value can be read simply by calling it as a function, there is no need to "subscribe" to it, and all of this happens synchronously. There are other functions that we will learn about later in this chapter that help us create new signals from existing ones or perform side effects when a value (or multiple values) changes. Let us see it in action now by familiarizing ourselves with the actual code necessary to deal with signals.

> **NOTE** If you are using Angular v16, signals are an experimental new feature that is in developer preview. We encourage readers to upgrade to newer versions as they have new features for signals and stable support.

6.2.1 Creating signals

First, before we start working with signals, we have to actually create one. Signals and everything necessary to deal with them have been added to the angular/core package. It turns out that to create a signal, we just need to import the `signal` function from the core package and use it to create a signal with an initial value:

```
import { signal } from '@angular/core';
const count = signal(0);
```

Here we have created a signal of a number whose initial value is 0. How can we see that value? As mentioned, the signal can be called as a function to extract the value, so we can just do the following:

```
import { signal } from '@angular/core';
const count = signal(0);
console.log(count());
```

This will log 0 to the console, as it is the latest (and incidentally, the very first) value of this signal. The value has not been updated yet, so it will always return 0 whenever invoked.

If we examine the `count` variable—for instance, hover over it in an IDE editor to see its type—we will see that TypeScript says its type is `WritableSignal<number>`. `WritableSignal` is a type of a `Signal` whose value can be changed (hence writable). There are other signals, typed as simply `Signal`, which are immutable, meaning they will lack the methods to update their value.

Both `Signal` and `WritableSignal` are generic types, and their type argument indicates the value that is stored inside of our signal. TypeScript is pretty smart, and the `signal` function is written in a way that allows TypeScript to infer the type of the signal from the default value. However, there are cases when inferring the value is not really possible. For instance, we want to create a signal of an array of strings but the default value is an empty array, so TypeScript has no way of guessing the overall type of this array. In such cases, we should provide the type manually:

```
import { signal } from '@angular/core';
const names = signal<string[]>([]);
console.log(names())
```

This will log [] and TypeScript will know that the names signal only accepts arrays of string.

There are two other ways of creating signals. One is by creating a computed signal: a signal derived from other signals. The other is by creating a signal from an observable. In both of those scenarios, we will have a `Signal` instead of a `WritableSignal`, which makes sense: their values entirely depend on either other signals or observables, so they should not be available for manual modification. Let's now see how we can update the value of an existing `WritableSignal`.

6.2.2 *Updating signals*

There are two ways of changing a signal: setting a value directly and updating the value using the previous value with a callback function. Let's examine each one in turn.

SETTING A SIGNAL'S VALUE

As signals are essentially wrappers around the actual values, there is a way to directly and manually set a new value. Here is how it's done:

```
import { signal } from '@angular/core';
const count = signal(0);
console.log(count());
count.set(1);
console.log(count());
```

Initially the console will log 0, as it is the default value of the signal, but the next time, after we invoke the set method, it will log 1, as we have set a new value afterward. As we mentioned, TypeScript inferred the type of this signal, so in the case of count, the set method will only accept numbers. If we invoke the set method in the names signal from the other example, it will only accept arrays of strings, as we explicitly provided the type of value that signal can hold, meaning signals are fully type-safe. We can also use other signals as values when setting a value of some signal; for instance, we can do the following instead:

```
const count = signal(0);
console.log(count());
count.set(count() + 1);
console.log(count());
```

As we can see, we passed the current value of the count signal + 1 as an argument to the set method, and it again produced 0 followed by 1 in the console. It turns out that updating a signal based on its previous value is a pretty common task, so we have a method for this too.

UPDATING A SIGNAL'S VALUE

The update method of a signal will accept a callback that works as follows: the argument to it will be the previous value of the signal, and whatever the callback returns will become the new value. Here we can use it to write an increment function that will increase the value of the count signal by 1 every time it's called:

```
const count = signal(0);
const increment = () => count.update(value => value + 1);
increment();
console.log(count());
```

Here, the previous value used to be 0, the initial value, and when we called count .update, what it did was invoke the callback function with the current value as argument (which was 0), and it returned 1, so 1 became the new value, which will be logged in the console.

The update method becomes very useful when working with arrays or objects when we want to modify a part of the array or the object without setting the whole value. For instance, we can write a function that adds a new name to the names signal:

```
const names = signal<string[]>([]);
const addName = (name: string) => names.update(value => [...value, name]);
addName('John');
console.log(names());
```

Here we used the update method to spread the existing items into a new array, with the new name appended in the end. This will log ["John"] to the console. Thus, we used the update method to change the value of the signal based on its previous value.

The callback for the update method can be any function, and we can perform a variety of operations and logical conditions here, provided they match the types. For instance, the callback for the update method when called on the count signal cannot return anything other than a number.

However, there are some guidelines for using the update method. A common best practice is to use pure functions as callbacks for it, meaning functions that always return the same value when called and do not have side effects. For example, it would be bad practice to change the value of some other property in the update callback, as it will be very surprising for other developers as to how that other property got changed. We should absolutely refrain from updating other signals in the update callback, as this could potentially cause systemic problems with how data flows through the app. If we want to update other signals based on one we have, there are other ways to do it cleanly, which we will explore further in this chapter.

So far so good: we learned how to create and update signals. Let's see how this fits into the rules we set up in section 6.1.2.

6.2.3 Creating signals vs. observables

Now let's briefly cover the rules that have already been fulfilled with signals.

VALUE CAN ALWAYS BE READ

As we have seen, we can always read the value of any signal by just invoking it as a function. So signals are compliant with this requirement, which already is a big plus when compared to observables.

READING THE VALUE DOES NOT AFFECT THE APPLICATION IN ANY WAY

Signals created manually are just wrappers around some value, and reading the value does not entail any "surprises," as compared to RxJS (which we saw might do something not very expected, like initiating an HTTP request). Thus, signals are also compliant with this rule.

VALUE CAN BE CHANGED ON THE FLY

There's not much to say here, as we spent the previous section elaborating on how to change signal values. We can safely tick this checkbox too.

EVERYTHING IS SYNCHRONOUS

While we did not explicitly say it, everything in our code suggested that signals work synchronously. Asynchronous signals do not exist, and even signals derived from async observables (we will learn how to do this later in this chapter) will work in a synchronous fashion and always have a value ready to be read. Thus, signals are compliant with this rule too.

UNSUBSCRIPTION WILL BE AUTOMATIC

This one is interesting, because we did not talk about what would happen after a component that uses signals gets destroyed (if anything, we haven't even explored such a component). However, signals that are created manually, as in our examples in the previous section, are just object wrappers around values, so they will be garbage collected the same way other, conventional properties are. As for computed signals and signals derived from observables, we will see how they work in the next sections. For now, this rule is fully complied with.

Now, with the knowledge of how signals can be created, updated, and read, we can move on and finally start creating an actual, practical Angular component that uses them.

6.3 Building Angular components with signals

In the HRMS application that we were building throughout chapters 2 to 5, we had several interrelated features concerning different management tasks for HR employees, like recruitment, employee management, vacations, and so on. One of the features was a "work" feature that dealt with employee affairs; for instance, there we had the employee list and employee details pages. Now we are going to add something more valuable for the HR administration—namely a page that helps handle time-off requests from employees. This page will display a list of time-off requests, allowing the HR admin to approve or reject them; it allows searching through requests by employee name and filtering approved/rejected/pending requests, and it shows statistical data about how many employees are off currently. We will do this by utilizing our newly acquired knowledge of Angular's signals and learning several new capabilities on the way too. Let's begin by creating our component.

6.3.1 Creating TimeOffComponent

First, let us define what a time-off request actually looks like and what properties that object will have. In the src/app/infrastructure/types folder, let's create a file named time-off-request.type.ts and put the following type there.

> **Listing 6.3 Time-off request type**

```
export type TimeOffRequest = {
    id: number;
    employeeId: number;
    startDate: string;
    endDate: string;
    type: 'Vacation' | 'Sick Leave' | 'Maternity Leave' |
     'Paternity Leave' | 'Other';
    status: 'Pending' | 'Approved' | 'Rejected';
    comment?: string;
};
```

Now, with the general idea of what a time-off request is, let's create a `TimeOffManagement Component`. In the src/app/pages/work folder, let's create a file named time-off-management.component.ts and put the actual component code. One note: we will use signals to represent the data there, and initially we will only use dummy data—without a service to load the actual data. We will add that in a further section in this chapter to illustrate interoperability with RxJS and async code. For now, the component will look something like the code in the following listing.

> **Listing 6.4 Time-off management component**

```
@Component({
    selector: 'app-time-off-management',
    template: `
        <h2>Time Off Management</h2>
        <table>
            <thead>
                <tr>
                    <th>Employee</th>
                    <th>Start Date</th>
                    <th>End Date</th>
                    <th>Type</th>
                    <th>Status</th>
                    <th>Comment</th>
                    <th>Actions</th>
                </tr>
            </thead>
            <tbody>
                <tr *ngFor="let request of requests()">
```

To read the value of a signal in the template, we will just invoke the signal, same as always.

```
                     <td>{{ request.employeeId }}</td>
                     <td>{{ request.startDate | date }}</td>
                     <td>{{ request.endDate | date }}</td>
                     <td>{{ request.type }}</td>
                     <td>{{ request.status }}</td>
                     <td>{{ request.comment }}</td>
                     <td>
                         <button *ngIf="request.status ===
        'Pending'">Approve</button>
                         <button
                           *ngIf="request.status === 'Pending'">
                           Reject
                         </button>
                         <button>Delete</button>
                     </td>
                 </tr>
             </tbody>
         </table>
     `,
     standalone: true,
     imports: [NgFor, NgIf, DatePipe],
})
export class TimeOffManagementComponent {
     requests = signal<TimeOffRequest[]>([
         {
             id: 1,
             employeeId: 1,
             startDate: new Date().toISOString(),
             endDate: new Date().toISOString(),
             type: 'Vacation',
             status: 'Pending',
         },
         {
             id: 2,
             employeeId: 2,
             startDate: new Date().toISOString(),
             endDate: new Date().toISOString(),
             type: 'Sick Leave',
             status: 'Approved',
             comment: 'Feeling pretty sick today :(',
         },
     ]);
}
```

We will add some actions that can be done with time-off requests next.

Signal that represents the array of time-off requests; the data is added manually for now.

One question we might have is about the part where we invoke the signal in the template like a function. We may have heard that calling functions in the template is a sort of bad practice, so why do this here? Note that Angular will call the function each time it suspects that there might have been a change in the data, which will need to be reflected in the UI, meaning whatever computation the function does, it will be re-executed. However, depending on a function, this might be something that is not important at all or something that will take lots of (unnecessary) time to complete, affecting performance. However, in the case of signals, this function call essentially immediately returns the value that is already there, meaning it is not something that will affect performance (reading signal values does some other things too; we will learn about them in the next chapter when we dive a bit deeper in their internal workings).

Next, let us practice our knowledge of updating signal values by creating the functions that will approve or reject time-off requests.

6.3.2 Handling signals in Angular components

Because we are working with arrays of objects, let us go forward and use the `set` and `update` methods to handle the data changes.

Listing 6.5 Changing signal values in a component

```
export class TimeOffManagementComponent {
  requests = signal<TimeOffRequest[]>([
    {
      id: 1,
      employeeId: 1,
      startDate: new Date().toISOString(),
      endDate: new Date().toISOString(),
      type: 'Vacation',
      status: 'Pending',
    },
    {
      id: 2,
      employeeId: 2,
      startDate: new Date().toISOString(),
      endDate: new Date().toISOString(),
      type: 'Sick Leave',
      status: 'Approved',
      comment: 'Feeling pretty sick today :(',
    },
  ]);

  approveRequest(request: TimeOffRequest) {        ◁──┐

    this.requests.update((requests) => {
      const index = requests.findIndex((r) => r.id === request.id);
      return requests.map(
        (item, i) => i === index ? ({
          ...item,
        status: 'Approved',
      }) : item);
    });
  }

  rejectRequest(request: TimeOffRequest) {         ◁──┐
    this.requests.update((requests) => {
      const index = requests.findIndex((r) => r.id === request.id);
      return requests.map(
        (item, i) => i === index ? ({
          ...item,
        status: Rejected',
```

We use update to approve a time-off request. We do it by mapping the existing array of requests to a new array, in which the exact request (corresponding to the index) is replaced by a new request object whose status is "Approved."

We do the same (but in reverse) when rejecting a request.

```
        }) : item);
      });
    }
                                              ┌─  When deleting a request, we can use
                                                  the update method and just filter
                                                  out the request with a particular id.
    deleteRequest(request: TimeOffRequest) {  ◄─┘
      this.requests.update((requests) =>
        requests.filter((r) => r.id !== request.id)
      );
    }
}
```

Now we have ourselves a workable component with basic functionality, and if we run this component, we will see how all of the UI gets updated when we click the buttons. However, there is more that we want to do with this component. For instance, we want to be able to search through requests by type, for example, and we also want to display some text that shows how many pending requests are left, so an HR admin can track their progress when reviewing multiple requests. Of course, those functionalities are dependent on the time-off request items and should be derived from that signal. Let us now see how it can be done.

6.4   Computed signals

With RxJS, we covered how observables are immutable and we can only create new observables from existing ones. With signals, we saw that they are mutable, but we haven't yet approached the topic of creating new signals from existing ones; so far, we only created new signals manually from scratch. However, as we saw, it is very important to be able to derive new values from existing signals that will be updated as soon as the source signal changes its value. With RxJS, we did it with a multitude of operators, mainly the map operator. With signals, it is far easier, as we do this just using a single, quite straightforward function called computed. Signals created with this function are called computed signals. Let's dive in and see how it works and how it improves our code readability and the flow of data across applications.

6.4.1   Creating computed signals

As mentioned, computed signals are created via the computed function. The function is very simple; it takes a callback, which has no arguments; and the value that this callback returns becomes the value of the resulting signal. Then the computed function returns that signal, which can be then used to read its value. Let us see it in action:

```
const count = signal(0);
const increment = () => count.update(value => value + 1);
const doubleCount = computed(() => count() * 2);
console.log(count());
console.log(doubleCount());
increment();
console.log(count());
console.log(doubleCount());
```

The count signal we are already familiar with and also with the increment function. Now what is new is the computed signal called doubleCount, which is defined as the value of the count signal times 2. This code will output 0, 0, 1, 2 in the console when executed. Now, 0 and 0 make sense, as the initial value of count is 0, and double count is just 0 times 2, which is still 0. What is fascinating about this code is that when we call the increment function, we only update the value of the count signal, but the doubleCount signal's value is updated automatically. What is even more fascinating is that we do not have to do any magical things here—just write the actual logic of how doubleCount is derived—and the value of that signal will always be automatically tied to the value of count. This drastically reduces the number of implementation details we need to code, only requiring us to write down the actual business logic.

We can also use the computed function to create signals derived from multiple other signals. For instance, we can calculate the sum of two different signals:

```
const a = signal(2);
const b = signal(3);
const sum = computed(() => a() + b());
console.log(sum());
b.set(7);
console.log(sum())
```

This code uses the signals a and b, and their sum is computed via the computed signal sum. This new signal will always have the value of the sum of a and b and will update automatically when one of them changes the value. In this instance, the console will log 5 and then 9.

Now we might wonder if just writing a function that returns this sum and calling it whenever we need the sum won't do the same job. However, that would mean the computation will run every time we read the value of the computed signal, even if the value has not changed at all, which might be quite costly. On the other hand, signals created with computed will recalculate their value when there are changes, and store it, so reading their value *does not* result in a new run of the calculation. We can check this by making a small modification to our computed signal and running the following code:

```
const a = signal(2);
const b = signal(3);
const sum = computed(() => {
  console.log('Recalculating');
  return a() + b();
});
sum();
sum();
sum();
```

Despite calling the sum signal three times, we only see Recalculating in the console once. This is because computed signals will rerun their computation only when one of the signals they depend on changes, meaning that reading its value will not (in general) trigger recalculation.

There is another important thing to pay attention to, and that can be seen if we just remove any reads to the computed signal:

```
const a = signal(2);
const b = signal(3);
const sum = computed((() => {
  console.log('Recalculating');
  return a() + b();
});
```

Now if we run this, we won't see anything in the console, as the computation callback will not be executed. This makes sense, as the `computed` function assumes there is no need to perform a computation if the value is not requested by anyone.

The final important thing to notice here is that `computed` returns a `Signal` and not a `WritableSignal`. This is completely in line with what we would expect, as a computed signal completely depends on other signals, and manually updating its value makes no sense whatsoever. Type safety is also guaranteed, as TypeScript will infer the type of the computed signal's value based on the return type of the callback we provided.

WE CAN CREATE NEW REACTIVE VALUES FROM EXISTING ONES

As we can see, the rule we set up earlier is now fulfilled, and this implementation of a reactive primitive is completely compliant with that rule. Moreover, if we try to draw parallels between signals and RxJS, we can notice that `computed` is somewhat similar to both the `map` operator and the `combineLatest` operator, with the main difference being that it always runs synchronously.

UNSUBSCRIPTION WILL BE AUTOMATIC

As computed signals "subscribe" to other signals, a question might arise as to what happens to that connection when it is no longer needed. Thankfully, Angular takes care of it all by itself: a computed signal will be destroyed when the context in which it was created is gone. For instance, if we create a computed signal in a component, it will be destroyed together with the component when the latter is removed from the DOM tree, meaning that computed signals continue to be compliant with this rule.

Next, let us explore how we can use the `computed` function in an Angular component.

6.4.2 *Simplifying complex logic in Angular components using computed signals*

As we previously already laid out our next objectives with the `TimeOffManagement` `Component`, let us start implementing them, beginning with a progress counter of how many resolved time-off requests are there versus the total number of requests, so that the users can keep track. We can easily accomplish this with computed signals.

Listing 6.6   Using computed signals in a component

```
export class TimeOffManagementComponent {
  requests = signal<TimeOffRequest[]>([]);
  resolvedRequests = computed(() =>
    this.requests().filter(
      (r) => r.status !== 'Pending',
    ));

}
```

⟵ **Mock data is omitted for the sake of brevity.**

A signal is computed from the whole list of requests to only include requests that are not pending anymore.

Other methods in the component are also omitted.

Now we have a signal that always contains only resolved requests, meaning ones that are no longer "Pending." We can simply drop this data somewhere in the UI—for example:

```
<h3>Resolved {{ resolvedRequests().length }} / {{ requests().length }}
    Unresolved </h3>
```

The UI will also gets updated every time the list of requests changes. We can check it by approving/rejecting or deleting some of the requests. Let us now move forward and implement something more complex—namely, a filtering functionality based on the type of requests. As we use signals for this, what we are going to create another signal that holds the type of request selected by the user and use a computed signal to combine it with the requests array to derive a list of filtered requests. Let's first create a simple signal that will hold one of the request types:

```
selectedType = signal<
    'Vacation' | 'Sick Leave' | 'Maternity Leave' | 'Paternity Leave' |
    'Other' | ''
  >('');
```

Here we are going with full type-safety and mentioning all possible variations of the request type, plus an empty string, which represents no filter selected (which is the default). Now let us add a select dropdown with all the options and bind it with this new signal using a `ngModel`:

```
<select [ngModel]="selectedType()"
    (ngModelChange)="selectedType.set($any($event))">
    <option value="">All</option>
    <option value="Vacation">Vacation</option>
    <option value="Sick Leave">Sick Leave</option>
    <option value="Maternity Leave">Maternity Leave</option>
    <option value="Paternity Leave">Paternity Leave</option>
    <option value="Other">Other</option>
</select>
```

There are two things worth paying attention to here: one is the fact that we wrote `(ngModelChange)="selectedType.set($any($event))"`. This is a bit unusual, as commonly we would write something like `[(ngModel)]="selectedType"`. However, we cannot do this in v16 because `[(ngModel)]="something"` is actually syntactic sugar, a shorthand syntax equivalent to `[ngModel]="something" (ngModelChange)="something = $event"`. However, with signals, we cannot just assign values to them and instead need to call the set method, which is why we have to spell the logic out explicitly. In Angular v17.3, this familiar way of binding signals to `ngModel` has been added, and we can use it as we always did, but as of Angular v16, there is no `signal NgModel` way of doing this, so, for now, we are going to use this syntax and will discuss the new approach in chapter 10.

Second, we used the `$any` helper function, which in Angular templates type-casts a value to type `any`. We do this because, while we explicitly stated all possible values of `selectedType` (which was narrower than just `string`), the `$event` here could be any `string` (from TypeScript's perspective), so we cast it to type `any` to let TypeScript know we understand what we are doing.

Now we have a signal that will update when the user changes the type from the dropdown. Finally, we need a computed signal, which will calculate the filtered users based on the selected type:

```
filteredRequests = computed(() => {
  const type = this.selectedType();
  return this.requests().filter(r => (type ? r.type === type : true));
});
```

Now we just check if some specific type is selected and return an array filtered based on that. In the template, we can replace `requests()` (which represent all the requests, without any filters) with the new `filteredRequests` computed signal:

```
<tr *ngFor="let request of filteredRequests()">
```

This will work the same way as with manually created signals. We can also compute new signals using other computed signals. For instance, the `resolvedRequests` signals can be modified to show the proportion of resolved requests among the ones filtered, as opposed to the total number of signals:

```
resolvedRequests = computed(() =>
    this.filteredRequests().filter((r) => r.status !== 'Pending')
);
```

Here the `filteredRequests` is treated like any other signal, so it is irrelevant whether it is computed or created manually.

Now that we have learned performing complex operations with signals, let us set up some basic rules and best practices:

- Always use computed signals instead of getter methods or functions for deriving new values.
- *Do not* write to signals in a computed callback, meaning do not ever call another signal's set or update methods in that callback.

- Try to refer only to properties that themselves are signals in the computed call-back unless absolutely necessary. While using nonsignal properties in a computed callback can sometimes be unavoidable, most commonly it is a code smell and can be a sign of deeper problems with the component's structure.

Let us move on and discuss executing side effects based on changes to signal values.

6.5 Effects

Sometimes, instead of calculating a new value that will dynamically change when a dependency changes, we just want to perform some "unrelated" action whenever a signal changes its values. For example, we might want to send an HTTP request that would track a user's action or maybe set a `FormControl`'s value based on some signal or something else.

6.5.1 Creating effects

Signals in Angular provide a special capability to execute side effects. This is accomplished via the `effect` function. Let's review it in code, which is a constructor of some Angular component:

```
constructor() {
    effect(() => {
        console.log(`Count is ${this.count()}`);
    });
    this.increment();
    this.increment();
}
```

The callback in effect will be called when the count signal's value changes, which it does via calling the `increment` function. However, as opposed to `computed`, it will only log `Count is 2`, skipping `0` and `1`. This is because signal effects are *always* asynchronous—no matter if the code inside the callback does not deal with any async logic. This means that if during one function execution the value of a signal that an effect watches changes several times, we will receive only the last one and perform the effect's logic on it once.

Let's use this to synchronize our selected type with `localStorage`. What we want is for the user who leaves the `TimeOffManagementComponent` to see what they selected previously from the request type dropdown and be able to continue doing what they used to do. The following listing shows how we can implement it.

Listing 6.7 Saving state to `localStorage` with an effect

```
constructor() {
    effect(() => {
        localStorage.setItem('selectedType', this.selectedType());
    });
}
```

As with computed signals, effects will automatically track the signals they depend on and run the `effect` callback again. So every time the user selects a new time-off request type, the `localStorage` will get updated and store the latest value. To bring that value back when the user visits the page, we can just change the default value of the `selectedType` signal:

```
selectedType = signal<
    'Vacation' | 'Sick Leave' | 'Maternity Leave' |
    'Paternity Leave' | 'Other' | ''
  >(localStorage.getItem('selectedType') as any ?? '');
```

Here we use the `as any` type-casting command because `localStorage.setItem` returns a value of type `string`, and we mentioned a narrower type; we did it to tell TypeScript we know what we are doing.

WE CAN PERFORM SIDE EFFECTS BASED ON CHANGES OF THE VALUE

As we can see, we ensured the new reactive primitive complies with this rule too. We are not only able to derive values but also perform loosely related logic based on other signals. Let's now take a deeper look at the effects and see how they function.

6.5.2   *Important things to know about effects*

While computed signals were more or less simple, effects have many restrictions that we need to be aware of. The following are the most important ones.

EFFECTS CAN ONLY RUN IN AN INJECTION CONTEXT

Similar to the `inject` function, we can only register effects in contexts where the DI tree is available. This is to ensure that Angular can then safely "unsubscribe" from the effect—for instance, when the component is removed from the DOM. If we *absolutely* need to register an effect in a method that is not the constructor, we can do this by passing a reference to the component's injector to the `effect` function:

```
private readonly injector = inject(Injector);
someMethod() {
    effect(() => {
      console.log(this.someSignal())
    }, {injector: this.injector});
}
```

This will ensure that the effect will be able to be destroyed when the component is gone.

EFFECTS CAN BE STORED IN COMPONENT PROPERTIES AND DESTROYED EARLIER

Instead of just spelling out the effect in the constructor, we are able to assign the reference to the created effect to a class property to be reused later. This accomplishes two things. First, the effect gets a name that future readers can use to immediately understand what it does without reading the code in the callback. Second, we can use that reference to terminate the effect *before* the component is removed from the DOM, based on an event or a condition.

Listing 6.8 Stopping an effect before the component is destroyed

```
@Component({
  standalone: true,
  template: `
    <button (click)="removeLogging()">Stop</button>
  `,
})
export class SomeComponent {
  count = signal(0);
  log = effect(() => {
    console.log(`Count is ${this.count()}`);
  });

  constructor() {
    setInterval(() => this.count.update(c => c + 1), 1_000);
  }

  removeLogging() {
    this.log.destroy();
  }
}
```

Stores the reference to the
effect in a component property

Logs a value of
the count signal

Increments
the count
every 1 second

Stops the effect from running using
the reference and the destroy method

Now if we click the "Stop" button, we will see that logging every 1 second to the console stops. This is useful for scenarios dealing with async events or streams that only need to be handled for a while.

WRITING TO SIGNALS FROM EFFECTS IS PROHIBITED

Sometimes we might be tempted to update some signal's value from the effect callback. However, code like this will result in an error:

```
export class SomeComponent {
  count = signal(0);

  constructor() {
    effect(() => {
      this.count.update(c => c + 1);
    });
  }
}
```

If we run this code, we will receive the following error:

```
Error: NG0600: Writing to signals is not allowed in a `computed` or an
`effect` by default. Use `allowSignalWrites` in the `CreateEffectOptions` to
enable this inside effects.
```

However, as we see, the error message offers a workaround. If we *absolutely* need to update another signal from an effect, we can allow it using the allowSignalWrites option:

```
effect(() => {
  this.count.update(c => c + 1);
}, {allowSignalWrites: true});
```

But it is important to remember that this is a very rare case. In most scenarios, what this means is that one signal is dependent on another one, meaning it probably can be derived from it using a computed signal instead of an effect.

Next let us talk about why we should, for the most part, avoid using effects too much and how to recognize scenarios where effects are really necessary.

6.5.3 When to use effects

As the name "side effect" suggests, effects are most useful in scenarios where we want to perform something that is out of the usual flow of a component. To better understand this, let's remember figure 5.1 from the previous chapter, which illustrated the life cycle of the component. It postulates that the UI is rendered based on the component's state; then the UI sends events to the component, which in turn updates the state, which again updates the UI, and so on. Thus, everything that falls out of this nice circle can be considered a side effect. Let's explore some examples.

WRITING TO EXTERNAL STORAGE

We already covered this example when we created an effect that stored a signal's value in `localStorage`. So local storage, session storage, cookies, indexed DB, and so on are part of neither the UI nor the component's state; thus we should use effects when interacting with them.

CALLING THIRD-PARTY APIS

We know that it is very common to work with reactive forms in Angular applications. Reactive forms work as a wrapper around form values, and we use methods like `FormControl.setValue` or `FormControl.disable` to handle the behaviors of our controls. There can be scenarios when we need to, for example, disable a `FormControl` based on a value from some signal. We cannot express this logic via a computed signal; thus we have to employ effects to handle such functionality. Any other third-party API that requires such interactions will be considered a side effect.

PERFORMING UI UPDATES THAT CANNOT BE EXPRESSED VIA ANGULAR'S TEMPLATE SYNTAX

The template syntax in Angular is very powerful and versatile, but there are still cases where it is not enough to perform some operations. For instance, we might want to set a dynamic title on the browser tab, and the only way to achieve this with Angular is by using the `Title` injectable. If we want to set the title based on some signal, we would need an effect.

> **Listing 6.9 Setting a tab title from a signal using an effect**

```
export class SomeComponent {
  name = signal('Tab name');
  title = inject(Title);

  constructor() {
    effect(() => {
      this.title.setTitle(this.name());
```

```
      });
   }
}
```

Any other DOM-related operation like this, when depending on signal values, should be implemented via an effect.

WORKING WITH CANVAS

Canvas provides a huge API to draw completely custom things outside of the usual flow of the DOM. We might be employing a third-party library to draw charts, for instance, or drawing an image ourselves based on values of some signals. As canvas cannot be drawn using just HTML tags, Angular's template syntax is powerless here, meaning we will have to resort to using effects to express relations between signals and whatever drawings are in the canvas.

As we saw, effects are something that we should avoid unless dealing with something that really falls out of the usual State → UI → Events → State flow. In the next chapter, we will explore more capabilities of effects and some pitfalls developers might stumble upon when working with them. Now let's move forward and finally try to reconcile RxJS with signals and see how the two can work together to achieve amazing functionality with just a few lines of code.

6.6   RxJS and signals interoperability

We began the chapter by listing several problems with RxJS, one of which was the problem that arises from the fact that observables can be asynchronous. We saw that signals are synchronous, meaning that RxJS will still have a job to do: handle all the async stuff. This raises a question: how do we make RxJS work with signals? There are two ways this is accomplished. One is being able to convert an observable to a new signal, which will always hold its latest value. The other is converting a signal to a new observable that will emit every time the signal changes its value. Let's examine those cases.

6.6.1   Converting observables to signals

In listing 6.4 we began building the `TimeOffManagementComponent`, and we made the initial value of the requests signal an array of mock requests. However, in real life, this won't be the case, and we will retrieve the requests from an API. We will have a service, which will utilize the `HttpClient` and return an observable of time-off requests. But if it is an observable, how do we use it as a signal in our code?

Another function, named `toSignal`, from the rxjs-interop package that we learned about in the previous chapter, will come to our rescue. This function will take any observable and return a signal that always contains the latest value from that source observable. Because signals are synchronous and observables can potentially be asynchronous and thus not have an initial value for some time, this function also accepts an options parameter, where we can specify an initial value until the observable emits. In our case, this will be an empty array. Let's see it in action.

Listing 6.10   Converting an observable to a signal

```
export class TimeOffManagementComponent {
  private readonly timeOffRequestService = inject(
  TimeOffRequestService,
);
  requests = toSignal(
    this.timeOffRequestService.getRequests(),
    {initialValue: []}
  );
  selectedType = signal<
    'Vacation' | 'Sick Leave' | 'Maternity Leave' |
    'Paternity Leave' | 'Other' | ''
  >(localStorage.getItem('selectedType') as any ?? '');
  resolvedRequests = computed(() =>
    this.filteredRequests().filter((r) => r.status !== 'Pending')
  );
  filteredRequests = computed(() => {
    const type = this.selectedType();
    return this.requests().filter(r => (type ? r.type === type : true));
  });

}
```

Injects the TimeOffRequestService, which will make HTTP calls and return observables

We make the HTTP call to retrieve the requests and convert the resulting observable to a signal using toSignal with an initial value set to an empty array.

All computed signals that used to depend on the requeests signal continue to work as expected.

Rest of the component code omitted for the sake of brevity

In this case, `requests` continues to be a signal that contains the array of requests, so we can use it as previously when deriving other signals from it, reading its value or displaying it in the template. However, all the methods where we changed its value via `update` will now throw errors. This is because the `toSignal` function returns a `Signal`, and not a `WritableSignal`, which is expected, because if we have created a signal from an observable, we expect it to depend entirely on the source observable and not to be able to change its value manually. In real life, we wouldn't do that anyway: when we approve or reject requests, we make HTTP requests to the backend instead of just changing the values in the UI.

Because observables can be async and have three states (working, error, and completed), this has to be reflected in some way in the signal derived from it. So if an error notification is received from the source observable, this error will be stored and thrown the next time we attempt to read from this signal. In case of observable completion, the signal will continue as usual and always return the last value emitted by the source observable before its completion.

Another important thing to remember is that, similar to the `effect` function, the `toSignal` function also only works in an injection context. This is because, under the hood, the function subscribes to the observable and injects the `DestroyRef` to unsubscribe from it automatically when, for example, the component in which it has been called gets destroyed. Again, as with effects, we can bypass this restriction by passing a reference to the component's injector and invoking the function in methods other than the constructor.

Because of this, we cannot just go assigning signals derived from observables to properties wherever we like. For instance, we could modify the `deleteRequest` method to update the requests array via an HTTP call:

```
deleteRequest(request: TimeOffRequest) {
  this.requests = toSignal(
    this.timeOffRequestService
      .deleteRequest(request.id)
      .pipe(switchMap(() => this.timeOffRequestService.getRequests())),
    { initialValue: this.requests(), injector: this.injector }
  );
}
```

While this seems right, in reality it will cause all of our computed signals to break, as we are reassigning the existing `requests` property to a brand-new signal derived from another HTTP call observable. To avoid such scenarios, we need to build our HTTP calls in a manner that will make the observable emit again (instead of completing after the response arrives) so that the signals derived from them update and show fresh data right away. Behavior like this already exists in state management systems that are based on observables, like NgRx, but in plain old Angular this does not work out of the box and needs to be implemented manually. However, this requires significant rethinking of our approaches and an architectural shift; thus, we will cover this topic in intricate detail in the next chapter, when we dive deep into how signals work and how we should build application architecture around them. For now, let's move on and see the reverse scenario: creating new observables from existing signals.

6.6.2 Converting signals to observables

While the previous approach is very popular, converting signals to observables is a bit less common as a development task. However, there are scenarios when this can be necessary. For instance, we might have a combined stream created from multiple observables and want to add another source only to discover that source is a signal, not an observable. In such a scenario, it would make more sense to convert that signal to an observable and just combine it with the rest of them, rather than convert the other stream to a signal and use `computed` or `effect`.

With the rxjs-interop package, another function is available to us to perform such a conversion: the `toObservable` function. This function operates as the reverse of the `toSignal` function, taking a signal as an argument and producing an observable that emits each new value of the source signal. The following is a basic example:

```
export class SomeComponent {
  count = signal(0);
  count$ = toObservable(this.count);

  constructor() {
    this.count$.subscribe(console.log);
```

```
    setInterval(() => this.count.update(value => value + 1), 1_000);
  }
}
```

Here count$ is an observable derived from the count signal. As the count signal is incremented by 1 each second, the output in the console will be 0, 1, 2,. . . and so on every second. Note that toObservable works similarly to toSignal in the sense that it can only be executed in an injection context (again this can be worked around by passing a reference to the component injector). This is because toObservable uses an effect under the hood to handle the connection between the source signal and the resulting observable, and effect itself requires an injection context to properly destroy itself on the component's destruction.

Another notable thing is the fact that while signals themselves are synchronous (we read their values in place, without subscribing via a callback), they propagate their changes asynchronously, meaning the updates to the source signal will only be emitted after the current stack frame stops executing synchronous commands. To better illustrate this point, let us consider the following modification to the previous example:

```
export class SomeComponent {
  count = signal(0);
  count$ = toObservable(this.count);

  constructor() {
    this.count$.subscribe(console.log);
    this.count.set(1);
    this.count.set(2);
    this.count.set(3);
  }
}
```

In this case, we will only see the value 3 logged in the console because the signal will wait until the current function (in this case, the constructor) stops executing before notifying subscribers about the update, and at that point the latest updated value will be 3. Also, if we completely remove the code that does updates to the count signal, we will still see 0 in the console: the observable will always emit at least the default value of the source signal when subscribed to.

IT SHOULD INTEROPERATE WITH RxJS

With this last section, we showed conclusively that signals comply with this rule too: we can easily integrate RxJS logic with signals, and vice versa, and decide when to use which in complete harmony with each other.

Now with the basics of signals already covered, we are ready to embark on the next part of our journey into the world of reactive programming: a deep dive into how signals function under the hood, learning about which tasks should be solved with RxJS and which with signals, how to manage state shared between components using signals (and should we do it at all), how to migrate certain parts of an Angular application from RxJS to signals, and how this all will affect Angular's performance and reusability.

6.7 Exercises for the reader

- Build a simple to-do list component from scratch using signals, with search, deleting to-do items and marking them as complete; additionally implement saving the data to local storage.
- Refactor previous components built in the HRMS application to use signals.
- Experiment with existing projects to try and find our cases where signals can be used to reduce complexity when dealing with reactive programming scenarios—for instance, large subscriptions to RxJS observables.

Summary

- RxJS is very powerful but is not fully compatible to solving all reactive programming tasks in Angular and comes with its own problems.
- The Angular core team proposed a new reactive primitive called a signal, which can be used to handle reactivity in Angular applications without RxJS observables.
- Signals are simple wrappers around values that notify other subscribers about their value updates.
- Signal values can be changed via Angular's `set` and `update` methods.
- New signals can be derived from existing ones using the `computed` functions; these new signals will be completely dependent on their source signals and won't be available for manual update.
- We can also register side effects as a callback that will be executed when signals in the callback change
- In both cases, Angular will automatically track dependencies and dispose of the subscriptions on the component's destruction.
- Signals fully interoperate with RxJS, allowing the conversion of observables to signals and vice versa.

Signals: A deep dive

7

This chapter covers

- Signal value equality and advanced manual cleanup of effects
- The internal workings of signals
- State management across components using signals
- Caveats of using signals with RxJS
- Migrating to signals
- The future of signals

In the previous chapter, we learned about the basics of working with signals: how to create them, change their value, derive new signals from existing ones, and make them work with RxJS observables. Now, as advertised in the title of this chapter, we will take a deep dive into the world of signals and learn about advanced options, best practices, and ways to migrate existing applications to use signals. Let's get started!

7.1 Advanced options when dealing with signals

So far, we have learned that signals are wrappers around values, which also notify us about the changes to those values. The process is pretty straightforward, accomplished via either the `computed` or `effect` functions. However, the default logic behind those computations is sometimes not enough to describe some complex processes and requires modification. Let's learn about those options and when we might want to use them.

7.1.1 Signal equality

In the previous chapter in section 6.4.1, we talked about computed signals and defined them as signals derived from other signals, which get re-evaluated whenever the original signal's value changes. One question we did *not* ask is: what constitutes a change to the signal's value? While the question indeed sounds superficial, in reality, it can get quite complex from time to time. Let's consider the code in the following listing.

Listing 7.1 Signal re-evaluating a value without an actual change

```
@Component({
  selector: 'some-component,          Uses a computed
  standalone: true,                   signal in the
  template: `                         template          The button will
    Full Name: {{ fullName() }}     ◄─                  change the signal's
    <button (click)="changeUser()">Change User</button>  ◄─  value when clicked.
  `,
})
export class SomeComponent {          A signal of an
  user = signal({               ◄─    object
    id: 1,
    firstName: 'Jon',
    lastName: 'Snow',
    age: 20,
  })                                              We log every time
  fullName = computed(() => {                      the computed
    console.log('Re-evaluating');      ◄─          callback executes.
    return `${this.user().firstName} ${this.user().lastName}`;
  });

  changeUser() {
    this.user.update(value => ({
      ...value,
      age: 20,              ◄─   Notice we do not actually change
    }));                         the value; this again sets the age
  }                              property's value as 20.
}
```

If we run this component, we can notice that the `Re-evaluating` text appears in the console every time we click the button, *despite* the fact that we did not really change anything in the original object, let alone the first or last names. This happens because `update`, for instance, will set a new value onto an object and just propagate a notification to all computed signals derived from the source.

In this case, the `update` method *does* in fact check for equality between the previous and current value, but in the case of objects, it just uses referential equality; that is, if we provide a new object, even if data inside matches the original 100%, it will treat it like a completely new one and propagate the changes.

So what do we do about this problem? It turns out Angular has us covered here: we can provide an equality-checking function when creating new signals! For instance, we might decide that a user is "changed" when its `id` property is mutated (a simplistic approach but could work in some cases in real life). Let's change our code a little so we get it working in the most efficient manner.

Listing 7.2   Using equality comparison for signals

```
export class SomeComponent {
  user = signal({
    id: 1,
    firstName: 'Jon',
    lastName: 'Snow',
    age: 20,
  }, {
    equal: (previous, current) => {          Provides an equality
      return previous.id === current.id;     checking function for
    }                                        the signal's value
  })
                                             The function will check if id is the same
  fullName = computed(() => {                for the new and previous values to
    console.log('Re-evaluating');            determine if the object has changed.
    return `${this.user().firstName} ${this.user().lastName}`;
  });

  changeUser() {
    this.user.update(value => ({
      ...value,
      age: 20,
    }));
  }
}
```

Now if we run the code, the `Re-evaluated` text will appear only once in the console: the very first time when the computed full name signal is evaluated.

This same logic can be applied to computed signals themselves, in case we are deriving new computed signals from them in turn somewhere down the line. So when we create new signals, we can define an equality comparison function to make sure we don't run costly computations too often. Next, let's optimize even further by ensuring computed signals only re-evaluate in the event of some of their dependency updates (only the important ones) instead of all the signals inside of the callback.

7.1.2 *Untracking dependencies*

In the previous chapter, we established that callbacks for `computed` and `effect` functions will be re-executed when one of the signals read inside them changes its value. This is great in and of itself, because we want the freshest available value, and this does the job without any friction. However, there are scenarios where we want to execute the callback only when *some* of the signals have changed but *not all* of them. Let's consider the code in the following listing.

Listing 7.3 Computed signal updated each second by an interval

```
export class App {
  user = signal({
    id: 1,
    firstName: 'Jon',
    lastName: 'Snow',
    age: 20,
  });
  dateTime = toSignal(interval(900).pipe(map(() => new Date())),
    {initialValue: new Date()});          ◁──────────┐
  fullName = computed(() => {                          │   Signal derived from an
    const {firstName, lastName} = this.user();         │   observable that emits about
    return `${firstName} ${lastName}, last modified at │   every second, converted to
    ${this.dateTime().toString()}`;   ◁──             │   that current date
  });

  changeUser() {                              Uses the date signal to show
    this.user.update(value => ({             when the user was last
      ...value,                              updated
      age: 20,
    }));
  }
}
```

Now we use the `dateTime` signal to show when the computed `fullName` signal was last updated, but we run into a problem: the "last updated" in the UI will show the current date and time to the current second. This is because this new computed signal also tracks (listens to) the changes on the `dateTime` signal, which in turn changes about every second. So how do we explain to Angular that we only care about the changes on the `user` signal and `dateTime` is only complimentary to it? It turns out that Angular has a tool for this, called the `untracked` function. Here is how we can use it in our scenario:

```
fullName = computed(() => {
    const {firstName, lastName} = this.user();
    const dateTime = untracked(this.dateTime);
    return `${firstName} ${lastName}, last modified at
    ${dateTime.toString()}`;
});
```

The `untracked` function will take a signal (important note: a *signal,* and *not* its value) and return its value without tracking it as a dependency for the derived computed signal. Now if we run the code, every time we actually change the user object, the computed signal will show the very "last modified time," but it won't change otherwise even though the `dateTime` signal does in fact notify about its new values.

This function is especially useful in effects, where we might want to run entire pieces of logic that interact with some signals, but only when a very specific signal notifies. For instance, we might have a complex form that runs a significant risk of users losing their progress if they spend too much time on it—for example, due to a timeout; in this case, we want to run an effect that will automatically save the progress every few minutes. However, because saving requires reading from the form signal, it will mean that the effect will also run whenever the user changes the values of the input fields, and we do *not* want that many re-executions. We can easily do this by providing a callback function to the untracked function, and whatever signals are read in the callback will remain untracked:

Listing 7.4   Using untracked callbacks in effects

Reads the dateTime signal, which notifies every 3 minutes, so we know when to save

Runs our saving/alerting logic in an untracked callback so that we do not save to localStorage every time the form is updated but instead only every 3 minutes

```
constructor() {
  effect(() => {
    const dateTime = this.dateTime();      ⟵
    untracked(() => {                      ⟵
      const formValues = this.form();
      localStorage.setItem('formValues', JSON.stringify(formValues));
      alert(`Your progress has been saved at ${dateTime}`)
    });
  });
}
```

As we can see, we can now run entire functions in an untracked environment, making them independent from the effect in which they have been invoked. It is also a good practice to wrap any calls to other functions in untracked, because they might possibly read other signals in the future if someone changes them, causing hard-to-find bugs. Finally, let us learn about the last advanced option signals have: the ability to manually clean up effects or signals derived from observables.

7.1.3   *Manual cleanup*

In section 6.5.2, we mentioned that we can manually end an effect cycle by storing it in a class property and calling EffectRef.destroy(). This could be useful if we want to terminate an effect way before the component that initiated it gets destroyed. However, there is a caveat: what if we invoke some asynchronous logic inside this effect—for example, something like a setTimeout? For example, let's modify the logic of our previous example. Now, instead of saving every 3 minutes, we will react to the change of the form, wait for a minute, and save it to localStorage. However, this effect will be canceled if the user clicks the Save button and outright saves their progress to the database. Let's see how this looks in the following listing.

Listing 7.5   Invoking asynchronous logic in effects

```
constructor() {
  effect(() => {
    const formValues = this.form();
    setTimeout(() => {
      localStorage.setItem('formValues', JSON.stringify(formValues));
```

```
    }, 1_000);
  })
}
```

In this case, we would run into another problem: when the user clicks "Save" and the effect is destroyed, the callback will be executed one last time. While in this scenario we may think "Not a big deal!", in general, such cases can cause really hard-to-find and hard-to-fix bugs. Also, we might want to clean the `localStorage`, as the values there have been saved to the database anyway. So how do we achieve this?

It seems we need to know the effect terminated so that the timeout callback does not execute, but how do we know the effect is done? For this purpose, `effect` callbacks have a special, optional argument, which lets us define another callback that will run whenever the effect is destroyed (regardless if it is terminated manually or because the component got destroyed). The following listing shows a simple modification to our code.

Listing 7.6   Cleaning up after an effect got destroyed

```
constructor() {
    effect(onCleanup => {                        ← Obtains the reference to
      const formValues = this.form();                the onCleanup function
      const timeout = setTimeout(() => {         ← Stores the reference to the
        localStorage.setItem(                        timeout so we can cancel
         'formValues',                               it later if necessary
         JSON.stringify(formValues),
        );
      }, 1_000);
                                           Invokes the onCleanup with a
                                           callback, which will be called
      onCleanup(() => {               ←   when the effect gets destroyed
        clearTimeout(timeout);       ←   Clears the timeout
        localStorage.clear();        ←
      });
    })                                  Clears the
}                                       localStorage
```

Now we can put aside our worries and rest assured nothing will "leak" out from our effect. Next, let's discuss ditching automatic cleanups and how to terminate signals created from observables.

In the case of effects, we already mentioned that they get destroyed automatically when their injection context gets destroyed (most commonly the component in which they have been defined). In very rare cases, we might want to override this behavior and fully assume control over when an effect should be terminated. This can be accomplished by providing a special option when defining an effect:

```
effect(() => {
    doSomethinWithASignal(someSignal());
}, {manualCleanup: true});
```

When setting `manualCleanup: true`, we essentially tell Angular that we will terminate the effect ourselves, so be careful when using it so as to not cause memory problems or bugs. A slightly more common scenario is wanting to terminate a signal created from an observable before the component is destroyed. Again, the `toSignal` function also accepts a `manualCleanup` option.

Note that both of these scenarios are extremely uncommon and might potentially indicate a problem within the structure of the code itself. For this reason, we do not provide a practical example here, as such use cases will arise from implementation details of a particular feature, rather than from business requirements. If we find ourselves in a situation where we want to use these options, the best course of action would be to first reconsider the code itself that resulted in such a necessity and do our best to avoid it. Next, let's discuss two other advanced options that signals in Angular provide before we move on to more in-depth knowledge.

7.1.4   *Readonly signals and synchronizing with RxJS*

Right at the very beginning of our journey into signals, we learned about the difference between a `Signal` and a `WritableSignal`—namely that the former cannot be modified, while the latter can. Sometimes we have a `WritableSignal` somewhere, usually in a service, which we want to be able to modify inside that class but not from the outside; from the outside world (for example, a component that injects this service), we want to be able to read only that signal's value. This can be easily achieved via exporting it as a readonly signal:

```
@Injectable({providedIn: 'root'})
export class SomeService {
  readonly #data = signal<Data>({});
  readonly data = this.#data.asReadonly();
}
```

> **NOTE** Calling the `asReadonly` method on a `WritableSignal` will return a signal, which will always have the same value as the original `WritableSignal` but can't be modified. In the case of this service, internally we will use `#data` to be able to modify the value, but other services or components will be able to read only the value, never to modify. This might seem like something very specific, but further in this chapter we will see how we can use it to our benefit when building component interconnections with signals.

One final thing left to discuss is requiring observables to be synchronous when we derive signals from them. In the previous chapter, we mentioned that if we do not provide an initial value to a signal created using the `toSignal` function, this signal can probably be `undefined`, so we have to either provide a default value or check the value every time we read it. This happens because observables can be asynchronous and not have a value at the moment of this signal's creation. However, if we are sure that the observable is synchronous, we can use the `requireSync` option, which will immediately use the first synchronous value of the observable as the initial value of the signal:

```
someSignal = toSignal(of(1, 2, 3), {requireSync: true});
```

In this case, the type of this signal will be `number`, rather than `number | undefined`, and we can use it without providing an initial value manually. We know this works because the `of` function produces synchronous observables by default; however, if we change it to, say, an `interval` observable, we will get the following error:

```
Error: NG0601: `toSignal()` called with `requireSync`
but `Observable` did not emit synchronously.
```

So this option both makes our lives a bit easier and ensures we don't inadvertently add undefined values to our signals.

Now that have covered the practical side, we can move on to the theoretical part, so we can better understand signals and how they function under the hood and use that knowledge to build complex features in real-life applications.

7.2   Signals under the hood

We began our journey into signals with a practical overview of what signals are, how to use them, what options we have to modify them, and so on. Now it is time to dive into their inner workings and find out how they fit into our view of reactive programming. Let's get started by figuring out what a signal is—not just as a wrapper around a value but as a tool for achieving reactive programming.

7.2.1   The nature of signals

When we discussed RxJS, specifically in section 5.1, we introduced the concepts of "push-based" and "pull-based" systems and illustrated that, for instance, functions are pull-based and RxJS Observables are push-based. Another important categorization that we have not yet mentioned is systems that have multiple values as opposed to systems that have a single value. For example, a function has a single value, while a generator function can have multiple values. Note that both are pull-based systems but can deliver solutions to different problems. The same goes for promises versus observables: both are push-based, but a promise delivers a singular value, while an observable can deliver multiple values. Again, this is something to consider when trying to categorize signals. Table 7.1 lists these distinctions.

Table 7.1   Categories of data access systems

	Single value	Multiple values
Pull-based	Functions	Generator functions
Push-based	Promises	Observables

So where do signals fit in here? The answer is "Probably somewhere in the center." The thing is, signals both deliver multiple values and allow us to read the one, latest value, and simultaneously they are both pull-based (we can just invoke them and read the value like a function) and push-based (we can "subscribe" to another signal to get notified about its changes). This placement makes signals very powerful, but that same versatility can be a source of problems down the line, as we will see in the next section.

Also worth reiterating is the fact that signals are side-effect free, as opposed to observables (observables can trigger, for instance, HTTP calls when subscribed to, but signals would never have such side effects). However, reading a signal's value, as we noticed, is not always confined to "just getting the latest value." If we do it in a random method, then that reading operation won't mean much in the large scheme of things, but as we have seen, reading a signal inside a `computed` or `effect` callback means that Angular will start following changes on those signals to recompute the value/re-execute the effect.

A final important thing to consider is that signals usually do not make much sense outside of Angular. Contrary to RxJS, which is framework-agnostic and can be used anywhere, Angular's signals are explicitly tied in with the framework's inner workings. We already saw that when we could not define an effect outside of an Angular component. This is an important thing to remember, especially when defining signals in services to be reused in multiple components, a goal we are steadily moving toward in this chapter.

Now, with this knowledge aside, we can move on and figure out how computed signals and effects work and track dependencies, which at this moment still might feel like a bit of magic.

7.2.2 *How changes to signals propagate*

In the previous chapter, when covering both computed signals and effects, we briefly mentioned that they automatically track dependencies from the callback function itself and then re-execute when the dependencies change their values. Let's expand on this and also discuss the order of execution of those operations.

HOW COMPUTED SIGNALS WORK

First, let's explore how computed signals operate and refresh their value. Figure 7.1 is a helpful graphic explaining the life cycle of a computed signal.

While this graphic might seem somewhat intimidating, what it actually conveys can be summed up in a sentence:

> *Computed signal's callback will start executing only when it is read for the first time, regardless of how many times the source signals might have changed previously, and then it will only execute when source signals change, regardless of how many times we read its computed value.*

Notice that in figure 7.1, the "dependency changes its value" event only joins the party *after* we have read the computed signal at least once, and afterward we do not mention reading the signal anymore.

This mechanism is super-optimized and uses the best possible strategy to prevent executing callbacks multiple times, as they might perform costly operations. Why execute the computation callback if its value is not even used anywhere? And why execute

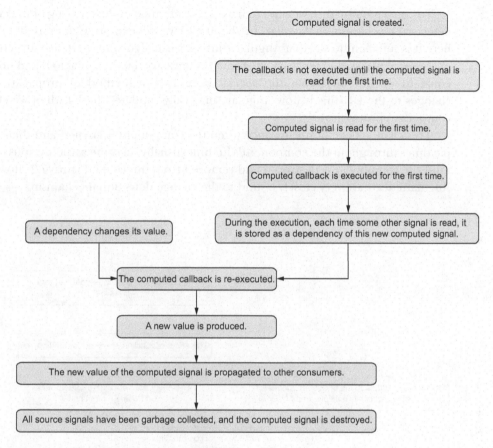

Figure 7.1   Life cycle of a computed signal

it every time the value is read when we can only execute it when a source value has changed (the *only* time the computed value could have possibly changed)? This makes signals *somewhat* similar to observables, as most observables will not start producing values unless subscribed to (there are exceptions, but the most common scenarios work like this). What is different, though, is that reading the value won't trigger any other commands down the line, an important point we have repeated multiple times in these last two chapters.

Now let's discuss how effects work, which is, a bit surprisingly, quite different from how computed signals work, and how they are more integrated into Angular's life cycle.

HOW EFFECTS WORK

From the perspective of code, effects seem to be the same as computed signals, differing only in not having a value and rather just performing some action "on the side." However, their behavior is very different from computed signals—and sometimes even a bit bizarre, as we will soon see.

To conceptualize this, we have to have a very minimal understanding of the change detection mechanism in Angular. In chapter 10 we will explore it in more depth, but here it is sufficient to say that Angular runs a special algorithm to detect any changes in components' states (for instance, some property used to be equal to 6 and now it is equal to 7) and then calls the special `refreshView` method to propagate those changes to the UI (this is how Angular "magically" updates the UI when we change component properties).

This change detection runs once when the component is created and then multiple times throughout the component's lifetime, usually on some asynchronous events, until the component is destroyed and removed from the DOM. Figure 7.2 shows how Angular effects are very closely bound to the change detection mechanism.

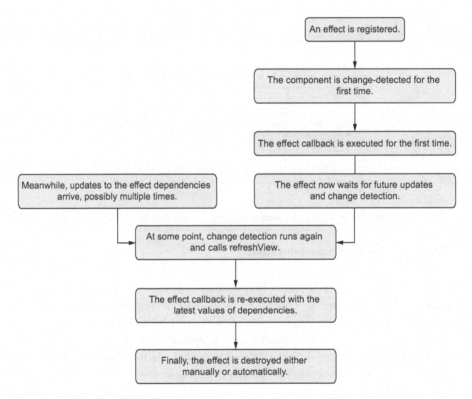

Figure 7.2   Life cycle of an effect

As we can see, the re-execution of effects, as opposed to computed signals, is closely tied to the change detection mechanism. This means that the following code will produce only the latest value:

```
export class SomeComponent {
  counter = signal(0);
```

```
constructor() {
  effect((() => {
    console.log(`Value is ${this.counter()}`);
  });
}

update() {
  this.counter.set(7);
  this.counter.set(11);
  this.counter.set(20);
}
}
```

This code will log Value is 0 and then log Value is 20 when the update method is called. This means we should be careful with multiple updates to a given signal in the same method (unless another update is scheduled asynchronously—for example, via setTimeout), as from Angular's perspective this will not make much sense.

Now that we've covered the deep corners of signals, it is time to expand our practice with them and build a custom state management approach using them. Let's dive in.

7.3   State management with signals

So far, we have only used signals in the context of a single component. However, the fact that signals are capable of notifying us of their updates lends us a powerful opportunity to build functionality that extends beyond a single component and allows us to manage data that is related to multiple parts of our application. This practice of sharing data and handling a global state of things in a frontend application is usually referred to as *state management*. While there are multiple state management libraries (some of which, like NgRx, we have already mentioned), for most of them, based on RxJS, with signals, we can create lightweight state management solutions best tailored to our application's needs. Let's build one!

7.3.1   State management: The task

In the previous chapter, we introduced a page into our HRMS application that actually does handle some employee-related jobs—in this instance, time-off management. In that scenario, an human resources employee will see lists of time-off requests and handle them on a case-by-case basis. However, it would be useful if employees in general receive notifications about tasks they have at hand. Of course, one type of such notifications would be the time-off requests, but users will receive other notifications too—for instance, their colleagues' birthday reminders, application maintenance notices, and more. Let's make some ground rules for our notifications system:

- Notifications can be used in multiple components of our application; for example, in the header we will see the list of all notifications with a counter, and in the sidebar we could see the list of notifications regarding certain features of our app (like a counter of time-off related notification on the sidebar link that navigates to the time-off management page).

- Notifications are real time, pushed from a server via a web socket connection. We are not going to implement that particular functionality explicitly, as it is out of the scope of this chapter, but we will assume a special `SocketService` that handles that functionality and exposes an RxJS observable that emits when new notifications arrive.
- Notifications can also be affected from outside; for instance, approving a time-off request will result in the corresponding notification being marked as read.
- Notification data will be stored in localStorage and brought back when the service is initialized; then it is updated via subsequent changes to the notification, either from the web socket or from the user's direct interaction.

With all of these conditions in mind, let's get started!

7.3.2 *State management: The implementation*

First, as we begin implementing the state management service, let's define what a notification is. Inside the HRMS project, in the src/app/infrastructure/types directory, let us add a new file named notification.ts and put the definition of the type shown in the following listing inside.

Listing 7.7 Notification type

```
export type Notification = {
    id: number;
    title: string;
    message: string;
    type: 'TimeOff' | 'Birthday' | 'Maintenance' | 'Other';
    read: boolean;
    date: string;
}
```

This is pretty straightforward. Now, to be able to share functionality between components, we need to create a service that hosts the relevant signals, so that different components can inject that service and make use of those signals. So far, we have only used signals in components, with one reason being that functions like `effect` and `toSignal` only work inside an injection context. However, services are also created in an injection context, meaning we can safely use signals in them. The following listing shows a first-time, somewhat simplistic implementation of the notifications service, without the socket connections (for now) in a new file located at src/app/services/notification.service.ts.

Listing 7.8 Notification service

```
@Injectable({providedIn: 'root'})
export class NotificationService {
    #notifications = signal<Notification[]>(          ◁──   A private signal that
                                                            holds all notifications
```

```
        localStorage.getItem('notifications') ?
          JSON.parse(
            localStorage.getItem('notifications')
          ) : [],
    );
    notifications = this.#notifications.asReadonly();
    readNotifications = computed(
      () => this.#notifications().filter(
        n => n.read,
      )
    );
    unreadNotifications = computed(
      () => this.#notifications().filter(
        n => !n.read
      )
    );

    constructor() {
      effect(() => {
          localStorage.setItem('notifications',
    JSON.stringify(this.#notifications()));
      })
    }

    addNotification(notification: Notification) {
      this.#notifications.update(value => [...value, notification]);
    }

    markAsRead(notification: Notification) {
      this.#notifications.update(
              value => value.map(
                n => n.id === notification.id ? {
                  ...n,
                  read: true,
                } : n,
              )
          );
    }

    markAllAsRead() {
      this.#notifications.update(
        value => value.map(n => ({
            ...n,
            read: true,
          }))
        )
      );
    }
}
```

The list of notifications is hydrated from localStorage.

Only a read-only version of the notifications signal is exposed to components to use.

Computed signals for read and unread notifications

An effect to store the latest notifications in localStorage

Methods to modify signals without explicitly changing them

Now we have a service that essentially acts as state management for the notifications' state in our application. Going forward, we can inject this service anywhere and use the data from it easily. Let's build a small HeaderComponent that will show the list of

the notifications in a dialog when the "bell" button is clicked. In src/app/shared/
components, let us add a new file named header.component.ts and put in the code in
the following listing.

Listing 7.9 Header component using signal-based state management

```
@Component({
  selector: 'app-header',
  template: `
    <header>
      <h2>HRMS</h2>
      <button
        (click)="notificationsOpen.set(true)"
        title="View Notifications">
        You have {{ unreadNotifications.length }} unread notifications
      </button>
    </header>
    <dialog [open]="notificationsOpen()">          ⟵⎯ Uses a local signal to open/
      <h3>Notifications</h3>                            close the notifications dialog
      <ul>
        <li *ngFor="let notification of notifications()">  ⟵⎯ Uses a signal from
          <h4>{{ notification.title }}</h4>                     the notification
          <span>{{ notification.message }}</span>              service to show
          <button                                              the list of
            *ngIf="!notification.read"                         notifications
            (click)="markAsRead(notification)"     ⟵⎯
          >
            Mark as Read                            If the notification is unread,
          </button>                                 we can mark it as read, so
        </li>                                       the counter will update.
      </ul>
      <button (click)="notificationsOpen.set(false)">Close</button>  ⟵⎯
    </dialog>                                        Uses the local signal to
  `,                                                 close the dialog
  standalone: true,
  imports: [NgFor, NgIf],                            Injects the notification service so
})                                                   we can access the data inside
export class HeaderComponent {
  private readonly notificationService = inject(NotificationService);  ⟵⎯

  notifications = this.notificationService.notifications;   ⟵⎯

  unreadNotifications = this.notificationService.unreadNotifications;
  notificationsOpen = signal(false);
                                                     Extracts
                                                     the full list of
  markAsRead(notification: Notification) {           notifications and
    this.notificationService.markAsRead(notification);  ⟵⎯  the list of unread
  }                                                  notifications to
}                         Updates a notification's   display in the UI
                          read/unread status
```

In this scenario, the HeaderComponent is fully bound with the live data of the notifications, as in, if we update the notifications from somewhere, the result will immediately be

visible in the HeaderComponent. Also, we can notice a local signal, notificationsOpen, living in harmony with a signal extracted from another service. From the perspective of the component, there is no difference between those two signals.

One important question that we might want to ask is: when are the signals from the service created? In the case of the local signal, it is fairly obvious: we put it in the constructor; that means whenever the component is created, its signals will be created too. In the case of the service, it is the same, but what is missing for us is when the service itself will be instantiated. We marked the service as providedIn: 'root', so this means it will be created the first time the service is injected in a component that is used somewhere in the UI. If we put the HeaderComponent in the AppComponent (which makes sense, as the header might contain navigation that we want to be visible on all pages), it will be created at the inception of the application itself.

However, this is not something that we would *always* want. In some scenarios, it makes sense to move the creation of those signals somewhere down the application structure. For example, the time-off request management feature we built in the previous chapter may need to have its own state management service (to share data only between its own components and not the whole application). In this case, we may provide a hypothetical TimeOffManagementService in the providers of the time-off management feature's routes, with the technique described in section 2.4.4, illustrated in detail in listing 2.15.

Now let's figure out how to make this connected to a socket service and what problems could arise when we try to interoperate signals with RxJS observables "a bit too much."

7.3.3 State management: The problems

In section 7.3.1, we mentioned that we are going to assume a service that handles the web socket connection and not actually implement it. This service will expose several observables that we can use to handle different socket connections. We will work with the one related to notifications.

In listing 7.7, we created the service for notifications and read the notifications just from localStorage. To make them real-time, we can use this socket service and derive the data for notifications from the observable it exposes. We can simply use the toSignal function to convert that observable to a signal, which we will then use (let's forget about the localStorage thing for now).

Listing 7.10 Using toSignal in a service

```
export class NotificationService {
    private readonly socketService = inject(SocketService);
    #notifications = toSignal(this.socketService.notifications$,
      {requireSync: true});                    ←─── Uses the observable as the source
                                                     for our notifications signal
}                    ←─┐
                       │ Rest of the service's code
                         omitted for brevity
```

For now, this will work; however, such an approach can pose certain problems in the long run. First, the `toSignal` will subscribe to the observable (remember: subscribing is the only way of reading values from observables), which in turn might cause side effects; for example, in our scenario, a web socket might be created as soon as we subscribe to this observable.

Presently this is not a big deal (we want to receive notifications via the web socket anyway). However, even if all the components that use notifications are destroyed, the subscription will continue to be active. This means the web socket will continue to be open, which will mean unnecessary load on both the user's device (for mobile devices this might mean a faster-draining battery) and the server (for maintainers it might mean higher monthly costs).

Another concern is that we can never manually terminate this subscription. We can, of course, expose the reference to the notifications signal (instead of it being private) and mark it as `manualCleanup: true`, but even in this case, because multiple components might be using it, there will be no way to truly tell when it is safe to terminate the connection. The only way would be if every component set up its own subscription, which would then be disposed of when it is destroyed, and when the last component using this subscription is gone, the connection will be closed. How can we achieve this? Let's rework our `NotificationService` and add a method that does exactly this.

Listing 7.11 Manually connecting a signal to an observable

```
@Injectable({providedIn: 'root'})
export class NotificationService {
    private readonly socketService = inject(        Injects the
      SocketService,                                socket service
    );
    #notifications = signal<Notification[]>(
        localStorage.getItem('notifications') ?
      JSON.parse(localStorage.getItem('notifications')) : [],
    );
    notifications = this.#notifications.asReadonly();    The notifications are
    readNotifications = computed(                         initially read from
      () => this.#notifications().filter(                localStorage; no direct
        n => n.read,                                      connection to the
      ),                                          socket/Observable here.
    );
    unreadNotifications = computed(
      () => this.#notifications().filter(
        n => !n.read,
      ),
    );

    constructor() {
        effect((() => {
            localStorage.setItem('notifications',
      JSON.stringify(this.#notifications()));
        })
    }
}
```

The connect method will provide that connection on a case-by-case scenario.

```
connect() {
    return this.socketService.notifications$.pipe(
        takeUntilDestroyed(),
    ).subscribe(notifications => {
        this.#notifications.set(notifications);
    });
}

addNotification(notification: Notification) {
    this.#notifications.update(value => [...value, notification]);
}

markAsRead(notification: Notification) {
    this.#notifications.update(
        value => value.map(
            n => n.id === notification.id ? {
                ...n,
                read: true,
            } : n),
    );
}

markAllAsRead() {
    this.#notifications.update(
        value => value.map(
            n => ({...n, read: true}),
        ),
    );
}
}
```

Manually sets the value of the notifications as they arrive via the websocket

Uses takeUntilDestroyed so we can automatically unsubscribe in the context in which we use this method

Subscribes to the notifications observable from the web socket

We might notice that while we define the connect method, we never call it inside the NotificationService itself. This is done on purpose, as we want consumers to manually set up the subscription if they need to listen to notifications. This way, they will be required to call the connect method in the constructor (otherwise the takeUntilDestroyed operator will throw an error, as we purposefully did not provide a DestroyRef), and then they will be able to store the subscription in a component property (in case they want to unsubscribe manually), and finally when that component is destroyed, this subscription will be automatically disposed of, resulting in the exact scenario we wanted to achieve.

We could also store all the subscriptions in an array and add a method to manually terminate them all, but this is out of the scope of this chapter. In addition, the notifications$ observable should be set up in a way that it shares the subscription between multiple consumers (so new components subscribing to notifications does not result in multiple web sockets being opened), but this is deep RxJS functionality and is again out of the scope of this chapter, so we will not implement it here.

Finally, what is left here is to call the connect method in a component that uses notifications; for instance, we can slightly modify our HeaderComponent.

Listing 7.12   `connect` method for signal/observable interop

```
export class HeaderComponent {
  private readonly notificationService = inject(
    NotificationService,
  );
  notifications = this.notificationService.notifications;
  unreadNotifications = this.notificationService.unreadNotifications;
  notificationsOpen = signal(false);

  markAsRead(notification: Notification) {
    this.notificationService.markAsRead(notification);
  }

  constructor() {
    this.notificationService.connect();
  }
}
```

> **Component code is essentially the same; no need to modify the way we use signals from services with this pattern.**

> **We just need to call connect from the constructor, and that is it.**

Now with all this complex knowledge in place, we are ready to fix one last outstanding problem. In section 6.6.1, we discussed converting observables to signals and used that in our `TimeOffManagement Component` to make HTTP calls but with a problematic solution that included passing down an injector reference and reassigning the signal itself (instead of its internal value). Let us now refactor that part with a state management solution based on interoperability between signals and RxJS.

7.3.4   *Advanced interoperability with RxJS*

Now we are going to build a state management service for time-off requests, which will host the entire data related to time-off requests, and all their behavior, and make that data flow only one way. This approach will have several benefits:

- Data can be easily shared with other components. For instance, we might have a page for non-human resources employees where they can view their own time-off requests, and that page can easily reuse this service.
- We can handle all asynchronous tasks inside this service.
- The components using this functionality will become incredibly simple. In the next chapter we are going to talk about unit testing, and having simple components is one of the best ways to make writing unit tests a pleasing activity.

Now let us take a look at this new state management service. It will use RxJS subjects to represent events of deleting, rejecting, and approving a time-off request.

Listing 7.13   State management with advanced RxJS interoperability

```
@Injectable({ providedIn: 'root' })
export class TimeOffManagementService {
  private readonly timeOffRequestService = inject(TimeOffRequestService);
```

The requests signal is now derived from events that occur when the user deletes, approves, or rejects requests or changes the selected type.

selectedType continues to be a signal that can be used anywhere.

Subjects that will propagate the events of user deleting, approving, and rejecting time-off requests

```
deleteRequest$ = new Subject<TimeOffRequest>();
approveRequest$ = new Subject<TimeOffRequest>();
rejectRequest$ = new Subject<TimeOffRequest>();
selectedType = signal<
  'Vacation' | 'Sick Leave' | 'Maternity Leave' | 'Paternity Leave' |
  'Other' | ''
>((localStorage.getItem('selectedType') as any) ??
  '');
requests = toSignal(
  merge(
    toObservable(this.selectedType),
    this.deleteRequest$.pipe(switchMap((r) =>
    this.timeOffRequestService.deleteRequest(r.id))),
    this.approveRequest$.pipe(switchMap((r) =>
    this.timeOffRequestService.approveRequest(r.id))),
    this.rejectRequest$.pipe(switchMap((r) =>
    this.timeOffRequestService.rejectRequest(r.id))),
  ).pipe(
    switchMap(() => {
      return this.timeOffRequestService
        .getRequestsByType(
          this.selectedType(),
        );
    })
  ),
  {
    initialValue: [] as TimeOffRequest[],
  }
);
resolvedRequests = computed(() =>
  this.requests().filter((r) => r.status !== 'Pending')
);

constructor() {
  effect(() => {
    localStorage.setItem('selectedType', this.selectedType());
  });
}

approveRequest(request: TimeOffRequest) {
  this.approveRequest$.next(request);
}
```

The merge function is used to combine all the events into one (we do not care about the nature of the event here, only that it happened).

We convert the selectedType signal to an observable to be able to merge it with other events.

Each particular event triggers its own HTTP call; for instance, deleteRequest$ Observable here calls the API that will delete a request.

Regardless of what the source observables did, when they are finished, we will refresh the data on the page.

The effect that stores the selected type in localStorage is also moved here.

Now approving (rejecting, deleting) a request is only a matter of triggering an event via the corresponding subject.

```
  rejectRequest(request: TimeOffRequest) {
    this.rejectRequest$.next(request);
  }

  deleteRequest(request: TimeOffRequest) {
    this.deleteRequest$.next(request);
  }
}
```

This might seem a bit intimidating; however, at a second look, this actually encapsulates the behavior we want to describe quite well. All we care about is the time-off requests, and the very definition of the requests signal *fully* describes what that array of requests is, what it is derived from, and what it can change. This also beautifully explains the difference in signals and observables. Signals are a reactive state, and observables are streams of events we can react to. Here, "the user decided to approve a time-off request" is an event, and the requests signal is an array of time-off requests that will react to that event; hence the first is an observable, and the latter is a signal derived from that observable.

Now all that is left to do is modify the `TimeOffManagementComponent` and just use this state management service. This will make our component super simple, and we don't even have to change the template!

Listing 7.14   State management with signals used in a component

```
export class TimeOffManagementComponent {
  private readonly timeOffsService = inject(TimeOffManagementService);
  requests = this.timeOffsService.requests;
  resolvedRequests = this.timeOffsService.resolvedRequests;
  selectedType = this.timeOffsService.selectedType;

  approveRequest(request: TimeOffRequest) {
    this.timeOffsService.approveRequest(request);
  }

  rejectRequest(request: TimeOffRequest) {
    this.timeOffsService.rejectRequest(request);
  }

  deleteRequest(request: TimeOffRequest) {
    this.timeOffsService.deleteRequest(request);
  }
}
```

Here we do not even have that much to comment about: we just inject the state management service, assign the signal from there to some local properties to use in the template, and define wrapper methods that delegate the functionality back to the service. This component is short, very easy to explain and understand, and, as we will see in the next chapter, extremely easy to test.

As we covered essentially everything we currently need to know about signals quite in depth, we can now explore the migration of existing applications towards using signals as their basic building block.

7.4 Migrating to signals

Before we begin, let's first briefly discuss how Angular applications handled reactivity previously. Of course, RxJS was the only available solution for this kind of problem; however, RxJS is *not* required by the Angular team (unless dealing with things that naturally are observables, like HTTP requests), meaning that we have roughly two types of Angular apps: the ones that already extensively use RxJS for reactivity and the ones that do not. Let's begin with the former, as it presents more different possibilities.

7.4.1 Migrating RxJS-heavy Angular applications

Angular developers who use RxJS in their applications beyond the built-in cases will probably enjoy a smoother experience when migrating to signals than the ones who do not. Let's illustrate several common scenarios that developers might encounter in such applications.

BehaviorSubjects

When learning about signals, we might have noticed that signals are suspiciously similar to BehaviorSubjects. They both have a default value, their current value can always be read, and they can propagate their changes. This makes the BehaviorSubjects in our code great candidates for conversions to signals. What we need to do is convert the BehaviorSubject to a signal (not using the `toSignal` function but directly, as in the property is a signal from the get-go); then all observables derived from it become computed properties, and if the `tap` operator is used for side effects, we just convert it to a separate `effect`.

RxJS-based custom state management

The state management solution described in the previous section can be easily implemented with RxJS observables instead of signals. In fact, this has been the unofficial approach to state management in Angular apps prior to the arrival of signals. Often in Angular apps, we would have a service that has a subject, or a BehaviorSubject, which would notify when a particular piece of data changes, and then different components would subscribe to it. This has been so common that content creators have named this approach "subject-in-a-service."

If we find ourselves with an app that uses such an approach, it can be easily converted to signals. Here we must replace source observables/subjects with signals, derived observables with computed signals, and usages of the `tap` operator to the `effect` function.

However, this scenario should be executed more carefully than the previous one, as only synchronous observables that hold state (rather than represent events, as explained previously) should be converted to signals. A good approach, in this case, would be to keep the initial subject in place, wrap it in `toSignal`, and see if the application continues to work as expected. If everything works just fine, we can continue and convert all derived observables to computed signals and so on.

RxJS INTEROPERABILITY ON A LOCAL SCALE

As we repeatedly mentioned, some existing Angular APIs, like `HttpClient`, use observables by default. In an Angular application, we often interact with such APIs and create lots of RxJS subscriptions. One example of this is using the `FormControl.valueChanges` observable to derive some value to then use in the template. This can easily be substituted by a simple call to the `toSignal` function and then using the value directly as a signal. This should be handled on a case-by-case basis. Next, let's focus on applications that do not extensively use RxJS.

7.4.2   *Migrating more traditional Angular applications*

In the case of more traditional Angular applications, we will have fewer calls to the `toSignal` function and more pondering to do. Let's examine some scenarios again.

PRIMITIVE RxJS

However remote an application is from RxJS, if it is sufficiently large, it will inevitably have some parts that use RxJS. A good practice, in this case, would be to search the application for usages of the async pipe and the subscribe method and then devise a strategy to convert this logic to use signals instead. Again, this should be done carefully, after an in-depth examination of the actual logic; no mechanical approaches would work here.

LOOKING FOR DERIVED VALUES

Often Angular apps that do not use RxJS rely on `getter` methods and `pipes` to convert some existing values to something else. It would be good to try to replace the `pipes` with computed properties and so with `getter` methods. In this case, we should begin from the top, convert the source of the data that gets transformed via a pipe/getter to signal, then remove the getters/pipes and create computed properties instead. Again, this is done on a case-by-case basis.

EVERY PROPERTY CAN BE A SIGNAL

This one applies to the RxJS-heavy Angular applications too. It is easy to see that any property can be a signal, rather than a plain value, and we can begin by converting simple properties to signals. Then we can explore what other properties and functionalities depend on that property we just converted and turn them into computed signals/effects. Finally, we might end up with an application that is fully based on signals. In chapter 10, we shall see how this might be a good thing for the future.

Finally, let's remember that signals themselves are only marked stable starting from v17, and some other more experimental features are still in the process of rolling out (we will talk more about them in chapter 10), meaning they are very much a work in progress. This means more changes are coming to the signals infrastructure, and this may result in even more changes to Angular as a whole. So let us briefly, without speculation, discuss signal-related features that we can reasonably expect to arrive in upcoming versions.

7.5 The future of signals

We could discuss at length the numerous scenarios of upcoming features that could further improve the developer experience of signals. However, we want to be as concrete as possible, so instead we will only discuss features already announced in some forms by the Angular teams in the official signals RFC (https://mng.bz/75xQ). Also, as the API for those features will probably change, we will not provide concrete code examples so as to not create a false impression of those features actually existing. Let's dive in.

7.5.1 Signal-based components

One of the more extreme features the Angular team proposes is the ability to mark components as signal-based (with a special flag in the component metadata). What this means is that such components will not employ traditional change detection and instead will rely on signal notifications *only* for UI updates. This will significantly improve runtime performance and application bundle size. In chapter 10, when we dive deep into the internals of Angular's current change detection mechanism, we will discuss signal-based components in more detail.

7.5.2 Signal inputs and outputs

One problem with signals as they exist in v16 is that there is no real way to make signals component inputs. We could, of course, mark a signal property with the `Input` decorator, but that won't work because the `Input` decorator assigns any new value arriving from a parent component that input property. This means that in the case of signals, the signal itself will be replaced by the value, rather than the signal's internal value updated.

Currently, we have a workaround for this by utilizing setter methods. The following listing shows how it can work.

Listing 7.15   Making `signal` into an input property

```
export class SomeComponent {
  #someSignal = signal('Name');

  @Input()
  set someSignal(value: string) {
    this.#someSignal.set(value);
  }
}
```

Obviously, this will work in case we are stuck with v16; however, it can become quite cumbersome when we have multiple input signals. Instead, the Angular team added a special `input` function starting from v17.1 (we will discuss this at length in chapter 10) that will create a signal that will also act as an input property out of the box. To also handle the two-way data binding, the team added a new `model` function in v17.2 that will create a signal that is both an input and output and can be used with two-way bindings (again, discussed in chapter 10).

7.5.3 *Everything else*

To keep all those changes in line, and for the sake of consistency, the Angular team also proposes to add signal-based functions to all the features that are currently achieved with decorators. These include the following:

- `output` function—This will create an EventEmitter (just as we used to do prior to signals), which can send events to parent components.
- `viewChild` and `viewChildren`—To access HTML elements from a component's template, these functions will be available and will return a signal of the HTML element or a signal of an array of those elements correspondingly.
- `contentChild` and `contentChildren`—To access HTML elements from a component's projected content, these functions can be used and will return a signal of the HTML element or a signal of an array of those elements correspondingly, as with the previous two functions.

Angular v17, v18, and future versions will show what other new developments might become available. Still, for now, we should keep these possibilities in mind, as they are likely to become part of the Angular framework.

Now we have reached an important milestone: we have covered all new code-level tools that modern Angular provides! In the next chapters, we will focus on other tools, like unit tests, application deployment on client and server, and future approaches to developing projects with Angular.

With the huge arsenal of such powerful tools, we are now ready to cover our next topic: writing unit tests in modern Angular applications.

7.6 *Exercises for the reader*

- Refactor the employee feature in the HRMS application to use signals and the state management approach from this chapter.
- Experiment with existing projects that utilize RxJS-based state management and try to convert them to a signals-based approach.

Summary

- Signals have a multitude of customization options.
- We can change the logic of signal equality checking to prevent unnecessary costly computations.
- We can untrack dependencies from computed signals and effects if we don't want to run updates on their changes.
- Effect and computed signal callbacks run in fundamentally different ways.

- Computed signals are lazy before first read and then run on every new arriving update.
- Effects run eagerly, are tied in with Angular's change detection, and will run whenever Angular refreshes the UI.
- State management solutions can be built using signals.
- Converting observables to signals in services can have significant effects on application performance, which can be mitigating by delegating the subscription logic to consumer components.
- Existing RxJS-heavy Angular applications can be converted to use signals in relatively easy steps.

Unit testing in
modern Angular

This chapter covers
- What unit tests are and how they work in Angular
- Setting up a unit testing environment
- Writing unit tests for Angular building blocks
- Unit testing classes that use the `inject` function
- Unit testing signals
- Third-party tools that facilitate unit testing of Angular applications
- AI tools to assist with unit testing

In previous chapters, we learned about all the modern code-level tools that Angular now provides out of the box to make developing large frontend applications as seamless as possible. All of those tools were confined to the code that we write itself, helping to solve business requirement-related problems. But what about building our applications, developer experience, deployment, search engine optimizations, and so on? Now it is time to explore all of these topics. However, before we can actually deploy our beautiful HRMS application, we need to ensure it works properly and is reasonably maintainable (as in "will not break easily when developers add new changes"). And this is precisely what this chapter is about: unit testing.

8.1 Unit testing: The what and the why

Before we begin, let's briefly discuss unit testing in more general terms, the reasons we need it, and how to achieve it.

8.1.1 Prerequisites

In chapter 1, we laid out some requirements for the reader, which included general knowledge of Angular and its building blocks, basic knowledge of RxJS, and so on. However, you might have noticed that we never mentioned unit testing or anything related to it. This was done on purpose; despite the fact that in this chapter we will focus more on the most modern tools that aid us in testing, we will still cover the entire topic quite in depth, so we do not require *any* particular knowledge of unit testing to unit testing of Angular applications specifically. Rest assured, this chapter is designed to be pretty easy to consume.

The reason for this is that despite the fact that unit testing is a great way to ensure an application's stability, thousands upon thousands of Angular applications (as well as applications generally) out in the world go on without it. Multiple factors contribute to this: often, projects are outsourced from other enterprises and the clients just do not want to spend budget on it; young startup teams want to "move fast and break things" and just deliver their product (such teams often make a promise to cover the codebase with tests later, and then this promise is broken); teams do not believe in automatic testing and leave everything for manual quality assurance. All of these stances are understandable; however, in the next few paragraphs we will try to convince ourselves that unit tests are, in general, quite useful and then move on to testing our application. To do this, let's first cover the basics.

8.1.2 What is a unit test?

As the name suggests, a unit test is an *automated* test that checks the functionality of some *programming unit* in *isolation*. What programming unit, we might wonder? Any basic building block can be a unit. A very small instance of a unit test might be a test that essentially checks the correctness of one single method of a class.

And what does "automated" mean, exactly? In this case, it means we will *describe* scenarios that might happen to our component/directive/service/etc. by, for instance, calling its methods with certain data, *expect* some results, and clearly define which results mean the functionality works as intended. All of this is done via functions that we will soon become familiar with (if you are not already). After describing the scenario, a special program can be called to execute those scenarios and ensure the program we want to test works correctly.

Finally, we mentioned that a unit test is a test in isolation. How is it isolated? A unit test kind of assumes that everything else in the world works fine, and we are just testing *this particular* component (or anything else). This means that if, for instance, a service is using Angular's `HttpClient`, we are not going to actually provide the real

HttpClient and perform real HTTP calls; we will just check if our own service properly calls the correct methods of the HttpClient and assume it will work correctly in the real world.

This makes sense on two levels: first, we don't really want to make our unit tests slower by actually performing HTTP calls (and possibly altering database data in unexpected ways); and second, the HttpClient is built and maintained by a team of professionals and is covered by its own unit tests. There is nothing that we can add to this reliability that may improve it, so it makes sense to just forget about it.

This also applies to our internal code blocks: if component A uses component B somewhere in its template, then component A's unit tests *do not* test if component B works properly. Component B has its own tests, and if they work fine, and A works fine, then from the perspective of unit tests both components are good to go. To achieve this isolation, we often provide empty substitutes for dependencies that our test subject has (so instead of the real HttpClient we might provide an empty service that has the same methods but does nothing) in a practice known as "mocking dependencies." We will learn about this and many other things in the next sections of this chapter.

Now that we've figured out what a unit test is, let's move forward and understand why unit tests are so important.

8.1.3 Why do we want unit tests?

After seven chapters, we already have an application at our disposal that is moderately complex. Of course, this application is far from being really big, but we have a lot of features and quite a lot of code—and, of course, more lines of code means a higher probability of bugs. How do we catch bugs? Obviously we test our application, to this point exclusively manually. However, unit testing can lend a helping hand in case our application grows (which any enterprise application very well can). Let's see some benefits we can draw from unit tests.

EARLIER BUG DETECTION
Unit testing will allow us to catch bugs and problems early in the development process. By writing tests for individual units or components of an Angular application, we can identify and fix errors, bugs, and impossible scenarios well before they escalate into more complex problems, saving time and effort in the long run.

EASIER REFACTORING
Refactoring is a common part of the development process; after all, we spent lots of time in this book describing various approaches for the migration of existing projects to newer Angular features; this is, in fact, a type of refactoring. Unit tests act as safety nets during such refactorings. With unit tests, we can confidently make changes, knowing that if any existing functionality is affected, the tests will fail, indicating the need for adjustments.

CONTINUOUS INTEGRATION AND DEPLOYMENT

In modern software development, continuous integration and deployment pipelines are the go-to approach for deploying and publishing applications. Unit tests make this process way easier, as they can safeguard us from various situations in which terrible bugs might appear in production environments. If unit tests pass, it indicates that the new changes haven't introduced regressions, allowing for confident automated deployments.

OVERALL IMPROVEMENT OF APPLICATION DESIGN

Writing unit tests often leads to more modular and loosely coupled code. Developers are encouraged to create components and services that are easier to test independently. This emphasis on testability naturally leads to better design decisions, resulting in a more maintainable and extensible codebase. We will notice that, say, a component that is easy to test is also quite simple to read and understand by a human developer.

Of course, unit tests also offer a plethora of other benefits, but these four points should hopefully be enough to convince you to start thinking about how to cover our HRMS application with tests. So, without further ado, let's get started!

8.2 Configuring a testing environment

Let's imagine the following scenario: we have been working on the HRMS application for a while, implementing cutting-edge features and being super excited about the future. We confidently report that the app is ready for an MVP release; however, upper management has some concerns.

One morning we gather during a standup and someone from management shows up to ask a question that feels a bit out of place initially: "Are we sure the application is ready? Is it tested enough?" We excitedly tell them what an amazing job the manual testing team has done and how many bugs have we identified and fixed. But the follow-up to it is this: "But the users *will* find some problems after the launch. Also, they will report things that aren't bugs, but just don't feel right, and they are expecting improvements. Are we sure we can deliver them? What if we break something while fixing something else? We want to apply those changes as fast as possible before the initial users are turned away." And, sure enough, someone comes up with the bright idea of covering the existing codebase with unit tests. An hour of discussions later, we are now tasked with setting up an environment in the project for developers to write and run unit tests. Let's see how it goes.

8.2.1 Choosing a test runner

First, we need to set up a test runner to actually execute tests. A test runner is a program that identifies test files and testing scenarios in them (usually called *specs*) and then runs them and reports their success or failure and whatever problems that were found. Different test runners exist for applications written in JavaScript, but for Angular applications, usually the choice boils down to Jest or Karma. Table 8.1 lists the differences between them.

Table 8.1   Karma vs. Jest

Karma	Jest
Developed by the Angular team	Developed by Facebook
Runs in a real browser	Runs in a NodeJS environment
Has to spin up the browser itself and then run the tests inside it, sometimes resulting in slower performance	Runs as an independent JS program, with no browser, and can be faster
No need to mock the browser's built-in functionality, as it already runs in a real browser	We can't directly use browser APIs here, as Jest runs in a NodeJS runtime; for instance, if our component calls `localStorage`, we will have to mock it for the tests to run correctly
Allows for cross-browser testing: if our application uses APIs that might not exist in some older browsers, we can configure Karma to use several different browsers and see if the tests pass on all of them	No real cross-browser testing

Despite the differences, these test runners also have a lot in common: both integrate easily with testing frameworks, have a vibrant community that provides tooling and libraries, and, most importantly, include aliases for commands from each other, meaning the tests written with Karma will *mostly* execute the same way with Jest.

However, here we should note that, despite being the default test runner for Angular applications for almost a decade, Angular is now moving away from Karma (https:// mng.bz/JNjz), as Karma is now deprecated (https://mng.bz/w5NB) and no longer adds improvements and newer versions. For this purpose. Angular is now looking for alternatives (which we will discuss later), and because Jest is already possible to be integrated into an Angular application manually (several community-driven projects already exist and are widely used), starting from v16 Jest has official, experimental support in Angular applications.

We say "experimental"; however, this test runner as it is currently will be sufficient for us to write and run the unit tests for our HRMS application, so we will be choosing Jest as our test runner. In the last section of this chapter, we will also discuss some other steps the Angular team is undertaking in regard to the test runners, but for now, let's focus on setting up our Jest-based testing environment.

8.2.2   *Setting up the test runner*

First, let us understand how we actually run our tests. For this purpose, the Angular CLI has provided a specific command. Let us spin up a command line terminal at the root of our HRMS application and run this command:

```
ng test
```

Let's see what it does. If we have not added or removed anything related to the tests in the app, we should see an error:

```
AppComponent should create the app FAILED
        NullInjectorError: R3InjectorError(Standalone[AppComponent])
        [AuthService -> AuthService -> HttpClient -> HttpClient]:
            NullInjectorError: No provider for HttpClient!
```

This is expected, as we developed some functionality in the `AppComponent` without updating their respective unit tests, which means the test has some problems creating an instance of the `AppComponent` class. But why does it run tests for AppComponent anyway? We surely have not written any tests, have we? Well, if we created the application without the `--minimal` flag (see chapter 1, section 1.3.1, table 1.2), then Angular automatically set up a default testing environment and some dummy tests for the `AppComponent` (the only component that existed at the time of the application's inception).

But how does Angular know where the tests are? Well, there is a specific configuration file, called tsconfig.spec.json at the very root of the project, which tells it how to function. The contents of the file are pretty simple, as shown in the following listing.

Listing 8.1 Testing configuration file

```
{
  "extends": "./tsconfig.json",          ◄─── This TypeScript configuration will
  "compilerOptions": {                        just use the same as the overall app
    "outDir": "./out-tsc/spec",               while adding some options.
    "types": [
      "Jest"                             ◄─── We switch to Jest types instead of
    ]                                         Jasmine, which was the testing
  },                                          framework that Karma used.
  "include": [
    "src/**/*.spec.ts",                  ◄─── All files that end with
    "src/**/*.d.ts"                           .spec.ts will be run.
  ]
}
```

As we can see, this config tells the test runner to grab all the files ending with .spec.ts and run the tests inside them. In our application, only one such file exists, located at src/app/app.component.spec.ts, which contains the tests that just failed when we first ran `ng test`. However, before moving to fix this problem, let's remember that this is the default configuration of the testing environment, meaning it runs Karma, and we have chosen to use Jest instead. Thankfully, this is an easy change. In the angular.json file we will find a section dedicated to unit testing. We need to alter it a bit to use Jest, so it will look like the following listing.

Listing 8.2 `angular.json` configuration to use Jest as test runner

```
{
                            ◄─── Rest of the file
                                 omitted for brevity
  "projects": {
```

```
"hrms": {
  "projectType": "application",
  "architect": {                    Other architect
                                    options also omitted
    "test": {
      "builder": "@angular-devkit/build-angular:jest",    We put build-
      "options": {                                         angular:jest:
        "polyfills": [                                     instead of build-
          "zone.js",                                       angular:karma.
          "zone.js/testing"
        ],
        "tsConfig": "tsconfig.spec.json"
                                Karma config included other
      }                         options like "assets," which
    }                           are not needed with Jest, so
  }                             we removed them.
}
}
```

Now if we try to run `ng test` again, we will get a new error:

```
Jest is not installed, most likely you need to run
`npm install jest --save-dev` in your project.
```

Continuing this, we will get other errors, so to jump to the point where the Jest test runner works, we need to run the following commands:

```
npm install jest --save-dev
npm install jest-environment-jsdom --save-dev
npm i --save-dev @types/jest
```

After, we can rerun `ng test` and see the same error (regarding the injection of `HttpClient`) that we saw when running tests initially; however, notice that the tests are now running with Jest (different format of reporting from the command). This means we successfully switched to Jest.

One concern for us down the line is being able to configure some options for our Jest test runner. To be able to do this, we need to provide a configuration file and a file that will do our custom setup. First, let's create a file named jest.config.ts at the root of our project folder, and put the following code there:

```
module.exports = {
  setupFilesAfterEnv: ['<rootDir>/setup-jest.ts'],
};
```

When we run the tests, Jest will automatically scan the root directory searching for a file named jest.config.ts, which we just created, and in it we tell Jest to look for a setup-jest.ts file and run it to get the additional supporting configuration. Let us also create this setup-jest.ts file at the root of our project and leave it empty for now (we will add some configurations later).

We are almost done setting up our testing environment; however, before we begin fixing the tests for the AppComponent, let us finalize our setup with the addition of some third-party tools that will become useful in the process of writing the actual tests.

8.2.3 *Installing third-party tools*

Angular provides many built-in tools for unit testing out of the box (as we shall soon see when we start interacting with the unit tests for the AppComponent). However, community-driven projects also provide a lot of functionality. Let's explore these.

MOCKING DEPENDENCIES

As mentioned in section 8.1.2, in unit tests, we test functionality in isolation, so a component is tested without actually testing the other components that it uses in its template or services that it injects. But how can we accomplish this if the component, for instance, calls a method from that service?

The way we do this is by *mocking* the dependencies of the particular class/function/ whatever we are testing. Mocking essentially means providing an empty, barebones replacement for a dependency, which has the same API but does nothing and only checks if our test subject calls the correct methods and properties of this "fake" dependency in the correct order. For instance, if our component uses another component, we can write a mock version of this component that has the same inputs and outputs and test the original component that way.

We will discuss doing this in code in the next section, but first we need to understand that this process can become quite cumbersome. A given component can use multiple other components and inject lots of services, so we would need to provide drop-in replacements for them both. In large projects, this can result in a *huge* amount of boilerplate code.

To counter this, a community project called ng-mocks has been developed, which provides functionality that allows to automatically mock existing services, components, pipes, and other Angular building blocks for unit testing purposes. Let's install it so we can use it next:

```
npm install ng-mocks --save-dev
```

Now, as we have it in place, let's discuss problems we may have when testing components specifically and what community solutions we can use to address them.

TESTING ANGULAR COMPONENTS

Testing most of the Angular building blocks boils down to creating an instance of the class we want to test (service, directive, pipe, and so on) and then playing with its methods in various scenarios. However, components do stand apart a bit in this case: they also have a template.

With Angular components, we don't just want to call some of the class methods and ensure they work properly but also to check if, say, some content has been rendered properly in the UI or some event caused the proper handler method to be called. While Angular provides built-in solutions for this, with them, we only work with prerendered instances of component classes and not the actual DOM nodes. The built-in approach also involves a lot of boilerplate.

We will begin with this approach and then move on to a community-driven solution known as the Angular Testing Library. Let's install it (and another relevant package we will use later) and then move on to fix our unit tests:

```
npm install @testing-library/angular --save-dev
npm install @testing-library/jest-dom --save-dev
```

Next, for Jest to actually pick up the new functionality from the Angular Testing Library, we need to add the following line in the setup-jest.ts file we created earlier:

```
import '@testing-library/jest-dom';
```

We will see what this affects in the next section. Now we can call our setting-up phase done and finally begin working with the unit tests! Let's fix our `AppComponent` unit tests.

8.3   Running Angular unit tests

As you recall, we left our exploration of unit tests at the point where running `ng test` resulted in errors when trying to run tests from src/app/app.component.spec.ts. Let's see what this file contains, how the tests there are structured, and what we can do to make them work.

8.3.1   What do unit tests look like?

Before we begin, let us remember what our actual `AppComponent` contains, which we can do by addressing the app.component.ts file in the HRMS project folder (the one we created in chapter 1, section 1.3, listing 1.1). We can easily see that the component is as simple as it gets—just a class that has a property called `title` and some imports in its metadata. We can also vaguely remember that some unit tests for this component were generated by the Angular CLI when we first created the project. Let's now see the automatic tests generated for it.

> **Listing 8.3   Automatic unit tests generated for `AppComponent`**

The "describe" block contains and groups multiple test cases.

```
import { TestBed } from '@angular/core/testing';
import { AppComponent } from './app.component';

describe('AppComponent', () => {
  beforeEach(() => TestBed.configureTestingModule({
    imports: [AppComponent]
  }));
```

Before each test, we need to configure a testing module, where we will either import or mock dependencies of the component we test. Otherwise, this block can also be used to set up different routines we may want to perform before each test case is run.

We create an instance of the component we want to test; here we
receive an instance of the component wrapped in a fixture, a special
object used for testing components.

A test case is described with an "it" block, which
has a name that describes what it does and then
a callback that implements the testing process.

```
it('should create the app', () => {
  const fixture = TestBed.createComponent(AppComponent);
  const app = fixture.componentInstance;
  expect(app).toBeTruthy();
});

it(`should have the 'hrms' title`, () => {
  const fixture = TestBed.createComponent(AppComponent);
  const app = fixture.componentInstance;
  expect(app.title).toEqual('hrms');
});

it('should render title', () => {
  const fixture = TestBed.createComponent(AppComponent);
  fixture.detectChanges();
  const compiled = fixture.nativeElement as HTMLElement;
  expect(compiled.querySelector('.content
    span')?.textContent).toContain('hrms app is running!');
});
});
```

An actual testing
expectation. Here we
expect the component
to be successfully
initialized.

As we can see, the tests follow a specific pattern: first, we initialize whatever we want to test in the `beforeEach` block; then in each testing scenario we take the testing instance, do something with it, and then expect a result with a function with the most descriptive name of `expect`. Also notice that test cases, or "specs" as they are more commonly referred to, follow a descriptive pattern that reads like actual English language: "It should render title," "It should create the app," and so on. Also, all of the specs are contained within a `describe` block that "describes" the `AppComponent`.

In general, running `ng test` will execute all the tests and their setup commands. It is done in a cyclic fashion where Jest finds the `describe` block, `beforeEach` and `it` commands (and many more) and runs them. Figure 8.1 illustrates the life cycle of the unit-testing process.

This test group contains three unit tests. The first one is just checking if Angular can initialize the component at all (commonsense check), and the second one checks for the existence and content of the `title` property. These two make sense, but the third one is a bit off: it does check in the template, and we can see that our `AppComponent` has moved very far from what the unit test expects here. However, we do not get that error, because our very first spec fails as it cannot initialize the `AppComponent`. Let's see why and how we can fix that.

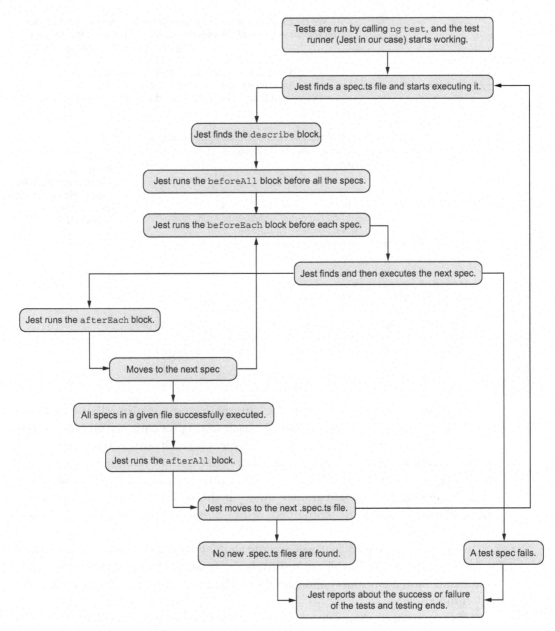

Figure 8.1   Execution of unit tests by the Jest test runner

8.3.2   *Providing mock dependencies*

When we first ran ng test, we encountered an error that was related to dependency injection, when our component tried to inject the HttpClient. However, if we take a look at the component code, we can see that nowhere do we attempt any injection of this service. So why this error?

If we open the src/app/app.component.html file, we can see that it contains a simple template:

```
<app-header/>
<router-outlet></router-outlet>
<app-footer/>
```

Now, the `FooterComponent` resides in the src/app/shared/components/footer.component.ts file (the one we created in chapter 3, section 3.2.2, listing 3.6), and is used here. If we look inside that component, we will see that it calls a function named `isAuth`, which in turn injects the `AuthService`, which finally injects the `HttpClient`, which is not provided anywhere (remember we set up a testing module that is independent of the applications itself, and it imports only the `AppComponent` at this point—nothing else).

So what do we do about this? We could provide the `HttpClient` in the `TestBed` `.configureTestingModule` command, but we do not really need to do this. It is sufficient to remember that unit tests are tests in isolation, so we not only do not need the `HttpClient` (it is already tested and trusted within the Angular framework), but we do not even need the `FooterComponent` and `HeaderComponent`, as they will have their own separate tests. Essentially, our component depends on these two components and `RouterOutlet`.

We can fix the `RouterOutlet` problems by using the `RouterTestingModule`, a specific module that mocks router-related building blocks for unit-testing purposes and the problem with the other two components using `MockComponents`, a special function provided by the ng-mocks library. This function will take a list of components and provide mock replacements for them—essentially components without templates, without injected dependencies, and with the same selectors and inputs/outputs as the components we provided, so we can use them and not bother about their problems when testing the `AppComponent`. Our tests will now look like the following listing.

Listing 8.4 Mocking dependencies to test `AppComponent`

```
import { TestBed } from '@angular/core/testing';
import {
  RouterTestingModule,                          Imports the router mock from
} from '@angular/router/testing';          ◁──  Angular router's testing package
import { MockComponents } from 'ng-mocks';
import { AppComponent } from './app.component';
import { HeaderComponent } from './shared/components/header.component';
import { FooterComponent } from './shared/components/footer.component';

describe('AppComponent', () => {
  beforeEach(() =>
    TestBed.configureTestingModule({
      imports: [                           Provides the        Mocking
        AppComponent,                      mock router         components that
        RouterTestingModule,          ◁──                      are used within
        MockComponents(HeaderComponent, FooterComponent),  ◁── AppComponent
```

```
    ],
  })                   Rest of the tests
  );                   omitted for now
});
```

Hopefully, this will at least fix the first two specs. Indeed, if we run `ng test` again, we will encounter a new error:

```
AppComponent
    √ should create the app (83 ms)
    √ should have the 'hrms' title (21 ms)
    × should render title (19 ms)

  ● AppComponent › should render title

    expect(received).toContain(expected) // indexOf

    Matcher error: received value must not be null nor undefined

    Received has value: undefined
```

As we can see, the first two specs did actually run successfully, and only the third one failed for obvious reasons: the template now contains references to some components and no text that reads "hrms app is running!" This is good news, as now we have a testing expectation fail and not a problem with how we set up the test. Let's move forward and explore how we can fix this.

8.3.3 Testing components

As mentioned previously, testing components is a bit different from other building blocks, because it involves also testing the template. There is a debate within the Angular community as to whether we should test the template of a component or not; however, Angular provides the necessary tools, and the template itself is a very important part of the component (probably *the* most important), so in this book, we will assume that the testing of the template is necessary.

TESTING COMPONENT TEMPLATE WITH ANGULAR'S BUILT-IN TOOLS

`AppComponent` class itself has a very simple implementation (essentially it only imports things to use in the template), so what is left for us is to test the template itself. The template is just calling three other directives, so to make sure `AppComponent` works properly, it should be sufficient to check if the proper components are rendered (only calls to them, without actually rendering them, as we use their mocked versions instead). Let's do exactly that by removing the third spec and writing a new one that checks the template.

Listing 8.5   Testing `AppComponent`'s template

```
it('should render header, footer and a router outlet', () => {
  const fixture = TestBed.createComponent(AppComponent);
```

Angular's change detection does not work
automatically in unit tests, so whenever we want to
check for new templates rendered, we need to call it
manually using the fixture object.

```
  fixture.detectChanges();        ⟵
  const header = fixture.debugElement.query(
    By.css('app-header'),                        Finds the reference to
  );                              ⟵              the header component
  expect(header).toBeTruthy();    ⟵
  const footer = fixture.debugElement.query(     Checks if it exists
    By.css('app-footer'),
  );                              ⟵             Repeats the same for
  expect(footer).toBeTruthy();                  other components
  const routerOutlet = fixture.debugElement.query(By.css('router-outlet'));
  expect(routerOutlet).toBeTruthy();
});
```

Now if we rerun our tests, we will see that all three execute successfully, meaning we just completed unit testing our first component! Congratulations are in order.

However, we can see that this code is a bit too wordy. We use different tools—for instance, the By object imported from @angular/platform-browser—to query the rendered DOM by a CSS selector, we manually trigger change detection, and so on. For now, we tested a routed component, which tends to be not so heavy on the template, often calling other, more reusable components to do the actual rendering (as in this case).

But what will happen when we test other components that accept inputs, call other components again, and change data and output events? Are we doomed to repeat the boilerplate code forever? It turns out, not really. Let's test one of our reusable components and see how the Angular Testing Library can help us reduce the noise and focus on checking the produced DOM.

TESTING COMPONENT TEMPLATE WITH ANGULAR TESTING LIBRARY

Previously, we built a ProjectCardComponent in the src/app/shared/components/project-card.component.ts file (see chapter 4, section 4.1.1, listing 4.1), which received a projectId as an input and made an HTTP call via the ProjectService to retrieve data about the given project and display it in the UI. The component itself is not particularly complex, but it is somewhat template-heavy: it uses the NgOptimized-Directive and injects a service that we built, so we need to learn to mock both and use the tools provided by the Angular Testing Library to easily check the DOM.

Let's see this unit test in action. In the src/app/shared/components directory, create a file named project-card.component.spec.ts and put the test shown in the following listing there.

Listing 8.6   Testing ProjectComponent's **template**

```
import { AsyncPipe, NgIf, NgOptimizedImage } from '@angular/common';
import { RouterLink } from '@angular/router';
import { RenderResult, render } from '@testing-library/angular';
import { MockDirective, MockProvider } from 'ng-mocks';
```

We use the render function provided by the testing library instead of TestBed to create and render our component.

In this variable we will store the reference to the rendered component created in the beforeEach block.

```
import { ProjectService } from 'src/app/services/project.service';
import { ProjectCardComponent } from './project-card.component';

let component: RenderResult<ProjectCardComponent>;        <—

describe('ProjectCardComponent', () => {
  beforeEach(async () => {
    component = await render(ProjectCardComponent, {        <—
      imports: [
        AsyncPipe,
        NgIf,            <—
        RouterTestingModule,
        MockDirective(NgOptimizedImage),        <—
      ],
      providers: [MockProvider(ProjectService)],        <—
    });
  });

  it('should create', () => {
    expect(component).toBeTruthy();
  });
});
```

We do not mock the AsyncPipe and the NgIf directive as we want to test the UI too and need conditional statements and observable values there.

We can just mock the NgOptimizedDirective as we do not need to test its functionality.

We use the MockProvider function from the ng-mocks library to mock the ProjectService; now, our component will receive a dummy version of this service with the same methods that do nothing when called.

If we run the tests now, they will execute successfully; however, we haven't yet tested for much—we only set up our testing space. What we really need to check is whether when the `projectId` property changes, the UI will update accordingly. To achieve this, we need a bit smarter version of the `ProjectService`, which will have the method `getProject` mocked separately and return some mock data for the UI to consume. Let's implement this in the following listing.

Listing 8.7   Mocking a service method separately

```
const mockProjects: Project[] = [        <—    An array of
  {                                            mock "projects"
    id: 1,
    name: 'Project 1',
    description: 'Project 1 description',
    image: 'path-to-image1.png',
    employees: [],
    subProjectIds: [],
  },
  {
    id: 2,
```

```
                name: 'Project 2',
                description: 'Project 2 description',
                image: 'path-to-image2.png',
                employees: [],
                subProjectIds: [],
        },
];

describe('ProjectCardComponent', () => {
    beforeEach(async () => {
        component = await render(ProjectCardComponent, {
            imports: [
                AsyncPipe,
                NgIf,
                RouterTestingModule,
                MockDirective(NgOptimizedImage),
            ],
            providers: [
                MockProvider(ProjectService, {
                    getProject(id) {
                        return of(mockProjects.find((project) => project.id === id)!);
                    },
                }),
            ],
        });
    });
});
```

> MockProvider accepts a second argument, with which we can provide mock implementations of any methods a given service has.

> Mock implementation will find the mock project with the corresponding id and return its observable (for the AsyncPipe to consume in the UI).

> ← Test omitted for now

Now we can imagine that an HTTP call is happening behind the scenes (which it is not) and we get the observable of these mock projects. What is left here is to test for the sequence of "id changed, then `ProjectService` was called, then the UI was updated." It turns out this complex scenario is pretty easy to implement with the testing library. First, let's create the component with an input given by default and check the UI.

Listing 8.8 Testing component UI with the Angular Testing Library

```
import { RenderResult, render, screen } from '@testing-library/angular';

let component: RenderResult<ProjectCardComponent>;

describe('ProjectCardComponent', () => {
    beforeEach(async () => {
        component = await render(ProjectCardComponent, {
            imports: [
                AsyncPipe,
                NgIf,
                RouterTestingModule,
                MockDirective(NgOptimizedImage),
            ],
            providers: [
                MockProvider(ProjectService, {
```

> Rest of the imports and mock data omitted

```
        getProject(id) {
          return of(mockProjects.find((project) => project.id === id)!);
        },
      }),
    ],
    componentInputs: {          ◁───    We can provide values
      projectId: 1,                     for component's inputs
    },                                  with "render."
  });
});

it('should render the project name', () => {
  expect(screen.getByText('Project 1')).toBeInTheDocument();    ◁───────┐
});                                                                       │
});                          A simple line of code checks the existence of the
                                 title in the UI generated by the components.
```

As we can see, testing this scenario boiled down to just a single line of code, thanks to the Angular Testing Library. However, this is the default scenario, and we also want to check that if the input changes, the component successfully updates the UI using the HTTP "call." Let's amend our test spec a bit.

Listing 8.9 Testing component UI when inputs change

```
                                    Tests the initial    │  Sets a new value
                                           scenario      │  for the input
it('should render the project name', () => {             │  using the Angular
  expect(screen.getByText('Project 1')).toBeInTheDocument(); ◁──  reference to the
  component.fixture.componentRef.setInput('projectId', 2);   ◁──  component
  component.fixture.detectChanges();                       ◁──┐
  expect(screen.getByText('Project 2')).toBeInTheDocument(); ◁─┤ Triggers change
});                                                            │ detection so
                                         Checks the UI for     │ that UI updates
                                         the latest text       │
```

With that we have a full scope of this component's functionality. From now on, it would be trivial to add checking for other cases (for instance, checking for an error). Next, we will explore another addition to Angular unit testing by diving into the unit testing process of Angular services.

8.3.4 Testing services

At this point, we should be able to deduce that the testing of services is going to be a simpler process than, say, components. After all, services do not have a template and usually incorporate some straightforward functionality. Let's now see in action what potential problems we might face.

Let's begin with a very foundational service in our application: AuthService. It is a good candidate for exploring here because it is both very important and contains some out-of-the-ordinary functionality like a BehaviorSubject that tracks the user's authentication status and also calls the localStorage object. We will begin by writing a simple test that just creates the instance of the service, and then we can play with it.

For this purpose, let's create a new test file in the src/app/services directory named auth.service.spec.ts and put the setup code from the following listing inside.

Listing 8.10   Setup for the testing of a service

```
import { AuthService } from './auth.service';

let service: AuthService;

describe('AuthService', () => {
    beforeEach(() => {
        service = new AuthService();
    });

    it('should be successfully instantiated', () => {
        expect(service).toBeTruthy();
    });
});
```

While this code looks both familiar and very understandable if we run the tests now, we will be confronted with an error:

```
NG0203: inject() must be called from an injection context
such as a constructor, a factory function,
a field initializer, or a function used
with `runInInjectionContext`.
```

Here we forgot that this service (as all others we authored in the project) uses the inject function to get its dependencies, and chapter 3 taught us that this function only works in specific places, so just calling new AuthService() will not work. What we have to do is set up a testing module, provide dependencies, and then use a special new method that allows us to run code in an injection context while unit testing.

Our service only uses the built-in HttpClient, but, as we mentioned previously, we don't really want to make HTTP calls inside unit tests, so it is better to mock it. For this purpose, Angular provides a special testing controller that allows us to emulate HTTP calls and check for the mocked data received. Let's configure it.

Listing 8.11   Initializing a service in unit tests

```
import { HttpClientTestingModule, HttpTestingController } from
    '@angular/common/http/testing';
import { TestBed } from '@angular/core/testing';          We will use the test
import { AuthService } from './auth.service';             controller in the next specs
                                                          to emulate HTTP calls.
let service: AuthService;
let httpMock: HttpTestingController;          ◄──────     Configures a module
                                                          for mocked providers
describe('AuthService', () => {
    beforeEach(() => {                                    Provides the HTTP testing
        TestBed.configureTestingModule({     ◄──────      module so we do not make
            imports: [HttpClientTestingModule],  ◄──────  real HTTP calls
```

```
    });
    TestBed.runInInjectionContext(() => {        ◁─┐  TestBed now supports calling some
        service = new AuthService();                  │  functions in its own injection
    });                                               │  context, which in our case allows for
    httpMock = TestBed.inject(                        │  the initialization of the AuthService.
      HttpTestingController,
    );                                  ◁──────┐   We also get the reference to the
});                                            │   testing controller to use later.

it('should be successfully instantiated', () => {
    expect(service).toBeTruthy();
});
});
```

Now we can see that our test here runs correctly, and the service is being initialized. Next, let us add a unit test that checks some real functionality—namely the `login` method. For this purpose, we have to send some mock token data via the `HttpTestingController` (we will soon see how), check that it arrived successfully, and also check that the `isAuth$` BehaviorSubject has been switched to true. Here is how we are going to do this in a new test spec, shown the following listing.

Listing 8.12   Testing an HTTP call

We call the method that handles
login and wait for its result.

```
it('should log the user is', () => {
    service.login({email: 'test', password: 'test'}).subscribe((res) => {  ◁─
        expect(res).toBe({token: 'mock token'});          ◁─
        expect(service.isAuth$.getValue()).toBe(true);    ◁─      We expect to
    });                                                            receive a mock
                                                                   token.
    const request = httpMock.expectOne({      ◁─
        url: '/api/auth/login',     ◁─                             We also expect
        method: 'POST',      ◁─                                    that the isAuth$
    });                                                            BehaviorSubject
                                                                   will be flipped to
    request.flush({token: 'mock token'});     ◁─                   true, as the user is
});                                                                 now authenticated.
```

Finally, we send the mock data that will   We use
be checked in the "subscribe" callback.   HttpTestingController
                                                     to check if the
We also check if the method is correct.   method we called
                                                     actually completed
We check if the URL is correct.   the HTTP request.

Now we know how we can unit test a service that makes HTTP calls. There is one thing left for us here to learn, and that is the `getToken` method of our service. We want to check if it really does return a token from `localStorage`. However, if we just write `expect(service.getToken()).toBe('mock token');`, we will be disappointed. Because (as we mentioned), Jest runs in Node.js rather than a browser (as opposed to Karma), `localStorage` doesn't really exist in this context. `localStorage` also isn't an Angular construct, so we have to come up with a custom way of mocking it. We can do this by utilizing some methods that Jest itself provides.

Listing 8.13   Mocking `localStorage`

```
let localStorageMock: Pick<Storage, 'getItem'>;

describe('AuthService', () => {
    beforeEach(() => {
        TestBed.configureTestingModule({
            imports: [HttpClientTestingModule],
        });
        TestBed.runInInjectionContext((() => {
            service = new AuthService();
        });
        httpMock = TestBed.inject(HttpTestingController);

        localStorageMock = {
          getItem: jest
            .fn()
            .mockImplementation((arg) => 'mock token'),
        };
        Object.defineProperty(window, 'localStorage', {
          value: localStorageMock,
        });
    });

    it('should return the token', () => {
        expect(service.getToken()).toBe('mock token');
    });
});
```

We define a mock abject for localStorage which only has the getItem method.

We create the mock object.

Jest provides utilities for mocking functions, and mockImplementation allows us to run any function when the function we want to mock is called.

We then override the localStorage and place our mock object instead.

Rest of the specs omitted

Finally, we check that our method does, in fact, return the mock data from the mock localStorage.

Finally, we have the full arsenal of both modern and existing tools to help us test services in Angular projects. Next, we are going to move to the biggest modern feature Angular has, the signals, and see how we can unit-test them.

8.3.5   *Testing signals*

Signals, as you remember, are a quite big topic (after all, we spent two chapters discussing them!). However, in this section, we will see that using signals actually simplifies the testing process. We already did ourselves good by creating a `TimeOffManagement-Service` in the src/app/services/time-off-management.service.ts file (we created it in chapter 7, section 7.3.4, listing 7.12), which acts as a state management service for components related to the time-off feature. This both simplified the respective component but also allowed us to encapsulate the logic in a service, which we already know is easy to test.

The fact that we can always retrieve the value of a signal plays a major role in this simplification: we can just call the value, then change it, then expect some new value, and that's it: our test is done! Let's see this on the example of this very service, after

which we will also move on and show how this approach simplifies testing the Tim-
eOffManagementComponent.

This service uses another service that makes the HTTP calls that are related to time-
offs. As we already know how to test such services; we will just assume it is already covered by unit tests and works properly, and we only need to mock it in a specific way to
test the TimeOffManagementService. While this service looks a bit intimidating, we can
see that after mocking its dependent service, testing its own functionality will become
extremely easy. Let us see it in action. First, let's mock the dependencies of the service.

Listing 8.14   Mocking the dependencies of a service with signals

```
const mockRequests: TimeOffRequest[] = [          ◁─── Some mock requests
    {                                                   to test with
        id: 1,
        type: 'Vacation',
        status: 'Pending',
        startDate: new Date().toISOString(),
        endDate: new Date().toISOString(),
        employeeId: 1,
    },
    {
        id: 2,
        type: 'Sick Leave',
        status: 'Pending',
        startDate: new Date().toISOString(),
        endDate: new Date().toISOString(),
        employeeId: 1,
    },
];

const MockTimeOffRequestService: Partial<          Mocks the
    TimeOffRequestService                          TimeOffRequestService
> = {                                  ◁──────────
    getRequestsByType: jest.fn()
                        .mockReturnValue(           Mocks this method to
                            of(mockRequests),       immediately return an
                        ),               ◁────────  observable of our mock requests
    approveRequest: jest.fn()
                        .mockImplementation(
                            (id) => {              ◁─── Mocks methods for
                                const request = mockRequests   approval/rejection/
                                                .find(          deletion of time-off
                                                (r) =>          requests to work with
                                                    r.id === id  the mock requests.
                                                );               We return an empty
        if (request) {                                           observable in the end
            request.status = 'Approved';                         for the service events
        }                                                        to work.
        return of({});
    }),
    rejectRequest: jest.fn().mockImplementation((id) => {
        const request = mockRequests.find((r) => r.id === id);
        if (request) {
```

```
                request.status = 'Rejected';
            }
            return of({});
        }),
        deleteRequest: jest.fn().mockImplementation((id) => {
            const index = mockRequests.findIndex((r) => r.id === id);
            if (index !== -1) {
                mockRequests.splice(index, 1);
            }
            return of({});
        }),
};

let localStorageMock: Pick<
  Storage, 'getItem' | 'setItem'          Mocks localStorage
>;                                        with a local variable
let selectedType = '';

let service: TimeOffManagementService;

describe('TimeOffManagementService', () => {
    beforeEach(() => {
        TestBed.configureTestingModule({
            providers: [
                MockProvider(
                    TimeOffRequestService,
                    MockTimeOffRequestService,
                )
            ],
        });
        localStorageMock = {
            getItem: jest.fn()
                        .mockReturnValue(        Getting from localStorage
                            () => selectedType,   should return that variable.
                        ),
            setItem: jest.fn().mockImplementation((key, value) => {
                selectedType = value;            Setting an item in
            })                                   localStorage will just
        };                                       change that variable.
        Object.defineProperty(window, 'localStorage', {
            value: localStorageMock,
        });
        TestBed.runInInjectionContext(() => {
            service = new TimeOffManagementService();
        });
    });

    it('should be successfully instantiated', () => {
        expect(service).toBeTruthy();
    });                                      Initialization of the service
});                                          will work fine now.
```

As we can see, while this seems a bit wordy, most of this code is pure boilerplate to set up the actual test, which, as we promised, is going to be quite simple. We will test the following scenarios:

- Initial mock requests are loaded.
- Changing the `selectedType` results in updates to the requests.
- `selectedType` is stored in `localStorage`.
- Rejection/approval/deletion of a request results in updates to the `requests` signal array.

However, when we implement the first test case, we will see that just doing `expect(service.requests()).toEqual(mockRequests);` does not yield the result we expect. So why is that? In the previous chapter, we learned that computed signals created from observables and effects are tied in with Angular's change detection, meaning in this case we need to trigger change detection to see the results update. In tests, we can only trigger change detection manually when we create a component to test, but we do not have a component now—we are testing a service!

The solution to this is creating an empty component for our testing purposes (such things are often called "stubs"), injecting our service into it, and triggering change detection on it to test the service. It can be achieved pretty easily, as shown in the following listing.

Listing 8.15   Using a stub component to test a service with signals

```
@Component({
    selector: 'app-stub',
    template: '',                            Our stub component is
    standalone: true,                        empty and only injects the
})                                           service we want to test.
export class StubComponent {          ←┘
    constructor(private readonly service: TimeOffManagementService) {}
}

describe ('TimeOffManagementService', () => {
    beforeEach(() => {
        TestBed.configureTestingModule({
            providers: [MockProvider(TimeOffRequestService,
    MockTimeOffRequestService)],
            imports: [StubComponent],        ←┤  We import the stub component
        });                                      into the testing module.
        localStorageMock = {
          getItem: jest.fn().mockReturnValue(() => selectedType),
          setItem: jest.fn().mockImplementation((key, value) => {
            selectedType = value;
          })
        };
        Object.defineProperty(window, 'localStorage', {
          value: localStorageMock,
        });
        service = TestBed.inject(                 We now use TestBed.inject to
                TimeOffManagementService,        get the reference to our service,
                );                          ←┤   so that the component's
    });                                          reference to the service is that
                                                 same as the one we are testing.
```

```
it('should be successfully instantiated', () => {
    expect(service).toBeTruthy();
});

it('should have all requests loaded initially, () => {
    const fixture = TestBed.createComponent(StubComponent);
    fixture.detectChanges();            ◄────────┐
    expect(service.requests())
        .toEqual(mockRequests);         ◄────┐
});
});
```

We call detectChanges before we check for the values in the computed signal.

This finally works.

As we can see, the only downside here is having to use the `TestBed` and manually triggering change detection before checking. Otherwise, all the tests are very simple, and we can just list them.

Listing 8.16 Unit tests for a service with signals

```
it('should be successfully instantiated', () => {
    expect(service).toBeTruthy();
});

it('should have all requests loaded initially', () => {
    const fixture = TestBed.createComponent(StubComponent);
    fixture.detectChanges();
    expect(service.requests()).toEqual(mockRequests);
});

it('should update requests when approved', () => {
    const fixture = TestBed.createComponent(StubComponent);
    service.approveRequest(mockRequests[0]);
    fixture.detectChanges();
    expect(service.requests()[0].status).toEqual('Approved');
});

it('should update requests when rejected', () => {
    const fixture = TestBed.createComponent(StubComponent);
    service.rejectRequest(mockRequests[0]);
    fixture.detectChanges();
    expect(service.requests()[0].status).toEqual('Rejected');
    expect(service.resolvedRequests()).toEqual([mockRequests[0]]);
});

it(`should write the values in
    localStorage when selectedType
    has change`, () => {
    const fixture = TestBed.createComponent(StubComponent);
    service.selectedType.set('Vacation');
    fixture.detectChanges();
    expect(selectedType).toBe('Vacation');
});
```

These tests are so straightforward we don't even need to dive that deep into them: we call a method on our service, detect changes, and ensure the signals have changed their values to whatever we expect them to be. As promised, other than the setup phase (which as we saw was a bit boilerplate-y), testing services with signals is easy, and there's no need to worry about asynchronous code, promises, or observables.

Next let us see how this testing approach will work with the `TimeOffManagement-Component`, which of course uses the service we just covered with tests. In that case, it will be even simpler: we only have to mock the `TimeOffManagementService` with some mock signal and then use the testing library to essentially test the DOM. For this purpose, we will create a new test file in the src/app/pages/work directory named time-off-management.component.spec.ts and put the tests shown in the following listing in it.

Listing 8.17   Unit tests for a component with signals

```
const MockTimeOffManagementService: any = {          ◁─────  Mocks the service that
    requests: signal(mockRequests),          ◁────┐          we already tested before
    selectedType: signal(''),                      │     We can just use the same mock
    resolvedRequests: computed(() => {             └──── requests from listing 8.13.
        return MockTimeOffManagementService.requests()
                                    .filter(          ◁──   We can implement
            (r: TimeOffRequest) => r.status !== 'Pending',       this signal here to do
        );                                                       the logic of filtration
    }),                                                          internally instead of
                                                                 making an HTTP call.
    approveRequest: jest.fn().mockImplementation((request) => {
        const index = mockRequests.findIndex((r) => r.id === request.id);
        if (index !== -1) {
            mockRequests[index].status = 'Approved';
        }
        MockTimeOffManagementService.requests.set(mockRequests);
    }),

    rejectRequest: jest.fn().mockImplementation((request) => {
        const index = mockRequests.findIndex((r) => r.id === request.id);
        if (index !== -1) {
            mockRequests[index].status = 'Rejected';
        }
        MockTimeOffManagementService.requests.set(mockRequests);
    }),

    deleteRequest: jest.fn().mockImplementation((request) => {
        const index = mockRequests.findIndex((r) => r.id === request.id);
        if (index !== -1) {
            mockRequests.splice(index, 1);
        }
        MockTimeOffManagementService.requests.set(mockRequests);
    }),
} as const;

let component: RenderResult<TimeOffManagementComponent>;

describe('TimeOffManagementComponent', () => {
    beforeEach(async () => { component = await render(
```

```
          TimeOffManagementComponent,
             {
providers: [
                  {
                      provide: TimeOffManagementService,
useValue:
                          MockTimeOffManagementService,
          },
          ],
          });
      });

      it('should render the component', () => {
          expect(component).toBeTruthy();
      });

      it('should render the requests', () => {
          expect(component.getAllByRole('row').length)
              .toEqual(3);
      });

      it('should update the UI with new buttons if a request is approved', ()
      => {
          const approveButton = component.getAllByText('Approve')[0];
          fireEvent.click(approveButton);
          expect(
              component.getAllByText('Approve').length,
          ).toEqual(1);
          expect(component.getAllByText('Reject').length).toEqual(1);
      });
  });
});
```

Simple setup of the testing environment

We can initially check that we have only three rows (one for the table column names + two for our mock requests).

We then expect the number of buttons to change accordingly; previously we had two of both as we had two pending requests, and now we have only one of each.

We use the utility functions from the Angular Testing Library to simulate a click on the first Approve Request button.

Evidently, with this state management approach and with the power of the Angular Testing Library, testing components essentially boils down to mocking services and checking for UI updates after simulated events. As we can see, the main problem for us so far has been the boilerplate: writing tests requires a lot of typing. Although we have finished covering the testing process of all the new features we explored in this book, it would also be helpful to consider a tool that may remedy the aforementioned tedium of writing tests. At the time of writing this book, AI tools have started popping up everywhere; most people are finding ways to integrate these tools into their workflow to make life easier and more productive. In the next section, we discuss how we can utilize modern AI tools to significantly cut down on some of the more laborious manual aspects of unit testing, which can cause us stress and lost time.

8.4   *Powers of AI with Angular unit tests*

The beginning of the third decade of the 21st century is marked by a rapid increase in the capabilities of AI-powered tools, ranging from text and image generation to problem-solving and, of course, writing code. Various tools now exist that can help developers, and, in the context of unit tests, we will soon see that those tools become extremely useful when trying to make the unit testing experience enjoyable (let's be honest, no one likes mocking dependencies!).

A multitude of coding-related tools exist nowadays, both as plugins for editors and as standalone tools; however, in this section, we will focus on two of the most popular—ChatGPT and GitHub Copilot—and see how they can be specifically tailored to our unit testing needs. Let's begin with ChatGPT, which is the more "brute force" way of writing unit tests.

8.4.1   *Unit testing Angular applications with ChatGPT*

ChatGPT is an online, AI-powered chatbot that can be accessed on any browser (https://chat.openai.com/). It has a very simple interface, where we can write any text (generally referred to as a "prompt") and ChatGPT will give us an answer. Prompts can vary a lot, but in general, we can ask any question, including those related to software development. ChatGPT can code in any programming language, but, of course, the addition of a reference to the technology we use will help it generate a more relevant response (i.e., "I am testing an Angular component, and ..."). So how can we use it? There are several approaches to it as related to unit tests.

MOCKING DATA

In listing 8.13, we wrote some mock time-off requests to unit-test our service. We wrote only two, for the sake of simplicity, but in general, we might want to have more to be able to exercise more testing scenarios. Typing that out (even when copy-pasting) is a bit of a hassle, so it might make sense to ask ChatGPT to do it for us. Let's craft a small prompt, using the type definition of the request, and see how ChatGPT might respond to us.

The prompt is

```
Provide an array of objects that conform to the following TypeScript type:

type TimeOffRequest = {
    id: number;
    employeeId: number;
    startDate: string;
    endDate: string;
    type: 'Vacation' | 'Sick Leave' | 'Maternity Leave' |
      'Paternity Leave' | 'Other';
    status: 'Pending' | 'Approved' | 'Rejected';
    comment?: string;
};
```

ChatGPT's output is

```
const timeOffRequests: TimeOffRequest[] = [
    {
        id: 1,
        employeeId: 101,
        startDate: '2023-11-01',
        endDate: '2023-11-03',
        type: 'Vacation',
        status: 'Approved',
        comment: 'Going on a short vacation'
    },
    {
        id: 2,
        employeeId: 102,
        startDate: '2023-11-05',
        endDate: '2023-11-07',
        type: 'Sick Leave',
        status: 'Pending'
    },
];
```

It actually provided some more text output (something along the lines of "here is the array you wanted") and yielded five objects in this array; however, we omitted the rest for the sake of brevity. We can also indicate how many results we want—for instance, "give me 10 objects like this."

> **NOTE**   ChatGPT is a nondeterministic AI tool that generates responses based on its own learning data, which changes constantly. Trying the same prompt can (and most probably will) yield at least slightly different results.

Of course, saving time on mocking data is very valuable, but what else can we do?

MOCKING DEPENDENCIES

As we saw, we spent most time mocking, say, services rather than data (the latter is mainly a mechanical job). On the contrary, mocking services involves some critical thinking on our part, so let us see if ChatGPT can handle it on the mock of the `TimeOffRequestService` we created in the same listing 8.13. The prompt is

```
Provide a mock object that mocks all of the methods in this service; use
Jest as the testing framework. Do not provide the tests, and do not make the
methods into spies, just provide mock implementations of the methods, and
use Observables
<the code of the service we want to mock goes here>
```

As we can see, we had to add some additional parameters to the prompt, asking it to skip tests themselves and to use observables. Let's see what we got in response (omitting all but the essentials for brevity):

```
export class TimeOffRequestServiceMock {
  getRequests(query = ''): Observable<TimeOffRequest[]> {
```

```
    // Mock implementation of getRequests method
    return of([]);
  }

  getRequestsByType(query = ''): Observable<TimeOffRequest[]> {
    // Mock implementation of getRequestsByType method
    return this.getRequests().pipe(
      map(requests => {
        return query === ''
          ? requests
          : requests.filter(r => r.type === query);
      })
    );
  }

  rejectRequest(id: number): Observable<any> {
    // Mock implementation of rejectRequest method
    return of({});
  }

  approveRequest(id: number): Observable<any> {
    // Mock implementation of approveRequest method
    return of({});
  }

  deleteRequest(id: number): Observable<any> {
    // Mock implementation of deleteRequest method
    return of({});
  }
}
```

Now we received something that is close to the mock object we created in listing 8.13. We can modify the getRequests method to return the mock time-off requests we created with the previous prompt, and we received a decent mock implementation of our service. So far, so good: but can ChatGPT write unit tests?

GENERATING UNIT TESTS
Large components (services, directives, etc.) that have specific business logic might be hard for ChatGPT to generate meaningful tests for; however, small and reusable components are good candidates. Let's try some with the ConfirmationDialogComponent from the src/app/shared/components/confirmation-dialog.component.ts file that we authored in chapter 2, section 2.4.5, listing 2.17. The prompt is

```
Generate unit tests for this Angular component,
use Jest and the Angular Testing Library
<component code goes here>
```

Now let's actually fly the generated unit tests generated by ChatGPT and create a new file named confirmation-dialog.component.spec.ts in the src/app/shared/components directory and put the tests generated by ChatGPT in response to the prompt there.

Listing 8.18 Unit tests generated by ChatGPT

```
import { render, fireEvent } from '@testing-library/angular';
import { ConfirmationDialogComponent } from './confirmation-dialog.component';

describe('ConfirmationDialogComponent', () => {
  it('should create', async () => {
    const component = await render(ConfirmationDialogComponent);
    expect(component).toBeTruthy();
  });

  it('should set isConfirmationOpen to true by default', async () => {
    const { component } = await render(ConfirmationDialogComponent);
    expect(component.isConfirmationOpen).toBe(true);
  });

  it('should close confirmation dialog on Cancel button click', async () => {
    const { getByText, component } = await
      render(ConfirmationDialogComponent);
    const cancelButton = getByText('Cancel');
    fireEvent.click(cancelButton);
    expect(component.isConfirmationOpen).toBe(false);
  });

  it('should close confirmation dialog on Confirm button click', async () => {
    const { getByText, component } = await
      render(ConfirmationDialogComponent);
    const confirmButton = getByText('Confirm');
    fireEvent.click(confirmButton);
    expect(component.isConfirmationOpen).toBe(false);
  });

  it('should have a dialog element with open attribute set to true',
    async () => {
      const { getByRole } = await render(ConfirmationDialogComponent);
      const dialogElement = getByRole('dialog');
      expect(dialogElement).toBeTruthy();
      expect(dialogElement.getAttribute('open')).toBe('true');
    });
});
```

Just by looking at these tests, we can see that they are pretty comprehensive. However, if we run them, we will see they cause a problem—mainly the last test. In the component, we set the dialog's `open` attribute to `true`, which results in the `dialog` element being rendered with a present but empty `open` attribute; however, the unit test expects the attribute to have a value of `'true'`. To amend this, we can simply change the very last expectation to the following:

```
expect(dialogElement.hasAttribute('open')).toBe(true);
```

Obviously, despite the results not always being completely perfect, ChatGPT can still be a great tool to help us skip many repetitive steps when writing unit tests and even just generate them outright. This comes with the caveat that the tool should always be used with caution, and the user must have an understanding of what they are asking ChatGPT to do so that any errors and problems in the output can be identified and resolved.

However, it is somewhat difficult to tailor the ChatGPT experience to the needs of our own projects, as ChatGPT treats every prompt as a separate question (to an extent, it still preserves the context of the chat window, but that's it), and oftentimes we have to provide a lot of context for it to generate a really relevant result. Next, let's discuss a tool aimed at solving that very problem.

8.4.2   Unit testing Angular applications with GitHub Copilot

GitHub Copilot (https://github.com/features/copilot) is an AI coding assistant developed by GitHub. It trained on public, open source repositories on GitHub itself, making it very proficient in a number of programming languages and frameworks, including, of course, JavaScript/TypeScript and Angular.

GitHub Copilot is a paid service (a free trial period might apply) that is used as a plugin installed in the developer's IDE of choice (VSCode, WebStorm, and so on). It acts as an enhancement to the code completion feature that most IDEs already have; however, it uses AI to infer the context of a given file or project and generate way more relevant completions. Later versions also include a built-in chat (like ChatGPT), which we can prompt with questions, generation of commit messages, and more. We won't dive too deep into it, and readers can try it out in their editor (unlike ChatGPT, it can be demonstrated only when actually typing out the code). Also, we already covered chatting with AI to generate code, so instead we will discuss some approaches that help GitHub Copilot generate better code in Angular applications specifically.

EXPLICIT TYPING IS BETTER FOR AI

Often, when we write code, especially unit tests, we tend to omit some typing declarations and either rely on TypeScript's (very powerful but still not perfect) type inference or leave some variable or property of type `any` altogether. For AI-powered tools like Copilot, this can pose a problem, as it may mean less context for it to infer and apply in the code that it generates. This is, of course, a relatively easy problem to fix, and the best approach here would be to provide explicit types for all mocks, component/service/etc. references, and so on.

GOOD SPEC NAMES WILL GENERATE BETTER TESTS

As we have noted previously when writing test specs with the `it` function, we provide a spec name (expectation of what the test subject, be it a component, service, or anything else we think should do) as the first argument. This spec name achieves several things, such as describing the spec in the English language to other developers who might read it, showing a meaningful report when the tests are run, and helping to locate a test that is failing. With Copilot, a good spec name also becomes a great way to hint at what we might want it to generate. Consider the second test spec from listing 8.17

that we generated with ChatGPT. Let's delete the implementation callback and just leave the spec name:

```
it('should set isConfirmationOpen to true by default', async () => {
```

This description itself is pretty much enough for Copilot to generate a meaningful test. This can work both in simple and very complex scenarios.

COMMENTS CAN HELP BETTER DESCRIBE TESTS

Sometimes, specs are too complex to be explained just by their name, so if we want Copilot to better understand exactly what we want, we can also use plain old comments. Copilot not only understands code but can also read the comments and treat them as inline commands. For instance, we might write something like the following:

```
// add a test spec that checks that when users log in or out,
// the footer component toggles the visibility of the links section
```

Copilot then can easily generate at least a simple spec (which we can modify further manually if necessary) for us to use. After we are done, we can remove the comment.

Comments are also great at explaining code. Sometimes a spec is hard, and a descriptive comment explaining some specific scenario can help Copilot generate more of those. On the other hand, code comments might also help Copilot generate more code like that or tests that cover that particular case.

Over the course of this section, we have built up an increasing awareness of the full arsenal of tools we have at our disposal when unit testing an Angular application, from built-in tools and third-party libraries to the power of AI. Now let us close this chapter with a brief discussion of what to expect next in the Angular framework in regard to unit tests.

8.5   *The future of unit testing in Angular*

At the beginning of this chapter, we discussed choosing a test runner and discussed Karma, the fact that it is deprecated, and the experimental support of Jest. When we combine these two facts, we will notice that at the time of writing this book (v16-17 of Angular), the framework does not have a stable and supported test runner that comes out of the box.

While Jest support will improve, and it will most likely become stable in the next versions of Angular, the Angular team itself thinks that running in a purely Node.js environment is still inferior to having them run in a real browser. With this in mind, the Angular team, in parallel with announcing Jest, has also announced future support for the Web Test Runner (https://modern-web.dev/docs/test-runner/overview/), a browser-based test runner that, by the words of the Angular team themselves, has quite impressive performance.

Support for this runner is still not available as default (although it can be set up manually in an experimental manner), but as its future addition is confirmed, it could be a good idea for the readers of this book to familiarize themselves with it and see how it can be used, what sort of performance it has, and so on.

Of course, as we mentioned previously, the choice of the test runner is ultimately up to the team of developers who are going to actually write the tests, so if your team thinks that, for example, Jest is enough, then most possibly Angular will have a variety of options in the future, Jest included.

As we developed our HRMS application and covered it with unit tests, it is now time to deploy it, so that users will be able to see it. In the next chapter, we are going to talk about building, deploying, and improving the performance of Angular applications, server-side rendering, and other modern tools that Angular now provides out of the box.

8.6   *Exercises for the reader*

When writing unit tests in this chapter, we skipped some scenarios. This was deliberate, as we want to provide the opportunity for the reader of this book to write those test scenarios.

- In the `AuthService` tests, add a spec that tests the logout method.
- Write unit tests for the HTTP calls in the `TimeOffRequestService`.
- Add a spec in the tests for `TimeOffManagementService` that checks that changing the selected type of requests the UI updates accordingly. (Note: you might want to change a bit both the mock data and the mock implementation of the `TimeOffRequestService` to achieve this.)
- If you have an existing project that runs unit tests on Karma, try to use the instructions from this chapter to switch it to Jest, and then study and resolve the problems that might arise.

Summary

- Unit tests are a great way to ensure the stability of Angular applications.
- Historically, Angular used Karma to run unit tests.
- Karma is deprecated, so Angular added experimental support for Jest.
- Libraries like `ng-mocks` and the Angular Testing Library can be a great asset when unit testing.
- Services that use the inject function can use the new `TestBed.runInInjection-Context` method to initialize.
- There are no serious differences in testing standalone and module-based components.
- AI tools can be used and tailored to provide a better experience when writing unit tests for Angular apps.
- The Angular team has announced future support of the Web Test Runner.

Modern Angular
everywhere

9

This chapter covers

- Server-side rendering
- Why server-side rendering can be necessary and the performance benefits it provides
- Building a project from scratch with server-side rendering
- Adding server-side rendering to an existing Angular application
- Configuring static site generation with page prerendering
- Configuring application build to use ESBuild for improved build time

Congratulations! During the previous eight chapters, we have successfully built an enterprise Angular application and even covered it with unit tests to ensure its stability. Next, we are preparing to go into production, so our concerns are now with building pipelines and application performance. Let's see how we move our application to a server and how we make it marketable.

9.1   *What is server-side rendering?*

While the developers working on the HRMS project we have been building so far rejoice in having completed a minimum viable product, the marketing team arrives with a big new task before we can move the project into production.

The team gathers with the marketing reps, and they lay out their vision of how the product will be promoted to potential buyers:

> *What we want is to have a separate, landing-page-style website that displays information about the product, and also uses statistics from the app itself; for example, we would like to have some banners that say that our product is used by X companies and has Y active users; that data, of course, has to be correct and reflect the situation in our databases.*

We might think, sure, it will be easy to throw around a new small Angular app that makes some requests for statistical data and largely displays static content. But the marketing team pushes on:

> *We also want lightning-fast performance. The performance of the HRMS product itself is decent, but it has terrible initial load time; this is not a problem for the users, as this is an enterprise tool used in offices; but for a landing page, we want almost instantaneous interaction. We are going to promote the platform online, and potential buyers will arrive at the landing page, possibly using mobile devices, so the initial load speed is of paramount importance.*

Then a discussion ensues, which inevitably ends with someone suggesting that the landing page website is built using server-side rendering (SSR). Is Angular capable of this? Well, it was capable of SSR for quite a long time with the separate Angular Universal package, but recently it received a powerful upgrade and got integrated with other Angular packages itself. So before we begin building this landing page, let's figure out what SSR is, what benefits it brings, and how it works in Angular.

9.1.1   *SSR: The what*

When the internet first began, it mostly consisted of servers providing static pages to a client's browsers. It was a pretty simple schema, exchanging HTML documents between computers, as figure 9.1 suggests.

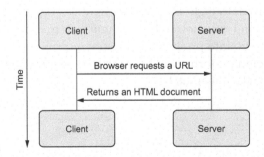

Figure 9.1   Serving static HTML documents

When in this sequence the client receives the HTML document, it is ready for consumption, and the browser renders the document and paints it as UI for the user to view. Even today many websites use this very schema of just serving static content. However, with time, both the server and the client sides became more and more dynamic.

First, a necessity arose for server-side dynamic pages; for instance, when a user navigates to a certain URL, depending on whether they are logged in or not, they should see different pages, meaning the server now has to "manually" generate an HTML document and serve it, instead of just grabbing a readily available one. Figure 9.2 shows how it looked with that approach.

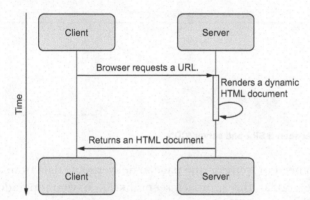

Figure 9.2   Rendering HTML documents on a server

Now the "Renders a dynamic HTML document" part is what we usually refer to as SSR. But what does it have to do with Angular? With the progress of rendering on the server side, the client side also received new tools. At this point, JavaScript was used almost everywhere to provide dynamic interactions in the browser (as continues to be the case to this day), opening popups, tracking user activity, validating forms, and so on. At some point, web developers figured we could just forgo the server part and render the page in the browser, with the backend only providing dynamic data as JSON. This is what we have been doing with Angular so far, and this is how single-page applications (SPAs) were born. They provided a number of benefits:

- Websites could now feel like mobile applications for users.
- Navigating from one page to another no longer involved destroying the entire previous page and repainting a new one.
- We could serve such single-page applications from static content servers like content delivery networks (CDNs) instead of large servers.
- The server and the client became very decoupled.

With SPAs, the process from figure 9.2 became more complicated, as evidenced by figure 9.3.

This approach ushered us into an era when all websites started looking like fully fledged applications and provided very powerful interactions and instantaneous

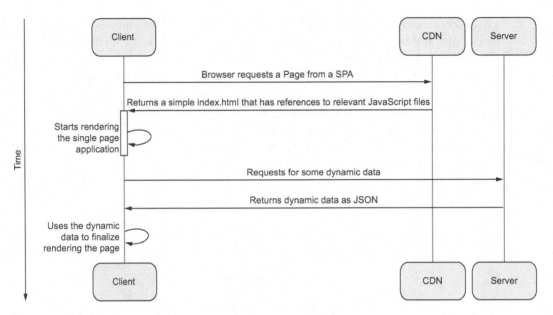

Figure 9.3   Life cycle of the relation between a SPA and server/CDN

feedback for the user (no need to "refresh" the page to deliver some data from a form to the server, for example). So far, this approach seems like an obvious upgrade from just SSR, so why are we discussing SSR in Angular in this chapter? Let's discuss what problems SPAs have.

9.1.2   SSR: The why

Despite all the aforementioned benefits, SPAs carry with them several problems that strike particularly painfully for websites intended to be accessed by millions that are dealing with marketing or are mobile-heavy. Let's discuss each of these in turn.

INFERIOR INITIAL LOAD TIME

If we take a closer look at figure 9.3, we will see that rendering the page now involves several steps; first, we need to load a page, which will contain some bare-bones HTML and links to relevant JavaScript files. In the case of Angular, applications by default are single-page, so if we build and serve them, every time someone accesses them, they will first receive this "initial" HTML. We can see this in action if we run `ng serve`, open the page, and inspect its source code. We can do this with the HRMS application we already have and will see the code shown in the following listing.

Listing 9.1   index.html file of an Angular single-page application

```
<!doctype html>
<html lang="en">

<head>
  <meta charset="utf-8">
```

```
    <title>Hrms</title>
    <base href="/">
    <meta name="viewport" content="width=device-width, initial-scale=1">
    <link rel="icon" type="image/x-icon" href="favicon.ico">
    <link rel="stylesheet" href="styles.css">
</head>

<body>
  <app-root></app-root>
  <script src="runtime.js" type="module"></script>
  <script src="polyfills.js" type="module"></script>
  <script src="styles.js" defer></script>
  <script src="vendor.js" type="module"></script>
  <script src="main.js" type="module"></script>
</body>

</html>
```

As we can see, the page is essentially empty, with just a reference to our root component (`AppComponent`) and some scripts. To render the actual content, in the next step,
the browser will have to load those scripts (some of which contain the code for Angular itself). Finally, the browser will execute those scripts, which will in turn render the
page the user really wants to see.

Obviously, this process is far more resource-heavy than what we described as SSR,
as, instead of just getting some prepared HTML and rendering it, the browser will
have to go through all of those steps, download the JavaScript files, and execute them,
and only then will the rendering even begin.

Obviously, this affects a number of important metrics, one of which is Largest Contentful Paint, which we discussed in relation to images in chapter 4, section 4.4. This
also makes the time-to-interactive (time that passes between the user navigating to a
page and them being able to trigger events like clicks in it) metric worsen by quite a
lot. Essentially, if we take any Angular SPA and run Chrome's built-in Lighthouse performance monitoring tool, we will see quite poor results.

All of these make Angular as a SPA an unappealing choice for websites aimed at
passing-by users. As we mentioned, for enterprise tools, such metrics can be not very
important (who cares how fast a page you load every day goes to interactive?), but for
websites like blogs, landing pages, marketing sites, and so on, poor performance in
such categories can mean reduced traffic, which in turn devolved into lost revenue.
However, such websites have an even bigger concern that is affected by SPAs.

WORSENED SEO
Search engine optimization (SEO) is a practice of making web pages more suitable
for search engines like Google, Bing, etc. Essentially, it means adding specific keywords and building websites in such a way that search engine web crawlers can easily
find and index them.

Search engines use these special programs, called crawlers, to automatically go
around the web and find new pages, extract information from them, and make

them related to keywords for which users might potentially search in the future. For instance, if we build a website for a legal company in Albuquerque, those web crawlers can find pages inside them and index keywords from them, and then when someone searches for "lawyer in ABQ," they will be presented with this particular website.

Obviously, having one's website on the Google search's front page is a huge boost to website traffic, which can and will translate to actual revenue. For this purpose, SEO has evolved into a huge science, where experts configure specific keywords, links, and structures to make websites easier to find.

However, all of those tricks and approaches are utterly defeated by the very nature of SPAs, because those web crawlers we talked about are not web browsers. They perform the initial load of a website, crawl it for keywords, index it in their database, and move to the links they found on the page; however, they will not execute any client-side JavaScript, and as we see from listing 9.1, our initial HTML file contains essentially nothing, and anything potentially useful for web crawlers is rendered by JavaScript.

These two points are already pretty bad from the financial perspective; however, they both become even worse when we consider that not all visitors to a website use desktop computers or laptops.

AFFECTED MOBILE EXPERIENCE

A worse initial page time for mobile users is even more damning for mobile users, as browsers on mobile devices tend to be a bit slower than their desktop counterparts. Also, users of mobile phones might get frustrated by a long page load far easier, as they commonly use mobile applications more often than websites, meaning they can be used to better load performance.

On the other hand, downloading lots of JavaScript (which as we saw was crucial for showing any content to the user at all) can negatively affect users with a sensitive data plan and quite literally cost them money, thus making SSR a preferable choice over a SPA for websites that want to be mobile-friendly.

With these strong arguments made for SSR, we can now discuss how it is possible to implement it within Angular applications.

9.1.3   *SSR: The how*

As we said, so far we have only run the HRMS application on the client side. For this purpose, when we run `ng serve`, Angular bootstraps a very simple server, which essentially only serves static files that we receive in the browser. Subsequently, if we then choose to deploy our app somewhere to become available to end users, we can run `ng build` and the command will generate some static HTML and JavaScript files, which we can easily host on some CDN (more on build commands later in this chapter).

However, for SSR, we are going to need a server. Traditionally, for Angular SSR, the role of such a server was played by Node.js and Express, a Node framework. Other setups can be configured; however, they are out of the scope of this book, as

Express is now the default choice for SSR in Angular. So let us talk a bit about Node.js and Express before we move to actually create an SSR Angular app.

We should already be at least a little bit familiar with Node.js, as Angular itself uses it to build and serve applications. We also use npm, the Node.js default package manager, to install and update dependencies like libraries, tooling, and Angular itself. While Node.js itself can be used to bootstrap a server that will render our Angular application, developers commonly use some frameworks to facilitate building backend applications. Express is one of the most common tools in this regard.

The good news about Express is that we don't need to know much about it. After all, we are not doing backend development here. However, we need to know a bit about it. As already mentioned, Express is a Node.js framework aimed at building backend applications of all kinds. It is particularly simple and easy to adopt. For instance, we can bootstrap a working Express backend with a couple of lines of code, as shown in the following listing.

Listing 9.2 Simple Express server

```
const express = require('express');
const app = express();

app.get('/', function(req, res){
   res.send("Hello world!");
});


app.listen(3000);
```

If we install Express using the npm install express command and run this file with Node.js, a server will start working and listening on port 3000. If we navigate to http://localhost:3000, we will see the "Hello world!" text rendered in the browser.

Express allows registering callbacks for different routes, and when an HTTP request arrives at that URL, those callbacks will be executed and some data will be sent as a response. Express can also be used to render HTML files and serve them dynamically, meaning it can be used for SSR, which Angular does.

Express applications also allow for so-called *middlewares*, functions that execute between requests and add some functionality to the existing application. Middlewares can be used to add plugins for Express-based applications and will be important in the next section, where we actually implement SSR and try to understand how it works.

Previously, Angular used Express to make SSR applications in a dedicated package called Angular Universal, which kind of existed outside of Angular itself (despite being developed by the same team). Starting from v17, however, SSR became a special package inside Angular itself, which we can either add to an existing project or use to begin a project with it from the very start.

Now, having all of this knowledge, let us build a promotional, landing-page-style Angular SSR application; explore it; find caveats; and prepare to build and deploy it with the HRMS app itself.

9.2   Building Angular apps with SSR from scratch

As already mentioned, previously we had to build an Angular app as usual, then add Angular Universal to it, and then configure it to be able to enjoy the benefits of SSR. However, now we can begin a new Angular app by following two simple steps:

1   Ensure we have Angular version 17 or higher.
2   Run the `ng new hrms-promo --ssr` command.

These steps will, as expected, generate a new Angular project for our promotional website. The `--ssr` argument will tell Angular to create an application that runs on the server side by default. Let us run this command, open the project in the editor of our choice, and explore it.

9.2.1   How is an SSR Angular application different from a SPA?

First things first: let's explore the package.json file. Not much has changed there; however, we might notice that dependencies now include "express" (naturally) and also a new package called @angular/ssr. This new package is where all the Angular functionality necessary to render the application on the server side resides.

Next, let's open up the angular.json file and see how it is different from what we might expect. For the most part, it is business as usual; however, the architect.build configuration now has some interesting properties.

Listing 9.3   angular.json file of an SSR application

```
"build": {
     "builder": "@angular-devkit/build-angular:application",
     "options": {
                                        ◄─────── The rest of the options are omitted.

         "server": "src/main.server.ts",          ◄──    Entry point for Angular
         "prerender": true,                 ◄──┐         when it runs on the server
         "ssr": {                              │         as opposed to the browser
           "entry": "server.ts"        ◄──┐    │
         }                                │    │         We will explore this option
     },                                   │    │         later in this chapter.
}                                         │
                                          │    This option indicates the file from
                                          │    which the server must start running
                                               to serve rendered Angular pages.
```

Evidently, these options pretty much tell Angular that this particular application is meant to run on a server and how to start it. The next thing foreshadowed by this file is that we have multiple main.ts files and that we also have a special server.ts file at the root of our application. Let us open it and explore it further in the following listing.

Listing 9.4   Configuring the server to render the Angular pages

Base HREF for the files to load correctly

**The CommonEngine will
be used to render the
page on the server.**

```
import { APP_BASE_HREF } from '@angular/common';
import { CommonEngine } from '@angular/ssr';
import express from 'express';
import { fileURLToPath } from 'node:url';
import { dirname, join, resolve } from 'node:path';
import bootstrap from './src/main.server';
```

**All node dependencies are
imported with the node: prefix.**

**This function will create a server and export
it for the case when developers want to use
Angular on a serverless function.**

```
export function app(): express.Express {
  const server = express();
  const serverDistFolder = dirname(fileURLToPath(import.meta.url));
  const browserDistFolder = resolve(serverDistFolder, '../browser');
  const indexHtml = join(serverDistFolder, 'index.server.html');

  const commonEngine = new CommonEngine();

  server.set('view engine', 'html');
  server.set('views', browserDistFolder);

  server.get('*.*', express.static(browserDistFolder, {
    maxAge: '1y'
  }));

  server.get('*', (req, res, next) => {
    const { protocol, originalUrl, baseUrl, headers } = req;

    commonEngine
      .render({
        bootstrap,
        documentFilePath: indexHtml,
        url: `${protocol}://${headers.host}${originalUrl}`,
        publicPath: browserDistFolder,
        providers: [{ provide: APP_BASE_HREF, useValue: baseUrl }],
      })
      .then((html) => res.send(html))
      .catch((err) => next(err));
  });

  return server;
}

function run(): void {
  const port = process.env['PORT'] || 4000;

  const server = app();
  server.listen(port, () => {
    console.log(`Node Express server listening on http://localhost:${port}`);
  });
}

run();
```

**Tells Express what engine to use when
rendering; different options exist, but
with Angular SSR just HTML is used.**

**Common engine is used to
render the HTML document.**

**All routes will invoke this callback, which will
render the corresponding Angular component
to an HTML document and return it.**

**All routes containing a dot will be identified as static
assets (like images we might have in the assets folder,
and a middleware will be used to serve them.**

**A server is bootstrapped
and listens on a port.**

While this file can seem a bit intimidating, the good news is we do not really need to understand all of it, as it is preconfigured and will work well, unless we want to heavily customize it. For the purpose of this chapter, we don't need to know more about it than we already covered, so we can move to explore the two main.ts files. The main.ts file is completely the same as with a common SPA setup:

```
import { bootstrapApplication } from '@angular/platform-browser';
import { appConfig } from './app/app.config';
import { AppComponent } from './app/app.component';

bootstrapApplication(AppComponent, appConfig)
  .catch((err) => console.error(err));
```

We already encountered such a setup in chapter 1, when we initialized the HRMS application itself, so we shouldn't have any surprises here. The main.server.ts file, on the other hand, has some minor differences:

```
import { bootstrapApplication } from '@angular/platform-browser';
import { AppComponent } from './app/app.component';
import { config } from './app/app.config.server';

const bootstrap = () => bootstrapApplication(AppComponent, config);

export default bootstrap;
```

As we can see, it is generally the same; however, it uses a different config than main.ts, and also, instead of bootstrapping the application outright, it just exports a function that does it. Again, this is done to help Angular run on any server environment, not just Express (although Express is the default).

Finally, let us see how the configs are different before we build some components and actually run the application. The app.config.ts configuration, unsurprisingly, is almost unchanged:

```
import { ApplicationConfig } from '@angular/core';
import { provideRouter } from '@angular/router';

import { routes } from './app.routes';
import { provideClientHydration } from '@angular/platform-browser';

export const appConfig: ApplicationConfig = {
  providers: [provideRouter(routes), provideClientHydration()]
};
```

The `provideClientHydration()` option is a new SSR-related feature that we will explore in more depth later in this chapter. As we can see, it is a best practice to use it, as it is included in an SSR setup by default. Otherwise, this file is mostly the same as the one we received when bootstrapping the HRMS application in chapter 1. Finally, let's see the app.config.server.ts file:

```
import { mergeApplicationConfig, ApplicationConfig } from '@angular/core';
import { provideServerRendering } from '@angular/platform-server';
import { appConfig } from './app.config';

const serverConfig: ApplicationConfig = {
  providers: [
    provideServerRendering()
  ]
};

export const config = mergeApplicationConfig(appConfig, serverConfig);
```

As we can see, this config provides SSR and merges itself with the normal config we have in the other file. Nothing else of interest is going on here, so we finish exploring the new files and move to run our application and then add some content to it.

9.2.2 Running an SSR Angular application

Previously we used the `ng serve` command to bootstrap a small server locally so that we could view and debug the Angular application that we were working on. Thankfully, nothing has changed, and with an SSR setup, we can just as easily run the same command and it will start serving the Angular application as rendered on the server. Before we run it, let's visit the `AppComponent` and change its template by removing the default blocks generated by Angular and putting some text in it for the time being.

Listing 9.5 `AppComponent` in an SSR setup

```
@Component({
  selector: 'app-root',
  standalone: true,
  imports: [RouterOutlet],
  template: `
    <div>This is the {{ title }} app!</div>
    <router-outlet></router-outlet>
  `,
  styleUrls: ['./app.component.scss'],
})
export class AppComponent {
  title = 'hrms-promo';
}
```

As we can see, we haven't done much to it and just used some plain text with an Angular binding. Let's now run it: go to http://localhost:4200 and view the page's source to see what we get with SSR.

Listing 9.6 SSR Angular app served in the browser

```
<!DOCTYPE html>
<html lang="en">

<head>
  <script type="module" src="/@vite/client"></script>
```

```
    <meta charset="utf-8">
    <title>HrmsPromo</title>
    <base href="/">
    <meta name="viewport" content="width=device-width, initial-scale=1">
    <link rel="icon" type="image/x-icon" href="favicon.ico">
    <link rel="stylesheet" href="styles.css">
</head>

<body><!--nghm-->
    <app-root _nghost-ng-c2553731897=""
      ng-version="17.0.0-rc.1" ngh="0"
      ng-server-context="ssr">
      <div _ngcontent-ng-c2553731897="">This is the hrms-promo
        app!</div><router-outlet
          _ngcontent-ng-c2553731897=""></router-outlet><!--container-->
    </app-root>
    <script src="polyfills.js" type="module"></script>
    <script src="main.js" type="module"></script>

    <script id="ng-state"
        type="application/json">{"__nghData__":[{"c":{"2":[]}}]}</script>
</body>

</html>
```

Again, for the most part, this is the same as what we received with the HRMS app in listing 9.1; however, there is a big difference: the `<app-root>` element is no longer empty, and it now contains the template of the AppComponent readily rendered and served directly to the browser! Thus, we know our SSR setup works correctly.

We can also notice that the Angular binding we used in the template also worked during SSR and displayed the application title in the resulting HTML. But what about interactivity? Will we be able to change component properties in the UI on the fly? Let's do a small experiment with the AppComponent and figure this out.

Listing 9.7   Interactivity added to an SSR Angular app

```
@Component({
  selector: 'app-root',
  standalone: true,
  imports: [RouterOutlet],
  template: `
    <div>This is the {{ title }} app!</div>
    <button (click)="changeTitle()">Change title</button>
    <router-outlet></router-outlet>
  `,
  styleUrls: ['./app.component.scss'],
})
export class AppComponent {
  title = 'hrms-promo';

  changeTitle() {
    this.title = 'Dynamic title';
  }
}
```

Here we added a button that will change the title property when clicked. If we rerun the application and click on that button, we will see the text change, as we would expect in a "normal" SPA Angular application. We can also check the source and see that the button itself is also rendered on the server.

This is enough to prove to ourselves that while with the SSR setup the application is initially rendered on the server and readily served to the browser, other Angular functionality works as expected. Let's explore building functionality in SSR applications and find some caveats that challenge this assumption.

9.2.3 *Building components in an SSR Angular application*

The most important question for us right now is whether our components will encounter any limitations when rendering on the server side. To understand this, we need to figure out how Angular renders UI in the first place.

Of course, we know that Angular provides us the opportunity to write HTML that is enhanced with Angular's special template syntax, allowing us to perform conditional checking, render lists of elements, bind attributes and textual values to component properties, and so on. What might elude us is that while we write those templates that are marked as .html, we don't usually deal with the DOM directly. We just write a declarative template showcasing what we want to see in the UI, and Angular takes care of the rest.

So how does it work? To run an Angular application, we first need to compile it. Compilation involves various steps, such as converting our .ts files containing our components, directives, and everything else into JavaScript, and many other things. But the key thing is the compilation of the templates. It's true that when an Angular application runs in a browser, *it does not deal with any HTML*. What it does instead is translate our templates written in HTML into JavaScript commands that it can then run in the browser to render our UI.

The process of translating it or the actual commands it outputs are not really important to us here; what matters is that the application has to be compiled before it can run. When we execute `ng serve`, it performs something known as *just-in-time compilation*, meaning it bootstraps the basic things the application needs to run and then it compiles the templates into those commands in the browser. This of course makes performance quite poor; however, the development process becomes way faster, and when developing the application the build time is the only thing we care about (later in this chapter we will discuss how we can improve it).

When deploying to production, however, we first run `ng build` to get a precompiled version of the application, where no HTML exists and the browser can execute the commands to render the UI outright. This is known as *ahead-of-time compilation*.

In both of these cases, we need to compile the template. The very nature of this step makes Angular capable of rendering pages on the server side. As long as the commands are the ones generated by Angular itself, it can verified that those commands are platform-agnostic and can run the same way both on the server and in the browser. So, at the end of the day, we cannot write any code in our templates that can cause problems on the server.

We can, however, write such code inside our components or directives, where we can deal directly with HTML DOM nodes and elements. Before we figure this out, let us first build some components and make our landing page more user-friendly and then try to implement some functionality that might push the boundaries of SSR.

We are going to implement four components for our application:

- Header and footer components (for the purpose of this chapter we can just copy-paste them from the HRMS application and remove the login/logout logic).
- An "About Us" page.
- A "Subscriptions" page where potential customers can find out ways of paying and using the HRMS product.
- In the `AppComponent`, several sections with detailed information about the product, a cover picture, and so on. The goal is to make the page large enough so that it has some scrolling on desktops.

We are only going to provide the code for the `AppComponent` template so that we can move forward. You can either author the other components as you see fit or use the ones from the example repository. The following listing shows how the `AppComponent` will look.

Listing 9.8   `AppComponent` **with content**

```
@Component({
  selector: 'app-root',
  standalone: true,
  imports: [
    RouterOutlet,
    HeaderComponent,
    FooterComponent,
    NgOptimizedImage,
    RouterOutlet,
    RouterLink,
  ],
  template: `
  <app-header />
  <div class="page">
    <div class="cover">
      <img ngSrc="./assets/images/cover-picture.jpg"
        alt="Cover Picture" width="1900"
        height="1000"/>                        ◁──┐  A large cover
    </div>                                         │  picture
  </div>
  <div class="information">
    <p>You can learn more about us <a routerLink="about-us">here</a></p>
    <p>
      Learn about our available subscriptions
      <a routerLink="subscriptions">here</a>
    </p>
```

```
        </div>
        <div class="container">
          <router-outlet />
        </div>
        <app-footer />
      `,
    styleUrls: ['./app.component.scss'],
})
export class AppComponent {}
```

Routed components will only begin in the middle of the application UI.

Now we have a workable component. As we have some content and a big cover picture, the page will get some scrolling on most desktop computers. What we want to do is for the user to be able to scroll back to the top of the page quickly. For this reason, let us implement a `ScrollToTopComponent` that will render a button that will become visible when the user has scrolled some distance from the top of the page and will scroll back when clicked. In the src/app folder let's create a new folder named components and put the scroll-to-top.component.ts file inside of it with the component code shown in the following listing.

Listing 9.9 `ScrollToTopComponent`

```
@Component({
    selector: 'app-scroll-to-top',
    template: `
        <button *ngIf="isVisible" (click)="scrollToTop()">Scroll To Top</button>
      `,
    styles: [
      `
            button {
                position: fixed;
                bottom: 20px;
                right: 20px;
                z-index: 99;
                font-size: 18px;
                border: none;
                outline: none;
                background-color: #333;
                color: #fff;
                cursor: pointer;
                padding: 15px;
                border-radius: 4px;
            }
      `
    ],
    standalone: true,
    imports: [NgIf],
})
export class ScrollToTopComponent implements OnInit {
    isVisible = false;

    scrollToTop() {
        window.scrollTo({ top: 0, behavior: 'smooth' });
    }
```

Button to scroll to top, only visible when the user has scrolled away from the top of the page

When the button is clicked, the page will be scrolled back to the very top.

```
ngOnInit() {
    window.addEventListener('scroll', () => {          ←─────  We listen to scroll events
        if (window.scrollY > 100) {          ←────────         to check if the user has
            this.isVisible = true;                              scrolled too far from
        } else {                                                the top of the page.
            this.isVisible = false;
        }                                                We use an arbitrary distance
    });                                                  to determine if we want to
}                                                        show the button already.
}
```

Other than the styles to make the button more appealing, the component is pretty straightforward: we listen to scroll events on the browser's window, and if the user has scrolled a bit too far, we toggle the button to become visible and vice versa. However, if we add this component to the AppComponent and run the application, we will receive the following compilation error:

```
ERROR ReferenceError: window is not defined
    at _ScrollToTopComponent.ngOnInit
```

Wait, this can't be right: why is window undefined? If we remember that the application is being rendered on the server side, we will realize that window (and other browser's built-in objects like document, location, and so on) are not available in that context. SSR will run all the component's life cycle methods, including ngOnInit, and encounter a reference to window and throw this error.

So how do we tell Angular that this code only needs to run on the client side? Here Angular has us covered. Starting from v16, the framework provides two special functions, afterRender and afterNextRender, which will take a callback and run it *only* on the client. As their names suggest, they both run after SSR is done; however, afterNextRender runs only once, while afterRender runs each time the application is rendered.

Let's modify our component to use afterNextRender and achieve our desired functionality.

Listing 9.10   Using afterNextRender in the ScrollToTopComponent

```
export class ScrollToTopComponent {
    isVisible = false;                                 We are going to need to manually trigger
    cdRef = inject(ChangeDetectorRef);   ←─────        change detection in afterNextRender.

    constructor() {                                    We call afterNextRender with
        afterNextRender(() => {          ←─────        our initialization callback in
            window.addEventListener('scroll', () => {  the constructor.
                if (window.scrollY > 100) {
                    this.isVisible = true;
                    this.cdRef.detectChanges();   ←───  Calls detectChanges
                } else {                                when we change the
                    this.isVisible = false;             visibility of the button
                    this.cdRef.detectChanges();
                }
```

```
        });
      });
    }

    scrollToTop() {
      window.scrollTo({ top: 0, behavior: 'smooth' });
    }
}
```

Now if we open our page and scroll, we will see that the button appears when we scroll a bit and vanishes when we get back to the top of the page, thus accomplishing our task.

We used `afterNextRender` because we wanted the callback to only run once, as we were essentially registering an event listener that would then work on its own. In scenarios where we want to, say, update the DOM manually (for instance, in structural directives) after the change of some state in the component, we should use `afterRender`, which will run each time. Other than that, there is no difference between these two functions.

Optionally, these functions can accept a second argument after the callback that will configure some options. We can provide an injector (if we intend to use dependency injection in the callback), or we can provide a special `phase` option. This option will configure *when* exactly in the life cycle of rendering will the callback be invoked, so changing it can positively affect the performance of our application. There are several options and some scenarios where they can be used (see table 9.1).

Table 9.1   Phase options for `afterRender`/`afterNextRender`

Option	Description	Scenario
EarlyRead	This option can be used to perform a reading from the DOM to render some UI that is not natively supported.	Implementing a custom scrollbar, calculating the previous position from the DOM
Write	This option should be used if we are only writing to the DOM. Never use it to read DOM elements or their attributes.	Updating the DOM when reacting to inter-section events; for instance, implementing infinite scrolling functionality
MixedReadWrite	This option is used when we can both read and write to the DOM. *This is the default option.*	Implementing a directive that shows a comparison between two instances of the same component; for example, an altered financial offer displayed side-by-side with another one, or a Git tree comparison
Read	This option is used when we only want to read from a DOM element. Never use it to update the DOM manually.	Implementing a directive that reads data from a third-party library to pass it to another component

Now that we have figured out how to run code meant for the client side in Angular applications that are generally rendered server-side and how to optimize that process, we can move forward and see what other options Angular SSR provides for the improvement of application performance.

9.3 Improving Angular SSR

Over the course of this chapter, we learned how to set up a new Angular project that uses SSR from the get-go. But, to be completely honest, outside the two functions we just used, we didn't do many new things: all the components we built were just regular Angular components, and the rest was generated by the `--ssr` option when bootstrapping the application. This is, of course, a good thing: this proves we don't have to care about lots of stuff when using SSR with Angular; however, there are several things worth exploring and ways to improve the performance or customize the behavior of an Angular SSR application. Let's dive into them now.

9.3.1 HTTP caching

So far we have built components that mainly just rendered some static content. However, if we remember the introduction to this chapter, we envisioned an application that would also make HTTP calls to display real statistics about the HRMS application. So now let us do exactly this, and see how Angular's `HttpClient` will perform when running on the server side.

For this purpose, in the src/app folder let us create a new file named api.service.ts. As we are only going to make a couple of HTTP requests, we can just create a simple service and put all those methods together. The following listing shows what that service will look like.

Listing 9.11 ApiService

```
@Injectable({
    providedIn: 'root',
})
export class ApiService {
    private readonly http = inject(HttpClient);

    getCompaniesCount() {
        return this.http.get<unknown[]>('/companies').pipe(
            map(items => items.length),
        );
    }

    getEmployeesCount() {
        return this.http.get<unknown[]>('/employees').pipe(
            map(items => items.length),
        );
    }
}
```

We don't really care about the type of objects we receive, only the count.

Maps the resulting array to the count of objects received

Now, with this service in place, we can move and create a component that displays statistics about our (arguably amazing) product. To do this, we will create a new file in the src/app/component directory named statistics.component.ts and put the component in the following listing there.

Listing 9.12   `StatisticsComponent` to display promotional data

```
@Component({
    selector: 'app-statistics',
    template: `
    <div class="container">
        <div class="block">
            <p>
                <span>
                    {{ companiesCount() }}
                    companies already use the HRMS platform!
                </span>
            </p>
        </div>
        <div class="block">
            <p>
                <span>
                    {{ employeesCount() }}
                    employees active on the HRMS platform!
                </span>
            </p>
        </div>
    </div>`,
    standalone: true,
})
export class StatisticsComponent {
    apiService = inject(ApiService);      ◁──┐  We are going to use the
    companiesCount = toSignal(               │  ApiService to get the
        this.apiService.getCompaniesCount(), │  statistics data in this
        {initialValue: 0},                   │  component.
    );                                    ◁──┐
    employeesCount = toSignal(               │  We make the HTTP calls and
        this.apiService.getEmployeesCount(), │  convert the results to signals
        {initialValue: 0},                   │  with default initial values.
    );
}
```

Here we make the HTTP calls we just created, convert the results to signals, and display it in the UI. Indeed, if we open the application now and take a look, we will see something like "3 companies already use the HRMS platform! 10 employees active on the HRMS platform!", meaning everything works as intended.

However, there is a catch: if we open the browser's developer console and go to the Network tab, we will see that there are no HTTP requests made to the URLs we used in our service. So how does the data appear in the UI? It turns out the requests to those endpoints have already been performed on the server, and the UI has been rendered as prepared HTML and delivered to the browser, thus eliminating the need to perform the request on the client.

This is a feature of client hydration that was already enabled in the app.config.ts file generated by Angular when we first bootstrapped the application (we will talk more about what hydration is in the next section). To verify this we can remove the `provideClientHydration()` line from the app.config.ts file and see that now those requests are performed on the client side and visible in the Network tab.

This is known as *HTTP transfer caching* (or simply *HTTP caching*), and it means that the requests are first performed during rendering on the server side; then their results are cached and passed onto the client, so the client does not have to re-execute those potentially costly operations. The HttpClient checks this cache and if it finds the results there, it just returns it without performing the actual request.

By default, only `HTTP GET` and `HTTP HEAD` method requests are cached. This makes sense, as we usually make other types of requests when the user triggers some operation (say, saving some data). However, there can be scenarios when an application makes a `POST` request to retrieve data rather than save it (for instance, some requests might require too many parameters that just don't fit as query parameters in the URL and the developers resort to using an HTTP `POST` request). In such cases, we can provide a specific configuration in the app.config.ts file to also cache the `POST` requests:

```
provideClientHydration(withHttpTransferCacheOptions({
  includePostRequests: true,
})),
```

The `withHttpTransferCacheOptions` we can configure the caching of `POST` requests and a number of other things. For instance, we can set the `includeHeaders` option and provide an array of specific header names that we also want to cache from the server; for instance, we might want to cache headers that provide metadata about some response (e.g., number of items in a collection passed as a header from some API, like "X-Total-Count"). By default, HTTP headers are not cached, and we have to provide a list of headers to cache manually.

Finally, we can also provide a `filter` option, which will take a function that receives the request object and return a Boolean that will indicate whether to cache some particular request. For instance, we might want to cache responses from our own API but not from third-party APIs like a cloud provider or others. The following is an example of how we can do it with the filter option:

```
provideClientHydration(withHttpTransferCacheOptions({
  filter: (req) => req.url.startsWith('https://our.api.com'),
})),
```

Now evidently all of these options given to the `provideClientHydration()` function are only possible because of said client hydration. So let us talk about it and finally understand what it means, how it improves performance, and why it is important to have it turned on in our SSR Angular applications.

9.3.2   *Client-side hydration*

In section 9.2.3 we discussed how Angular works on the server side as opposed to the client side. We mentioned that it involves a compilation step, and on the client, Angular actually executes JavaScript code that will render the UI. During that rendering process, Angular will not only paint the UI but also apply its bindings on certain elements, so that future changes in the application state result in an updated UI. This is what happens, for instance, when we bind a property of an HTML element to a property in our component class with the bracket syntax, as follows:

```
<input [placeholder]="customPlaceholder"/>
```

As we know, those bindings are the essence of Angular and the reason why we have interactive web apps built with it at all. This happens in the client, but what about SSR? With SSR, the browser is already served with a prepared HTML page, so how does Angular function then? We already saw that Angular apps rendered on the server continue to work as usual on the client, but how is that achieved if Angular on the client didn't render the DOM items itself? Well, it turns out that before SSR, it did, again and from scratch in the browser!

Figure 9.4 is a diagram illustrating how SSR worked *before* the arrival of client-side hydration.

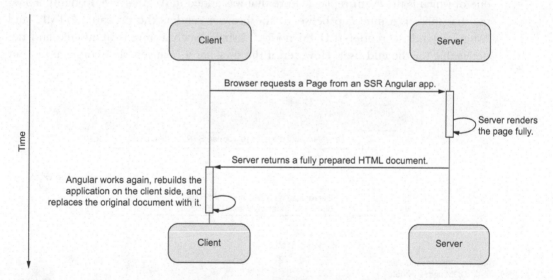

Figure 9.4   Angular in the client with SSR before client-side hydration

Obviously, this is not a very performant operation. Essentially, we render the application twice (and also hit the backend APIs twice!), once on the server and then on the client. Of course, even with this more primitive approach, we get benefits like improved

Largest Contentful Pain and better SEO support, but the application's own performance in the browser is still not great. So how can we improve this?

Enter client-side hydration. *Client-side hydration* is the practice of reconciling Angular and its bindings with the DOM that has been rendered on the server. Essentially, when the server-rendered DOM arrives, Angular performs a series of clever tricks to attach itself to the existing DOM nodes and make bindings work without destroying and then recreating the DOM in the browser again.

This significantly improves client-side performance, user experience, and other metrics we discussed previously. For instance, the application will become stable sooner and users won't see flickering screens and too many loadings. As we already saw, this option also allows us to limit the number of unnecessary HTTP requests to the same endpoint: when performed on the server side, the request's response will be cached and then just simply reused on the client side.

The best thing about hydration is that outside some (not even required) options we already explored, it does not require anything from the developer—only to drop `provideClientHydration()` in the application configuration. As this option is easy to adopt and leads to better performance, it is good practice to *always* use it when doing SSR; as we saw, Angular itself generated this new application with the client-side hydration enabled by default.

While hydration itself is a very useful feature, it has some room for improvements, one of which is the event replay feature that was added in Angular v18. In figure 9.5 we see that there is a time gap between "the browser renders the prepared HTML" and "Angular binds to rendered DOM nodes." Usually, such a time is minuscule and not noticeable for the end user. However, if the user has a relatively slow connection, they

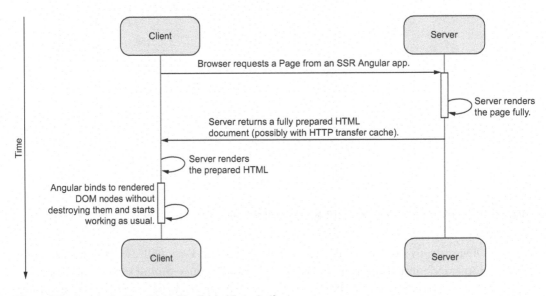

Figure 9.5   Angular in the client with client-side hydration

might trigger some events on the UI (for example, click a button or input some text) before hydration completes, and the UI actually becomes interactive. In this scenario, these events will be lost, and the user will (and rightfully so!) think that the UI is lagging.

However, to prevent this, a new option has been introduced called *event replay*. What it does is record the events that the user triggers before the completion of client-side hydration and, when it is done, replays them in the same order, so no user interaction is lost. It is very simple to set up: the only thing needed is to include it when providing client-side hydration:

```
provideClientHydration(withEventReplay())
```

Now that we have explored HTTP transfer caching and client-side hydration to improve client-side performance, we can move forward and next discuss an option that, this time, improves SSR itself.

9.3.3   Prerendering

So far we have actually only created one component that the user can see: the `AppComponent` (the rest were used inside it in some way), although we promised to create two more (`AboutUsComponent` and `SubscriptionsComponent`). If we had those components, connected to the application via defined routes, that would mean the server would have more tasks to do. When the user enters, say, the "about-us" route, it will have to render that component every single time. While this approach provides all the benefits we mentioned earlier, it can be optimized even further using a technique called *prerendering*.

Prerendering is the practice of rendering (mainly static) pages from Angular applications *at build time*, rather than on user's demand. This can be achieved by setting a `prerender` option in the angular.json file. In fact, if we revisit listing 9.3 we can see that this option is set to `true`. This means that if we build our application, Angular should look into our routing system, discover what pages exist within our application, and prerender them into static HTML, which can be served right away.

To check this, we would first need to have at least one route. For this purpose, let us create two files in the src/app/components directory named about-us.component.ts and subscriptions.component.ts and put these two components into them, shown in the following two listings, respectively.

Listing 9.13   `AboutUsComponent`

```
@Component({
  selector: 'app-about-us',
  template: `
    <div class="container">
      <div class="block">
        <p>
          <span>
            HRMS is a platform that allows companies to manage their employees.
          </span>
```

```
        </p>
      </div>
    </div>
    `,
  standalone: true,
})
export class AboutUsComponent {}
```

Listing 9.14   SubscriptionsComponent

```
@Component({
  selector: 'app-subscriptions',
  template: ` <div class="container">
    <div class="block">
      <p>
        <span>Subscriptions</span>
      </p>
    </div>
  </div>`,
  standalone: true,
})
export class SubscriptionsComponent {}
```

These are of course very simplistic implementations, but for this experiment, it won't
matter anyway. Next, we need to connect them via routing, so, in the src/app/app
.routes.ts file we should put the config in the following listing.

Listing 9.15   Application routing config

```
import { Routes } from '@angular/router';
import { AboutUsComponent } from './components/about-us.component';
import { SubscriptionsComponent } from
    './components/subscriptions.component';

export const routes: Routes = [
    { path: 'about-us', component: AboutUsComponent },
    { path: 'subscriptions', component: SubscriptionsComponent },
];
```

Now all we need to do is run `ng build` and observe. Angular will build the application
and output a dist folder in the root of our application. This folder contains all the artifacts we need to deploy and run our application. Let's look inside that folder. Immediately, we can see two nested folders, server and browser, with the former containing
JavaScript files necessary to run the server that will render and serve our pages and the
latter containing prerendered HTML files. Indeed, in the dist/hrms-promo/browser/
about-us folder we can find an index.html file that is actually a prerendered version of
the "About Us" page, ready to be immediately served.

Of course, the "About Us" page is a quite simple page that just displays static content. But how about more complex cases? For instance, our routes can have path
parameters that might be dynamic. In this case, we might have a page named "Product

Details," which is not actually a single page but rather a collection of a multitude of pages, like "/products/1," "/products/34," and so on.

In this case, by default, the prerendering won't work for obvious reasons: Angular cannot guess what parameters are there, and the possibilities are nearly endless. However, if we personally know all the variations of a parameter, we can help Angular discover those dynamic routes and still prerender them. For this purpose, we have to slightly modify the prerender option in angular.json and, instead of just setting prerender to true, provide a configuration object with the following options:

```
"prerender": {
  "routesFile": "routes.txt"
},
```

Next we can create this routes.txt file at the root of our application and put any route variations there:

```
/products/1
/products/2
/product/17
```

Obviously this approach can't work if we really do have a plethora of parameters, but it can really help when we have a predetermined set of options as a route parameter.

As we already mentioned, the prerendering approach has *all* the benefits of the usual SSR (that's why it is enabled by default), but it also improves another key metric that the usual SSR cannot: time-to-first-byte (TTFB). This metric shows how much time passes since sending an HTTP request for a particular page and until the very first byte of the response arrives. In the case of SSR, when the server receives a request for a page, it starts rendering it before it can send the resulting document back, which takes time, affecting the TTFB. However, with prerendering, lots of pages can be served right away, resulting in an incredibly great TTFB.

Now that we now know all the specifics of SSR, it is time to discuss our last topic—actually building our application and preparing it for deployment—and see how Angular also improved these processes in versions 16 and 17.

9.4   Building an Angular application

Unsurprisingly, this whole section is going to revolve around a single command: ng build, the command that is used to compile our application down to such files that can be deployed on some server or device so the end users can access and use it. Such files are usually called *build artifacts*. First, let's see what building an Angular application means in general terms.

9.4.1   What does building an Angular application mean?

In most frameworks of the modern web, developers usually code in a setup that is quite drastically different from what will be eventually shipped to the browser. For instance,

React developers create components using JSX, Angular has its own template syntax and uses TypeScript, and other frameworks and libraries have other approaches.

However, the browsers only understand HTML, CSS, and JavaScript. This means that to actually run applications in the browser, we need a build process that will convert our source files (TypeScript, template syntax, etc.) to HTML, JS, and CSS files. It would also make sense to minify the JS and CSS files to make them load faster and apply other optimizations.

For this purpose, different frameworks use different programs, all of which are known as *bundlers*: programs that produce a bundle that can be deployed somewhere and served. While there are multiple different bundlers for the web, up until v16, Angular has been using Webpack, a quite successful tool used by a wide community of web developers. However, with time, even better bundlers emerged, so now Angular is in the process of adopting new approaches for this. Let us discuss them next.

9.4.2 *ESBuild and Vite*

While Angular was still running on Webpack, a number of modern frameworks adopted Vite, a new tool built around ESBuild, a super-fast web bundler. Vite provides a superior experience and faster build time, so, starting from v16, Angular added experimental support for it.

The good news here is that we don't have to do much to activate it. We can do it on the example of the HRMS application. All we need to do is slightly change one line in the angular.json file, so instead of the following:

```
"builder": "@angular-devkit/build-angular:browser"
```

we have

```
"builder": "@angular-devkit/build-angular:browser-esbuild",
```

This will make the `ng serve` command use the ESBuild bundler. If we go on and run our application locally, we will see a vastly improved build and serve time.

> **NOTE** Please keep in mind that as of v16, support for ESBuild is only experimental and meant for developer preview. It will only be possible to use when serving the application locally for development, so please refrain from using it in any production build pipelines.

With improved build time, there is one last concern to address before deploying the application: environments.

9.4.3 *Configuring environments for Angular applications*

In any real-world application, especially if it is a bit large, it is common practice to have it deployed to multiple places for various purposes. Of course, there is the production itself, where real-life users actually use the application. But there might be other places, like one for internal testing, one for user acceptance testing or beta testing, and so on.

These "places" are usually called environments, and the thing about them is that, depending on the environment, an Angular application might need to behave at least slightly differently. For example, on the developer's computer, we would like to have the HttpClient call the http://localhost:5000 API, while on production we want the HTTP calls to go to https://our.application.example.com/api.

For this very purpose, Angular has the concept of environment files. If we had worked with older Angular versions, we might have already encountered them—say environment.ts or environment.prod.ts and so on—as Angular used to generate those files out of the box when we first bootstrapped an application. However, starting with v15, default environment files have been removed, and we now have to add and configure them manually.

To do this, we need to use the Angular CLI to first generate a folder for environment files and a base environment. This can be done with a simple command. Let's run it on the hrms-promo application:

```
ng generate environments
```

This command will generate an environment folder in the src/app directory, with two files inside: environment.ts and environment.development.ts. Both files contain the same single line of code:

```
export const environment = {};
```

This object is the environment configuration. Note that we only ever import this object from the environment.ts file, not the other ones. This works as when using a different environment, Angular replaces the file with the contents of the other environment—the one that we are targeting. This is achieved with angular.json, which now has a configurations option that contains all of our environments. If we take a look at the angular.json file in the hrms-promo application, we shall find a new configuration named development, with the following options:

```
"development": {
  "optimization": false,
  "extractLicenses": false,
  "sourceMap": true,
  "fileReplacements": [
    {
      "replace": "src/environments/environment.ts",
      "with": "src/environments/environment.development.ts"
    }
  ]
}
```

The fileReplacements option will tell Angular which environment file to sweep instead of the base one. We can easily add new environments by copy-pasting this config, making necessary adjustments, and adding a new environment file with its own configuration. Then we can run a specific environment by specifying its configuration; for instance, if we have a "qa" environment, we can run the following command:

```
ng build --configuration qa
```

This will make Angular run the build process using the contents of the environment .qa.ts file. Note that the `--configuration` option can also be used when just serving the application locally (for instance, to debug problems that only happen in a certain environment). Finally, as we have everything ready to build our app, let's briefly discuss what we need to know before we deploy it.

9.4.4   *Preparing to deploy Angular applications*

While we are not going to discuss the specifics of the deployment process itself (this is a book about Angular and not, say, Google Cloud Platform, after all), we will briefly discuss some scenarios to be prepared for deployment on any platform or cloud provider. There are several types of deployment.

CLIENT-SIDE RENDERING

This is, of course, the most "classic" scenario. We already have an example of a CSR Angular application (the HRMS platform), so let's build it and see what we need to do to deploy it:

```
ng build
```

This will generate a dist folder, so let's explore it and pay attention to the most important details. Inside we can see an hrms folder, which contains JavaScript, HTML, and CSS files. This means our application has been bundled and is ready to be deployed. As this is a CSR app, what we essentially need to do is just deliver the index.html file to the client browser, and everything will work correctly from there. So, at the end of the day, irrelevant from the hosting service we chose, we would just need to copy this hrms folder to a designated place from where the server can respond with these files when users navigate to our application, and that will be it.

One small concern relates to the way single-page applications work. They first need to serve the index.html file and load the JavaScript, and only then can they figure out the routing and how to show a particular page. However, if the user directly navigates to a particular route, say, /products, the server that hosts our files will itself try to load that route and serve a (nonexistent) products.html file, resulting in a 404 error. This can be mitigated by configuring the server itself, usually done through a configuration file at the root of our application, to make it return the index.html file whenever a route is not found, instead of throwing a 404 error. This will make the routing work on the client side (see figure 9.6).

The configuration file itself will differ from server to server, so we are not going to provide an example; however, it is mostly a simple process to add that configuration. Next, let us discuss an even simpler scenario.

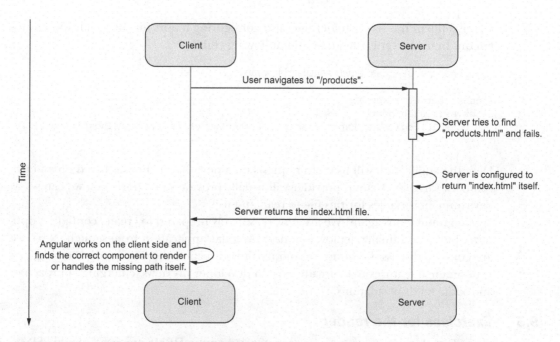

Figure 9.6 Server + Angular handling a direct request to a particular route

PRERENDERED STATIC WEBSITE

Prerendering, which we discussed in the previous section, is also often known as static site generation. This makes sense, as the fact that we serve already rendered pages means we have a fully static website. We also have an example of this; as `hrms-promo` does not have dynamic routes and is mostly just text and images with prerendering configured, it can be considered a static website. We already mentioned that it generates a browser folder when we run `ng build`. If we look inside that folder, we will find something that is quite similar to the previous CSR example, except it will be more HTML files and less JavaScript. Again, this is all we need to deploy it the same way we did in the CSR scenario. One thing we need to note is that the "404 error" scenario also applies here and can be addressed in the same way. This leaves us with the final, most complex scenario.

SSR

With SSR, we indicate that our application is going to be (at least partially) dynamically rendered before being served. Of course, with prerendering enabled, some of the pages will be served immediately from the browser folder as mentioned earlier, and some routes (say, routes with dynamic parameters) will need to be rendered on the server on a per-request basis. This means we will need a hosting or cloud provider that will be able to run Node.js. There are, again, a multitude of possibilities here that prevent us from really discussing the deployment process itself; however, it is worth keeping in mind that most often it will boil down to making the server run the generated server.js file in the server folder and also configuring a port for the application to listen on. In the server.ts file we saw the following code:

```
const port = process.env['PORT'] || 4000;

  const server = app();
  server.listen(port, () => {
    console.log(`Node Express server listening on http://localhost:${port}`);
  });
```

Here the application will listen to requests on a port that it chooses based on an environment variable. A cloud provider will usually provide some ports that we can set as environment variables for this file to read and use.

Congratulations again! We are now reasonably prepared to create, configure, optimize, build, and finally deploy a modern Angular application from scratch. Next, we are going to discuss the future of Angular: the direction the framework is taking, *very* experimental features that already exist in developer previews, emerging approaches, and some mild speculations.

9.5   Exercises for the reader

- Run the ng add @angular/ssr command on the HRMS app itself to add SSR on it and fix any emerging problems.
- Configure environments for the HRMS application.

Summary

- SSR can provide better performance and SEO for Angular applications than classic client-side rendering.
- SSR by default runs on a Node.js server.
- Applications can now be built with SSR from scratch.
- Client-side hydration can improve the reconciliation of client-side Angular with the DOM rendered on the server.
- HTTP transfer cache can prevent making the same HTTP call twice.
- Prerendering can be used to serve HTML documents generated at build time to improve TTFB.
- Angular apps can now be built faster with ESBuild + Vite.
- Environments can be configured manually to support different needs like testing, debugging, beta testing, and production.
- Build artifacts can be deployed in different ways depending on the scenario we choose (CSR, static-site generation, SSR).

10

What's next in modern Angular?

This chapter covers

- New template syntax
- Built-in conditional expressions in templates
- Deferred views and advanced lazy loading of components
- Change detection in depth
- Building zoneless applications

So far, almost everything we have discussed has involved stable, ready-to-use modern tools provided by the Angular team for cutting-edge solutions. Now, in this last chapter, it is time to enter the experimental realm and discuss the direction that the Angular framework will be taking in the near future and the features that are currently available for us in the "developer preview" status. Let's begin!

10.1 New template syntax

We have already built and deployed not one but two modern Angular applications, and now we are in the sweet period of maintaining that application. Of course, maintaining it means following the new releases of all dependencies (framework, libraries, build tools, and so on) and trying our best to keep our application as up-to-date as possible.

If we had started the HRMS application when Angular v16 was the latest version, then by the time of this book's release it would have already had two newer versions: v17 and v18, which brought with them some powerful new features. In fact, we have already discussed things from v17 in previous chapters [mainly things in relation to server-side rendering (SSR)], but there is more to explore.

> **NOTE** If you are using Angular v16 or lower, you can use the official Angular update guide (https://update.angular.io/?v=16.0-17.0) to upgrade to v17 or v18; otherwise, feel free to continue with this chapter.

As of v17, Angular introduced massive additions to the existing template syntax in an effort to make it both easier to read and learn and more performant. These changes are experimental for now; however, the changes will definitely become stable and the go-to solutions to the problems they are addressing. All the changes are related to conditional statements (`if`s, `for` loops, and so on) in the template; that's why it is also referred to as the new control flow syntax. So let us explore these new control flow statements and see how they transform our templates.

> **WARNING** All features and approaches relevant to the template syntax described in this chapter are *experimental* in v17 and are marked for developer preview by the Angular team. In Angular v18 they are marked as stable. If using Angular v17, we discourage using these features in production-ready applications and encourage using them in testing or experimental applications. For versions higher than 17, please refer to the latest Angular documentation to get information on how to upgrade to those versions to be able to use those features in production applications.

10.1.1 Goodbye ngIf!

When learning Angular, we quickly encounter the concept of structural directives—directives that not just alter the behavior of their host elements but manipulate entire DOM structures. Immediately we are introduced to directives like `*ngFor` and `*ngSwitch`, but of course, the first one we usually encounter is `*ngIf`—the all-too-familiar directive that empowers us to add or remove DOM elements (part of UI) depending on some conditions.

In chapter 2 we learned that `NgIf` is a standalone directive now, so all we need to do is import it into our component directly and use it. So far so good; however, this still brings some disadvantages:

- The directive still needs to be imported.
- The directive itself has some code that will be added to our final application bundle.
- Implementing if-else-if-else blocks can quickly become very messy.

The last point is especially painful, as it requires using ng-templates that increase the level of nesting in our templates, are not very readable, and are not required to be placed after each other in the actual template. The following is a hypothetical example of implementing such a block:

```
<div *ngIf="condition1; else template2">Content 1</div>
<ng-template #template2>
    <div *ngIf="condition2 else template3">Content 2</div>
    <ng-template #template3>Content 3</div>
</ng-template>
```

As we can see, simply expressing "if condition 1, show Content 1, else if condition 2 show content 2, else show Content 3" quickly devolved into having two ng-templates and lots of custom expressions. Of course, in the case of real-life examples, such code will become even messier, as it will involve way more content and possibly even more conditions. Such code is not very readable and can potentially be hard to debug and maintain.

One natural question we might have here is: what if we could just use JavaScript if-else statements in the template? Of course, this is a perfectly valid question; after all, an Angular template is a syntax invented by the Angular team, and it already has custom features like bindings, interpolation, and template variables, so why not just have the capability to also directly use conditional statements?

It turns out the Angular team was thinking the same thing, and starting from v17, we have access to a special form of template syntax that allows for built-in conditional statements. To be able to preview this feature, we need to move our HRMS application to v17. To do this, run the following command at the root of the project (skip this step if you already use Angular v17 or higher in the HRMS project):

```
ng update @angular/core@17 @angular/cli@17
```

> **TIP**   If you are using the Angular Language Service extension with VSCode, make sure to upgrade it to the latest version to enjoy syntax highlighting with the new control flow statements. In addition to this, if you wish to work directly with Angular v18, after running this command, rerun it with the number "17" changed to "18." This is *not* necessary to continue reading this chapter and running the example project.

Now we have the 17th version of Angular installed, with all the new things coming along. To preview the new syntax, let us choose an existing component that shows parts of its UI conditionally and switch its template to the new approach. For instance, in chapter 7 we added some functionality to the `HeaderComponent` (located at src/app/shared/components/header.component.ts) so that it displays notifications, and when a notification is unread, we show a button that allows the user to mark it as read. Let's change that logic to use the built-in control flow syntax.

Listing 10.1   `@if` **control flow statement example**

```
@Component({
  selector: 'app-header',
  template: `
```

```
<header>
  <h2>HRMS</h2>
  <button (click)="notificationsOpen.set(true)" title="View
Notifications">
    You have {{ unreadNotifications.length }} unread notifications
  </button>
</header>
<dialog [open]="notificationsOpen()">
  <h3>Notifications</h3>
  <ul>
    <li *ngFor="let notification of notifications()">
      <h4>{{ notification.title }}</h4>
      <span>{{ notification.message }}</span>
      @if (!notification.read) {
        <button (click)="markNotificationAsRead(notification)">
          Mark as Read
        </button>
      }
    </li>
  </ul>
  <button (click)="notificationsOpen.set(false)">Close</button>
</dialog>
`,
standalone: true,
imports: [NgFor],
})
export class HeaderComponent {

}
```

We now use a new built-in syntax @if and curly braces to show or hide a block of UI.

No more *ngIf on the button itself.

No import for NgIf either; the new statements are built-in.

The rest of the component code is omitted for brevity.

This new syntax works the same way as NgIf and will dynamically add or remove the elements inside of the curly braces when the condition changes. However, it has a number of benefits:

- There are no imports, as we have seen.
- We can place multiple unrelated DOM elements inside the curly braces, while NgIf only worked on a single element.
- It is more readable.
- There is no confusion as to where an if statement starts and ends.

Now let's see some even more powerful benefits. Let's suppose we have a new task at hand: when the notification is read, instead of showing nothing, we show a small "tick" icon to let the user know they have already covered that task; with the new syntax, it is going to be as easy as an if-else statement in conventional JavaScript.

Listing 10.2   @else control flow statement example

```
<header>
  <h2>HRMS</h2>
  <button (click)="notificationsOpen.set(true)" title="View
Notifications">
    You have {{ unreadNotifications.length }} unread notifications
```

```
      </button>
    </header>
    <dialog [open]="notificationsOpen()">
      <h3>Notifications</h3>
      <ul>
        <li *ngFor="let notification of notifications()">
          <h4>{{ notification.title }}</h4>
          <span>{{ notification.message }}</span>
          @if (!notification.read) {
            <button (click)="markNotificationAsRead(notification)">
              Mark as Read
            </button>
          } @else {
            <span title="Notification is read">?</span>
          }
        </li>
      </ul>
      <button (click)="notificationsOpen.set(false)">Close</button>
    </dialog>
```

@else block is used to display content in case a condition for @if is not satisfied.

Displays a "tick" symbol if the notification is read

With this approach, we now have a template that is more readable and easier to digest. Also, in fact, this syntax also supports @else if statements, just like regular conditional statements in JavaScript, so we can create multiple interdependent conditions. We can also easily nest more conditional statements inside, making for high-level code structure in the templates.

On top of this, we are still able to use the as syntax, which is handy when using the async pipe. We use this approach with NgIf in the ProjectCardComponent we built in chapter 4 (you can find it in src/app/shared/components/project-card.component.ts), so let us refactor it with the new syntax and use the as modifier.

Listing 10.3 @if with the as keyword

```
@Component({
  selector: 'app-project-card',
  template: `
    @if (project$ | async; as project) {
      <div class="card">
        <img
          [ngSrc]="project.image"
          width="100"
          height="100"
          loading="eager"
          sizes="100vw, 50vw"
        />
        <div class="card-body">
          <a [routerLink]="['/work/projects', project.id]">{{
project.name }}</a>
        </div>
      </div>
    }
  `,
})
```

We can extract the value from an observable via the async pipe with an @if statement. Note the semicolon!

```
  imports: [AsyncPipe, RouterLink, NgOptimizedImage],
  standalone: true,
})
export class ProjectCardComponent implements OnChanges {
  private readonly projectService = inject(ProjectService);

  @Input({ required: true }) projectId!: number;
  project$: Observable<Project> | null = null;

  ngOnChanges(changes: SimpleChanges): void {
    if (changes['projectId']) {
      this.project$ = this.projectService.getProject(this.projectId);
    }
  }
}
```

As we can see, the new syntax has the same benefits as NgIf used to have but solves essentially all the problems the former approach had. Next, let us learn about the new syntax for creating loops in templates and improve this component's code even further.

10.1.2   *Hello @for!*

When displaying lists of data, our go-to tool for almost a decade has been the NgFor directive. Of course, it did its job reasonably well, but it suffered from the same problems as those we discussed with NgIf in the previous section. In addition, it had the trackBy problem, wherein, for optimization reasons, we had to provide a callback function that allowed the directive to differentiate between DOM elements rendered in a loop to update the UI faster. However, many Angular developers just skipped the trackBy function, and providing it was a bit cumbersome when we had to declare a simplistic method that essentially just returned a property of the object we were rendering in a loop.

Now there is a new syntax available for rendering DOM elements in a loop, and it not only solves the trackBy problem but also adds some new benefits. Let us refactor the HeaderComponent even further to see the new approach.

Listing 10.4   @for loops in Angular templates

```
@Component({
  selector: 'app-header',
  template: `
    <header>
      <h2>HRMS</h2>
      <button (click)="notificationsOpen.set(true)" title="View Notifications">
        You have {{ unreadNotifications.length }} unread notifications
      </button>
    </header>
    <dialog [open]="notificationsOpen()">
      <h3>Notifications</h3>
      <ul>
        @for (
```

```
          notification of notifications();
          track notification.id
      ) {                                    ◄┐  @for syntax now requires
        <li>                                  │  a "track" property.
          <h4>{{ notification.title }}</h4>
          <span>{{ notification.message }}</span>
          @if (!notification.read) {
            <button (click)="markNotificationAsRead(notification)">
              Mark as Read
            </button>
          } @else {
            <span title="Notification is read">?</span>
          }
        </li>
      }
    </ul>
    <button (click)="notificationsOpen.set(false)">Close</button>
  </dialog>
  `,
  standalone: true,           │  No more imports, as the entire
                             ◄┘  control flow is built-in now.
})
export class HeaderComponent {
                              ┌─  The rest of the component's
                             ◄┘  code is omitted for brevity.
}
```

As we can see, providing the property by which we can track the objects rendered is even simpler now thanks to the special syntax: we can directly point to the very property, as we have done here by telling Angular to use the id of a notification to differentiate between two notifications.

In addition, we can now choose to show some UI if the list we try to render is empty. In this case, if the user has no notifications, it makes more sense to display some text about that fact rather than just an empty dialog. The following listing shows how we can accomplish this.

Listing 10.5   Showing default UI when the list is empty

```
<header>
    <h2>HRMS</h2>
    <button (click)="notificationsOpen.set(true)" title="View Notifications">
      You have {{ unreadNotifications.length }} unread notifications
    </button>
  </header>
  <dialog [open]="notificationsOpen()">
    <h3>Notifications</h3>
    <ul>
      @for (notification of notifications(); track notification.id) {
        <li>
          <h4>{{ notification.title }}</h4>
          <span>{{ notification.message }}</span>
          @if (!notification.read) {
            <button (click)="markNotificationAsRead(notification)">
```

```
          Mark as Read
        </button>
      } @else {
        <span title="Notification is read">?</span>
      }
    </li>
  } @empty {
    <li>No notifications to display</li>
  }
  </ul>
  <button (click)="notificationsOpen.set(false)">Close</button>
</dialog>
```

@empty contains the UI that will be displayed if there are no notifications.

The message to show when empty

Now this is already a serious upgrade over NgFor; furthermore, we can even use contextual variables to determine the current index of an iteration, whether it is the first or last element, or more. Let's use this knowledge to provide more context to the user and display a counter next to each notification that will display the index of the current notification as opposed to all notifications left (like "2/17").

Listing 10.6   Using @for block contextual variables

```
<ul>
  @for (notification of notifications(); track notification.id) {
    <li>
      <h4>
        {{ notification.title }}
        {{$index + 1}}/{{$count}}
      </h4>
      <span>{{ notification.message }}</span>
      @if (!notification.read) {
        <button (click)="markNotificationAsRead(notification)">
          Mark as Read
        </button>
      } @else {
        <span title="Notification is read">?</span>
      }
    </li>
  } @empty {
    <li>No notifications to display</li>
  }
</ul>
```

$count represents the total number of items in the array, and $index represents the number of the current iteration (starts at 0).

While these variables prefixed with $ are available everywhere inside a @for loop, we can also choose to extract them into a local variable:

```
@for(item of items; let i = $index, count = $count)
```

This can be useful if we have nested @for loops so we do not confuse the variables of one loop with ones from another. Table 10.1 shows a full list of all the contextual variables available within @for loops.

Table 10.1 Contextual variables in `@for` **loops**

Variable Name	Description	Potential use cases
`$count`	Number of items in the array	Can be used if we do not want to reference "array.length" inside
`$index`	Index of the current iteration (starts at 0)	Can be used to pass it to component methods that need to know which item they are working with
`$first`	Boolean that indicates if the current item is the first one in the array	Can be used to display a title before the first iteration or apply specific styles to only the first item
`$last`	Boolean that indicates if the current item is the last one in the array	Essentially the same use cases can apply as with `$first`
`$even`	Boolean indicating if the current iteration `$index` is an even number	Can be used to dynamically apply styling to differentiate between rows in a table, for instance, showing some lines as they are, and some lines as grayed out
`$odd`	Boolean indicating if the current iteration `$index` is an odd number	The same use cases apply as with `$even`

With this knowledge, we can now address the final control flow improvement that allows us to choose between multiple UI blocks.

10.1.3 @switch

To dynamically choose between multiple UI items, the `NgSwitch` directive has been the go-to tool for Angular developers. Yet again, it has the same problems as `NgIf`, and with the new syntax, we can now ditch the directive and use a built-in approach.

In chapter 4, we worked on the `CandidateDetailsComponent` and had a case of complex logic to select which child component to show in the UI. To avoid clutter in the template, we used a method on the component itself to retrieve the reference to the correct component and then render it dynamically in the template. However, with the new syntax, we can refactor our component, simplify the TypeScript code, and put the switch statement directly in the template. Let's open the component's file located at src/app/pages/recruitment/candidate-details.component.ts and change it as shown in the following listing.

Listing 10.7 Using `@switch` **for complex template logic**

```
@Component({
  selector: 'app-candidate-details',
  template: `
    <div class="candidate-details">
      <div>
        <h2>{{ candidate.firstName }} {{ candidate.lastName }}</h2>
```

```
        <p>Email: {{ candidate.email }}</p>
        <p>{{ candidate.position }}</p>
      </div>
      @switch (candidate.status) {        ←————  @switch works just like JavaScript switch-
        @case ('CV evaluation') {                case construct but in an Angular template.
          <app-cv-evaluation [candidateId]="candidate.id" />   ←——┐  Cases can be
        }                                                           matched with the
        @case ('Interview preparation') {                          @case keyword.
          <app-interview-preparation [candidateId]="candidate.id" />
        }
        @case ('Interview Feedback') {
          <app-interview-feedback [candidateId]="candidate.id" />
        }
        @case ('Rejected') {
          <app-rejection-letter [candidateId]="candidate.id" />
        }                                     ┌—  We can easily nest blocks with
        @case ('Approved') {                      the new template syntax.
          @if (candidate.offerAccepted) {   ←——┘
            <app-onboarding-preparation [candidateId]="candidate.id" />
          } @else {
            <app-candidate-finalization [candidateId]="candidate.id" />
          }
        }
        @default {                          ←——┐  @default can optionally be used
          <span>Unknown candidate status</span>  to show a block of UI when no
        }                                          condition has been matched.
      }
    </div>
  `,
  standalone: true,
  imports: [
    CvEvaluationComponent,
    InterviewPreparationComponent,
    InterviewFeedbackComponent,
    RejectionLetterComponent,
    OnboardingPreparationComponent,
    CandidateFinalizationComponent,
  ],
})
export class CandidateDetailsComponent {
  @Input() candidate!: Candidate;
}
```

As we can see, this approach greatly simplified the component, which is now just reduced to getting a candidate object and rendering the UI, and the complex logic is eloquently described in the template itself. And, of course, we do not need to import `NgSwitch` anymore to enjoy this functionality!

> **WARNING** `@switch`, despite looking a lot like the native switch-case block of JavaScript, does not support fall-through and has no break statement. In cases where this might be preferable, opt in for the usage of `@if`-`@else if`-`@else` constructs instead.

One other benefit of this new template syntax is the performance improvement. Rather than directly performing the operations at runtime via the structural directives, Angular is now capable of generating template code ahead of time in such a way that it already incorporates these statements as native JavaScript into the application's flow itself.

Now that we have covered all the new template syntax options, let us discuss migrating existing codebases to using this new approach.

10.1.4 *Migrating to the new template syntax*

As with other migration guides in this book, it is always possible to migrate codebases manually, in an incremental fashion (do one migration at a time, test, deploy, repeat). However, in this case, we also get an Angular schematic that allows us to easily migrate (while being a bit cautious about it).

To automatically change our codebase from structural directives to the new syntax, all we need is to ensure that our project runs Angular v17 or higher and then run the following command:

```
ng generate @angular/core:control-flow
```

This is a specific command that will modify our templates to fully use the new syntax. The command will prompt us to choose a directory that is to be changed (by default it will begin from the very root of the project so conversion will affect *all* HTML files and inline templates). This allows us to adopt an incremental strategy when instead of converting the entire project and dealing with a big mess, we can convert only some subdirectories, see how it goes, fix problems, maybe even deploy, and then address another subdirectory, and so on until the entire project is converted.

> **WARNING** The schematic will only affect HTML files and inline templates. We will still need to manually remove imports for NgFor, NgIf, and NgSwitch directives.

While the semantic works impressively well, on larger projects we still need to verify that the correct fixes have been applied. One easy tip for this can be to initially search for references to *ngIf in the codebase, remember the count, and then, after the schematic runs, search for references of the @if keyword to verify those counts are the same.

> **TIP** As the @for syntax requires a track modifier, if a trackBy function was not provided for an NgFor directive, the schematic will automatically put the reference to the object itself as a tracking item. This is not very useful, so a good practice would be to run through @for instances and provide more meaningful properties for tracking, for instance "item.id."

Because the process is automatic, it is also important to perform some regression testing to figure out if new bugs have not emerged. If the project has unit tests, it is very important to run them first to try to catch new bugs. It is worth noting that if the tests use references to `NgIf` or other structural directives in component tests (not a good practice anyway), we will also need to manually modify those tests, so running tests is even more important than just "finding bugs" in this case.

> **WARNING**   The `@switch` syntax is using strict equality checks (`===`) for matching cases, while `NgSwitch` has been using loose equality checks (`==`). This might cause problems if our `NgSwitch` clauses have been relying on loose checking prior to migration, so it is worth checking and testing the switch cases to ensure their correct operation

Regardless of the problems that might arise, this migration schematic is a powerful tool that will help us to easily convert our projects to conform to the best standards and improve performance, so I strongly recommend using it.

Now with the knowledge about this new template syntax, we are ready to learn about a template keyword that offers completely new functionality: deferring UI loading.

10.2 *Deferrable views*

In chapter 2, we discussed some techniques to improve the bundle size and loading times of our application related to the concept of lazy loading of components, when we load some components either when the user navigates to a certain route or in a customized fashion directly in the template. Recall that it involved some boilerplate code and wasn't very flexible in general.

However, with the new template syntax, the Angular template introduced a special new keyword, "defer," which will help us to lazily load components directly in the template and provide amazing flexibility as to how, when, and in what fashion the lazy loading should be performed. Let us spend this section discussing this new keyword.

10.2.1 *Deferring a simple component*

In chapter 2 we created a reusable component named `ConfirmationDialogComponent` (located at src/app/shared/components/confirmation-dialog.component.ts) and used it in the `EmployeeListComponent` (src/app/pages/employees/employee-list.component .ts) while also loading it lazily, only when the user clicked a button to delete an employee record. Let us introduce this new keyword and make the confirmation dialog lazy-loaded using defer.

Listing 10.8   Simply deferring the loading of a component

```
@Component({
  selector: 'app-employee-list',
  template: `
    <h2>Employee List</h2>
    <table>
      <thead>
        <tr>
          <th>Full Name</th>
          <th>Position</th>
          <th>Actions</th>
```

```
        </tr>
      </thead>
      <tbody>
        <tr *ngFor="let employee of employees$ | async">
          <td>
            <img [ngSrc]="employee.profilePicture" width="20" height="20" />
            <a [routerLink]="['/employees/details', employee.id]">
              {{ employee.firstName }} {{ employee.lastName }}
            </a>
          </td>
          <td appTruncate [limit]="10">{{ employee.position }}</td>
          <td>
            <button (click)="isConfirmationOpen = true">Delete</button>    <——┐
          </td>                                              Converts a Boolean to
        </tr>                                                 open the dialog
      </tbody>
    </table>                              ┌ Using the
    @defer {                    <——┘      │ @defer block
      <app-confirmation-dialog                           ┌ We use the
        [isConfirmationOpen]="isConfirmationOpen"/>  <——│ component here as if
    }                                                    │ it is already loaded
  `,
  standalone: true,
  imports: [
    AsyncPipe,
    NgFor,
    NgIf,
    NgComponentOutlet,               Notice we still import the component in the
    RouterLink,                      component's metadata; Angular will then
    TruncateDirective,               use the @defer keyword to determine in
    EmployeeNotAvailableDirective,   what bundle to include and load a
    NgOptimizedImage,                particular component.
    ConfirmationDialogComponent,  <——┘
  ],
})
export class EmployeeListComponent {
  employeeService = inject(EmployeeService);
  employees$ = this.employeeService.getEmployees();
  isConfirmationOpen = false;
}
```

Now if we open the browser's console and go to the Network tab, among the usual JavaScript files like main.js of polyfills.js we will also see a confirmation-dialog.compo-nent.js, meaning Angular bundled this component separately and only served it when the user navigated to this page.

WARNING Only standalone components can be deferred, as the non-stand-alone components will be loaded with their respective `NgModules`. We can still put non-standalone components inside `@defer` blocks; however, this will not change the manner in which they are loaded.

Because we did not specify any specific clause, Angular deferred the loading of this component in the simplest possible way: it started loading it as soon as we visited this page. But previously, this component used to be loaded dynamically, when the user clicked on the Delete button. Now let us see how we can achieve this with the new keyword.

10.2.2 *Deferring depending on a condition or trigger*

There are actually two ways of achieving this in our case. Let's first see how we can do it with a Boolean.

Listing 10.9   Deferring a component until a condition is satisfied

```
<h2>Employee List</h2>
  <table>
    <thead>
      <tr>
        <th>Full Name</th>
        <th>Position</th>
        <th>Actions</th>
      </tr>
    </thead>
    <tbody>
      <tr *ngFor="let employee of employees$ | async">
        <td>
          <img [ngSrc]="employee.profilePicture" width="20" height="20" />
          <a [routerLink]="['/employees/details', employee.id]">
            {{ employee.firstName }} {{ employee.lastName }}
          </a>
        </td>
        <td appTruncate [limit]="10">{{ employee.position }}</td>
        <td>
          <button (click)="isConfirmationOpen = true">
            Delete
          </button>
        </td>
      </tr>
    </tbody>
  </table>
@defer (when isConfirmationOpen) {
  <app-confirmation-dialog [isConfirmationOpen]="isConfirmationOpen" />
}
```

The when keyword is used to indicate that the block needs to be loaded when the condition becomes true.

WARNING   Defer-loading conditionally with a Boolean only works one time, and if the Boolean becomes false again in the future, the component will *not* disappear; if we want it to be removed in that case, we will need to use a combination of `@defer` and `@if`.

This solves our problem, but here we have to rely on a Boolean, meaning, in this case, some other functionality has to change it, making the connection somewhat indirect. Thankfully, Angular provides a way of achieving this directly.

Listing 10.10 Deferring a component until a UI interaction

```
<h2>Employee List</h2>
    <table>
      <thead>
        <tr>
          <th>Full Name</th>
          <th>Position</th>
          <th>Actions</th>
        </tr>
      </thead>
      <tbody>
        <tr *ngFor="let employee of employees$ | async">
          <td>
            <img [ngSrc]="employee.profilePicture" width="20" height="20" />
            <a [routerLink]="['/employees/details', employee.id]">
              {{ employee.firstName }} {{ employee.lastName }}
            </a>
          </td>
          <td appTruncate [limit]="10">{{ employee.position }}</td>
          <td>
            <button (click)="isConfirmationOpen = true" #deleteButton>
              Delete
            </button>
            @defer (on interaction(deleteButton)) {
              <app-confirmation-dialog
                [isConfirmationOpen]="isConfirmationOpen"
              />
            }
          </td>
        </tr>
      </tbody>
    </table>
```

We put a template variable on the delete button so we can reference it later to load the component when it is clicked.

The on keyword allows specifying events for when to start the deferred loading; in this case, we specify that it should load when the delete button is interacted with.

The `interaction` option here helps define an event, which will trigger Angular to load the deferred component. Interaction in this context for Angular means either a `click` event or a `keydown` event. A hover event can also be specified instead to load the component when the Delete button is hovered.

Another popular scenario could be loading a component when the page is scrolled so far that it should become visible, a scenario that is usually referred to as "entering the viewport." Angular now provides a way of doing this directly with the defer block. To see this, let's entertain the following scenario: in chapter 4, we built a `Footer-Component` (you can find it at src/app/shared/components/footer.component.ts), which displays some information about the HRMS application. If we want to supercharge our application's performance, we might consider deferring its loading up until the point when the user actually scrolls down to see the footer. The following listing shows how we can accomplish it in the `AppComponent`.

Listing 10.11   Deferring a component until it is in the viewport

```
<app-header/>
<router-outlet></router-outlet>
@defer (on viewport) {          ◁───┐  The viewport trigger will
    <app-footer/>                    │  activate as soon as the
}                                    │  component enters the view.
```

However, if we do it just like this, we will get the following error:

```
"viewport" trigger with no parameters can only be placed on an @defer that
    has a @placeholder block
```

If we think about this error, it makes perfect sense: we mention the component coming into the viewport, but the component is not even loaded: it obviously *is not in the viewport!* So how can Angular know the user scrolled this far and it is time to load the component? We have two options: either we provide an argument to the viewport trigger as we did with the interaction trigger, or we provide a special @placeholder block, which will be displayed before the deferred component loads and replaces it. Now when this placeholder block comes into the viewport, it will trigger the loading of the component.

Listing 10.12   Deferring a component with a placeholder

```
<app-header/>
<router-outlet></router-outlet>
@defer (on viewport) {              The placeholder content to
    <app-footer/>                   show before the deferred
} @placeholder {          ◁─────┘   component is loaded
    <div>Footer</div>     ◁───┐  We display the "Footer" text, which will
}                              │  be then replaced by the actual footer.
```

This provides us with a high level of flexibility in choosing our scenarios for deferred loading. We will talk more about other defer blocks (there are more than just @placeholder) in the next section when we explore very custom scenarios. For now, let's finalize our knowledge of deferred loading triggers with table 10.2, which illustrates all the possible triggers.

Table 10.2   Triggers for deferred loading

Trigger Name	Description	Potential use cases
on idle	Will trigger loading when the application becomes idle (no animations, painting, and current HTTP requests). Uses the `requestIdleCallback` API (https://mng.bz/q0KN) under the hood. This is the default behavior.	Can be used to simply defer the loading of some components to reduce the final bundle. For example, we can defer large but not very important components near the application root so that they load when possible but do not block the main functionality of the application.

Table 10.2   Triggers for deferred loading *(continued)*

Trigger Name	Description	Potential use cases
on viewport	Loads when the placeholder content enters the browser's viewport. Can also be used with another element provided via an argument. Uses the `Intersection-Observer` API (https://mng.bz/75oV) under the hood.	Can be used to load components far from the top of the pages dynamically, as we did with the `FooterComponent`.
on interaction	Loads when the placeholder content is interacted with (click, keydown). Can also be used with another element provided via an argument.	Can be used to load a component on the user's demand, as we did with `ConfirmationDialogComponent`.
on hover	Loads when the placeholder content is hovered. Can also be used with another element provided via an argument.	The same scenarios apply as with on interaction.
on immediate	Loads when the parent component finishes rendering.	Can be used to simply reduce the bundle size for some heavy components that are needed anyway.
on timer	Loads when the indicated timespan has elapsed. Accepts time in milliseconds or seconds [on timer (500 ms) or on timer (2 s)].	Can be used to apply time-related logic to deferred loading; for instance, we can choose to wait a while before loading a component that is in the viewport but does not depend on an external trigger and is not too important to load right away.

Now that we have explored all the possible triggers and conditions for deferred loading, we can dive even deeper and make the best possible user experience for people using the application.

10.2.3   Customizing deferred loading

There are several ways of improving the UX when using deferred loading, which means covering two important scenarios: handling different loading scenarios and prefetching. Let us explore both.

LOADING AND ERROR STATES

We already explored the `@placeholder` block, which allowed us to display some content before it is replaced with the actual deferred component. We can, however, add further blocks to display some UI when the loading is in process and also display some fallback content when the deferred loading has failed (for instance, the user got disconnected from the internet while loading). This can be achieved with two blocks with pretty telling names.

Listing 10.13   Deferring a component with error/loading

```
<app-header/>
<router-outlet></router-outlet>
```

```
@defer (on viewport) {
    <app-footer/>
} @placeholder {
    <div>Footer</div>
} @loading {                          This content will be
    <div>Loading...</div>    ◁───┘    displayed while loading.
} @error {
    <div>An error occurred when trying to display the application's
    footer</div>
}                            ◁───┐   This content will be displayed
                                  │   if the loading fails.
```

Now, having provided the users with detailed messages about the loading of the components, let us try to customize the loading process itself.

PREFETCHING

To understand this concept better, let's again explore the FooterComponent's loading. At this point, we have deferred its loading to the moment when the user scrolls down to the placeholder; however, this might not be the best strategy in terms of UX. This means the user will always have to see the placeholder first (especially on a slow connection), and if this component is something that we always want present (we have no other conditions for its loading), then it might make sense to defer its loading but start the loading anyway under the hood after some time.

This strategy is known as prefetching, and the @defer block also provides instruments to add it to our deferred loading flow. For instance, we can signify that we want to load the component either when the placeholder enters the viewport or after a given amount of time regardless of user interactions. This means that the component will be defer-loaded, but if the user scrolls to the footer later, they will see the component itself already and not the placeholder. This can be achieved by one simple modifier.

Listing 10.14   Prefetching of a component with timer

```
<app-header/>
<router-outlet></router-outlet>
@defer (on viewport; prefetch on timer(2s)) {      ◁───┐   Prefetch trigger added
    <app-footer/>                                       │   to the defer clause
} @placeholder {
    <div>Footer</div>
} @loading {
    <div>Loading...</div>
} @error {
    <div>An error occurred when trying to display the application's
    footer</div>
}
```

Now with a single, simple command we added prefetching and maximized our UX improvements; let us also note that everything we did in this section we did in the template, without any code added to the component's code itself. Such is the power of the @defer block.

TIP We can use both on and when clauses with prefetch and apply any of the triggers listed in table 10.2

As we close in on our learning journey of the latest features already available (at least for developer preview), it is now time to venture into the unexplored territory of massive performance optimizations that are planned to arrive in Angular that may finally make us able to ditch Zone.js. So next let us consider what Zone.js is, why we want to get rid of it, and what Angular might look like without it.

10.3 Zoneless Angular applications

One of the most important Angular-related concepts that we have touched on very little so far is *change detection*. We have referenced it once or twice (mainly in chapters related to signals), but in general, for an Angular developer who has not dived too deep under its hood, change detection is a mysterious engine that makes Angular's magic work. So, in this section, let's explore what change detection is, how it works, how it is interconnected with Zone.js, and how we (and the Angular team!) want to improve it.

10.3.1 How change detection works in Angular

First and foremost, let us begin with the very concept itself to understand what it means and why we need it. Let's begin by examining (or maybe re-examining) how frontend applications work so that we can figure out where the change detection comes in the grand scheme of things.

WHAT IS CHANGE DETECTION?

In chapter 5, we presented a simple diagram that explained the relation between the three core components of any frontend application (figure 5.1): the application state, events, and the UI itself. Next we explained that the state is used to render the UI, UI can send events, and event handlers can modify the state to rerender the UI again, and so on. We did this in the context of RxJS + Angular; however, we did not focus too much attention on the fact that this process works the same way even without RxJS. Consider the following code:

```
@Component({
    selector: 'app-some-component',
    template: `
      <p>{{name}}</p>
      <button (click)="name = 'Alex'">Change name</button>
    `,
    standalone: true,
})
export class SomeComponent {
    name = 'John';
}
```

Of course, we don't have to have years of experience to understand that an Angular component like this one will first display the name "John" and then, when the button is clicked, display the name "Alex". But we didn't use any reactivity like RxJS or signals, so how does Angular know that the name property has changed and the UI needs to be updated?

Here is where change detection comes in. When the state is updated, Angular checks the bindings that we have in a given component and applies changes to the UI. In the previous example, we have binding in the template {{name}}, which Angular will check, see that the name has changed, and apply the new name. Figure 10.1 is a revised version of figure 5.1.

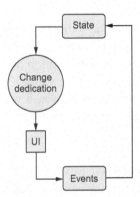

Figure 10.1   Change detection's role in the life cycle of a component

Change detection in this loop is what actually propagates the changes to the UI, resulting in something new that the user will see on their screen. So now we understand that after the state changes, Angular will perform template binding checks and render a new UI if necessary. But one question remains unanswered: how does Angular know that the state has changed at all?

WHY DO WE NEED ZONE.JS?

In a classic, "vanilla" if you will, JavaScript application, there is no concept of change detection; all we can do is render some UI and manually listen to events. This means we will need to react to some asynchronous events to rerender the UI—for example, "the user clicked this button, let's now render a popup that will appear in the middle of the page." Of course, in Angular, we do not do this directly but change some state to update the UI using the logic declared in a template. Actually, if we think about it, it is easy to see that this always happens without change detection, and Angular's change detection just allows us to skip the middle step (manually updating the DOM).

The Angular team thought that, after initially rendering the application's UI, the only way it might ever change is as a result of some asynchronous operation (browser event, promise resolved, timeouts, or intervals). So why not listen to those events, see how many there are, and check the existing DOM to see if any bindings have been changed and start rerendering from that point? Here is where Zone.js comes in.

Zone.js is a JavaScript library that allows developers to create special execution contexts (called *zones*) and run some code inside those zones. Whatever code runs in a zone, we can easily track asynchronous events happening in that context and react to things that we haven't even explicitly subscribed to. Zone.js accomplishes this by monkey-patching the browser's async-related APIs (like promises and others) and notifying about events within a zone.

Angular uses Zone.js heavily for the purpose of change detection. What essentially happens is the entire Angular application runs inside a zone, and we can react to asynchronous events and perform change detection (it is more complex than this, but for the purpose of this chapter, it is good enough to understand change detection).

What Angular then does is listen to Zone.js, receive notifications, and start performing change detection each time there has been such a notification. It is very important to note that regardless of where the notification originated, Angular will perform a checking *top-down*, meaning it will start from the very root component and change detect every single component in our application. Figure 10.2 visualizes that process.

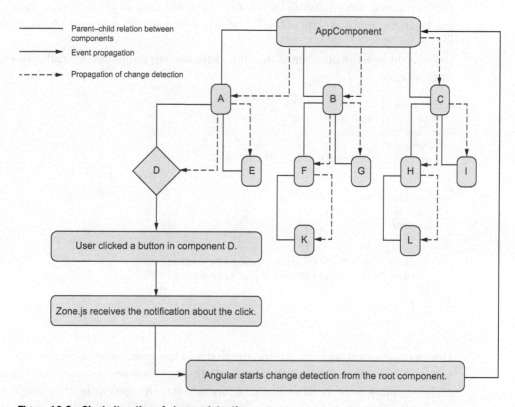

Figure 10.2 Single iteration of change detection

From the diagram alone we can see some problems with this process, but Zone.js-based change detection has worked relatively well for Angular applications so far, so let us spend some time discussing the problems that exist within this implementation and see what a working solution to those problems must entail.

10.3.2   *Why change detection in Angular needs to improve*

The process we just described can seem like a bit of overkill if we consider the magnitude of checking that Angular might perform on a sizable application. What's worse is that all those checks are performed in an "erratic" fashion; Angular often has no idea whether a change really happened but has to check the view anyway because Zone.js has notified it that an async event has happened; whether the event handler resulted in some relevant state change is yet to be seen. This means additional load on the runtime, unnecessary pollution of memory, and potentially race conditions—situations where something depends on another thing being executed previously but that other thing fails to execute.

Another concern is the checking itself; because Angular also reacts to changes to deeply nested properties inside objects, this means that the algorithm might have to perform a very long and deep introspection of multiple large objects (and, as per the previous point, this might still be for nothing!), resulting in poorer performances and a delay to the actual update of the UI (which is the only thing we care about at the end of the day).

Next there is the problem with calling functions in templates. Consider this simple Angular code:

```
@Component({
  selector: 'app-root',
  standalone: true,
  template: `
    <p (click)="handle()">{{ fullName() }}</p>
  `,
})
export class App {
  firstName = 'John';
  lastName = 'Doe';

  fullName() {
    console.log('This function has been called');
    return `${this.firstName} ${this.lastName}`;
  }

  handle() {}
}
```

Here we use a function to combine the first and last name, and while it works, we can notice the function is being called multiple times. This is because Angular has no way of determining if the return value of a function has changed without calling it, meaning it will call the `fullName` function on every change detection cycle. Because change detection is triggered on async events, clicking on the full name in the UI will result in new multiple calls to the `fullName` function, despite the fact that the `handle` function is literally empty and can't possibly modify the value of the full name. This is why we have pipes in Angular—mainly to overcome such change detection problems (more on that later).

Finally, Zone.js itself is a bit of a problem: it adds to our final bundle, and because it is how change detection functions, it means the user has to download it and execute it, and only then will the application function properly, resulting in a pretty poor time-to-interactive metric.

So far, we have established a number of problems with the existing approach to change detection. Now the stage is set to discuss what a potential solution to this problem might look like. Please keep in mind the following is the approach that the Angular team publicly adopted; however, it might go through a number of modifications until it is stable and ready to replace Zone.js.

10.3.3 ChangeDetectionStrategy.OnPush

To better understand what is going on, we first need to revisit the only optimization technique we currently have in Angular in regard to change detections: the `OnPush` change detection strategy. When performing change detection, Angular has two strategies for approaching the task: one is the default strategy, which we already discussed, and the other is `OnPush`. Let us see what optimizations this approach brings us. When a component is marked as `OnPush`, Angular will do the following:

- Trigger change detection on changes to `@Input` properties.
- Trigger change detection on events *from inside* the component.
- Trigger change detection when explicitly called for via `ChangeDetectorRef`.
- Check `@Input` properties only via references (in case of objects).
- Check only the ancestor of the component instead of the entire component tree.

It's easy to see how this can significantly limit the amount of change detection cycles and improve performance. In figure 10.3 we revisit figure 10.2 but with a component that is now marked as `OnPush`.

As we can see, now only three components get change-detected instead of all of them. We can see this in action if we run the following simple components:

```
@Component({
  selector: 'app-some',
  standalone: true,
  template: `
    <p (click)="handle()">{{user.firstName}}</p>
  `,
  changeDetection: ChangeDetectionStrategy.OnPush,
})
export class SomeComponent {
  @Input({ required: true }) user!: { firstName: string; lastName: string };

  handle() {}
}

@Component({
  selector: 'app-root',
  standalone: true,
  template: `
```

```
    <app-some [user]="user"/>
  `,
  imports: [SomeComponent],
})
export class App {
  user = { firstName: 'John', lastName: 'Doe' };

  constructor() {
    setTimeout(() => {
      this.user.firstName = 'Alex';
    }, 1_000);
  }
}
```

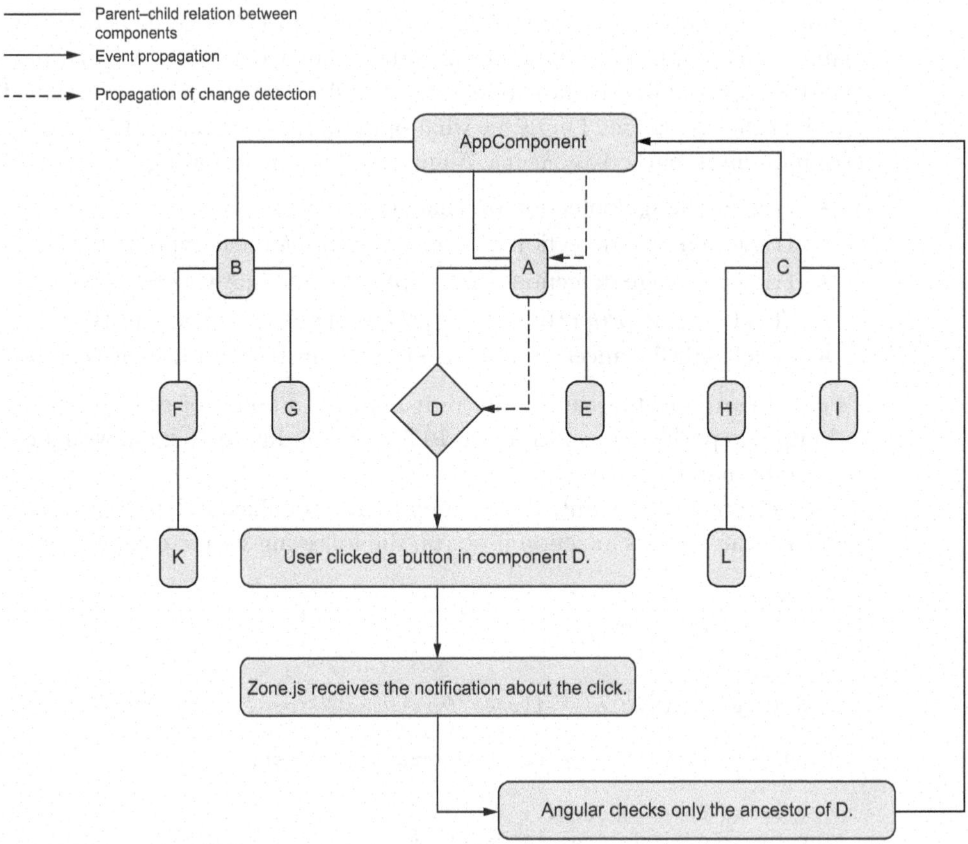

Figure 10.3 Change detection when a component is marked `OnPush`

Here, if we wait for 1 second, the UI will *not* get updated. This is because the event of updating happened in the parent component of a component that is marked `OnPush`, and despite it being passed via an input, its reference has not been changed, thus not triggering a change detection cycle. However, if we click on the text in the child component, the first name will get instantly updated. To have updates immediately from the parent, we can simply change the logic of changing the first name to change the entire reference of the object:

```
this.user = {...this.user, firstName: 'Alex'};
```

The OnPush strategy, as we can see, offers some improvement over the default change detection; in large applications, it might make sense to mark the heaviest, most inter-active components as OnPush to cut down the amount of unnecessary change detection cycles at runtime. Some teams go so far as to make all components OnPush to enjoy the best runtime performance.

However, the OnPush strategy is not something new in and of itself; so what changed in more recent versions of Angular? Having the necessary knowledge of change detection, we can now discuss the new benefits and some upcoming approaches that will further optimize the process of updating the UI in Angular applications.

10.3.4 Introducing granular change detection

In this section, we will discuss two new concepts that have become possible with the advance of signals in Angular. One approach already exists and does not require any particular changes, and the other is an overhaul of how we think about Angular change detection and might possibly help us ditch Zone.js for good.

LOCAL CHANGE DETECTION

So far we have discussed the OnPush strategy with the usual Angular components, which has simple properties for which Angular could not possibly automatically learn about their updates (hence the need for Zone.js and all that). However, a massive game-changer landed in v16, which we discussed extensively: the signals. While signals are wrappers around the same values we stored as simple properties previously, they also have the massive advantage of being able to tell Angular about their own updates, meaning they can potentially result in us not needing Zone.js anymore (more about that in the next section).

While this prospect is still looming in the future, right now we already can enjoy some of the benefits of signals in regard to change detection. Here we are referring to a concept added in Angular v17 known as *local change detection*. Essentially, now if we mark our component with OnPush, and use only signals, then those signal changes will update the UI but will *not* trigger change detection for parent components (if they are also OnPush).

This update is both a massive improvement in performance and also easy to adopt. We can iteratively bring our components to this state to be able to enjoy runtime opti-mization while not disrupting the logic of our applications. All we need is to adopt the "all components should be OnPush" strategy, and with time the entire application will be OnPush. The approach of using signals exclusively can also bring us closer to the zoneless future, which we will discuss soon. However, before we can proceed, we must address a problem that arises if we want to turn *everything* into signals, and that problem is: how do the component inputs work then?

SIGNAL INPUTS

So far, whenever we talked about component inputs, we perceived them as simple component properties that just have been marked with the @Input decorator. This allows Angular to work its magic and pass the value from the parent component right into the child component.

However, this also comes with some downsides. First, it gets somewhat hard to react to changes to input properties; we have to use either ngOnChanges or a getter/setter mechanism. For instance, in chapter 4, listing 4.6, we used the ngOnChanges approach to build the ProjectDetailsComponent, which received an id as an input property (it utilized component-input binding to get a parameter from the URL) and then used ngOnChanges to make an HTTP call to retrieve the project details data and display in the UI. It looked like the following:

```
export class ProjectDetailsComponent implements OnChanges {
  @Input({transform: numberAttribute}) id!: number;
  private readonly projectService = inject(ProjectService);
  project$: Observable<Project> | null = null;

  ngOnChanges(changes: SimpleChanges): void {
    if (changes['id']) {
      this.project$ = this.projectService.getProject(this.id);
    }
  }
}
```

As we can see, this has a lot of code that is essentially boilerplate and can become tedious to maintain when the component gets bigger. Another downside to this approach is that when working with observables and signals, properties that are neither can become hard to maintain; in the real world, we might want our signals and observables to interact with input properties and also react to their changes, which is hard to accomplish with simple, nonreactive properties.

However, with Angular v17.1, a new concept has been added that will make this very easy to achieve: *signal inputs*. This is a new way to declare input properties on components, which uses a function instead of a decorator and creates an input that is already a signal! This allows us to use a host of tools like effects, computed properties, and RxJS interoperability with inputs, making it easy to switch between inputs, signals, and observables. Let us refactor the ProjectDetailsComponent and see it in action.

Listing 10.15   Component using signal inputs

```
import { Component, input, inject, numberAttribute } from '@angular/core';
import { toObservable, toSignal } from '@angular/core/rxjs-interop';
import { switchMap } from 'rxjs/operators';
```

```
import { ProjectService } from 'src/app/services/project.service';
import {
  ProjectCardComponent,
} from 'src/app/shared/components/project-card.component';

@Component({
  selector: 'app-project-details',
  template: `
    <div class="project-details">
      <h3>Project Details</h3>
      @if (project(); as project) {
      <div>
        <span>Project Name: {{ project.name }}</span>
        <span>Project Description: {{ project.description }}</span>
        <span>Logo: {{ project.image }}</span>
        <div class="subprojects">
          <span>Subprojects:</span>
          <app-project-card
            *ngFor="let subProjectId of project.subProjectIds"
            [projectId]="subProjectId"
          >
          </app-project-card>
        </div>
      </div>
      }
    </div>
  `,
  standalone: true,
  imports: [ProjectCardComponent],
})
export class ProjectDetailsComponent {
  private readonly projectService = inject(ProjectService);
  id = input(null, { transform: numberAttribute });
  project = toSignal(
    toObservable(this.id).pipe(
      switchMap(id => this.projectService.getProject(id!))
    )
  );
}
```

Now we use "project" as a signal instead of an observable and ditch the async pipe.

Using signal inputs and built-in control flow allows us to only import other components instead of NgIf, AsyncPipe, NgFor, and so on.

"id" is now a signal input with a default null value, and incoming string values get transformed into numbers. TypeScript automatically infers the type.

Next, we can create an observable for the HTTP call that will retrieve the project details and convert it to a signal to use in the template.

We convert the "id" input signal to an observable to perform an HTTP call.

We switch the observable of "id" to the Observable of the HTTP call that will then get converted back to a signal.

As we can see, this approach made our code more understandable, everything flows in one direction, and our component has fewer lines of code and also only properties (no methods). This results in a codebase that is easy to debug, reason about and, ultimately, maintain in general.

In this case, we used a nullable signal input, meaning the type of id will be number | null, and that is why we used `this.projectService.getProject(id!)` to perform the HTTP call (notice the ! operator). If we, however, are assured that the id will not be null, we can define a required input:

```
id = input.required({ transform: numberAttribute });
project = toSignal(
  toObservable(this.id).pipe(
```

```
      switchMap(id => this.projectService.getProject(id))
    )
  );
```

The parameters object (the one we passed the transform attribute to) also accepts the `alias` option from the `@Input` decorator, making signal inputs equivalent in functionality to the decorator input, with the distinction of only producing signals.

> **NOTE**   While conventional input properties allow us to modify their values in the child component, signal inputs *disallow* this, and they do not have `set` or `update` methods, so their only source of new data is the parent component. Be careful when refactoring to use signal inputs.

Now a sensible question arises: what about outputs? Of course, outputs are event emitters and do not store data, so they are not signals. However, for the sake of consistency, the Angular team introduced a function for creating output properties instead of relying on the `@Output` decorator. Let's see it in action next.

SIGNAL OUTPUTS

In chapter 4, listing 4.4, we created a `FileUploadComponent` (src/app/shared/components/file-upload.component.ts) to explore transforming inputs. It also had an output named selected, which transferred the `FileList` of the files that the user had selected. Of course, this is a prime candidate for refactoring both its inputs and outputs. We will use the new `output` function, introduced in Angular v17.3, to achieve this.

Listing 10.16   Component using signal outputs

```
import { Component, input, output } from '@angular/core';

@Component({
  selector: 'app-file-upload',
  template: `
    <div class="file-upload">
      <label for="upload">{{ label }}</label>
      <input type="file" id="upload" (change)="onFileSelected($event)" />
      @if (errorMessage) {
        <span class="error">
          {{ errorMessage }}
          Only following file types are permitted:
          <ul>
          @for (let type of accept(); track type) {        ⟵   "accept" is now
            <li>{{ type }}</li>                                  a signal input.
          }
          </ul>
        </span>
      }
    </div>
  `,
  standalone: true,
})
```

```
export class FileUploadComponent {
  label = input.required<string>();
  accept = input([], { transform: (value: string) => value.split(',') });
  selected = output<FileList>();                    ◄─┐
  errorMessage = '';                                   │

  onFileSelected(event: any) {
    const files: FileList = event.target.files;
    this.errorMessage = Array.from(files).every((f) =>
      this.accept().includes(f.type)
    )
      ? ''
      : 'Invalid file type';

    if (this.errorMessage === '') {
      this.selected.emit(files);                   ◄─┤
    }
  }
}
}
```

> **The output function is used to define the "selected" property as en EventEmitter and output.**

> **Nothing changes in the syntax of sending an event to the parent component; we just call "selected.emit()".**

As we can see, this change is mainly cosmetic and does not break anything; all code and logic for component intercommunication remains the same. However, we do have an edge case. It might not be very popular, but with the @Output decorator, it is possible to turn any observable into a vehicle for sending events to the parent component, not just the EventEmitter. To do this, we could just add the decorator to an observable property:

```
@ViewChild('containerElement') containerElement: ElementRef<HTMLDivElement>;
@Output() clicked = fromEvent(this.containerElement, 'click');
```

In this case, we pick the reference to a div element in the template and, using RxJS, transfer it to the parent component, where we can just read those clicks with the usual (clicked)="handleClick($event)" syntax. However, with these new outputs, it is a bit different. We can still use this observable, but we have to resort to another function instead of output, and that is the outputFromObservable function, which is (and this is *very* important) imported from the @angular/core/rxjs-interop package and not directly from @angular/core. As we mentioned in chapters 5 and 6, Angular is working toward reducing its dependency on RxJS (with the goal of eventually making it fully optional), so having the output function work with observables would introduce a dependency from @angular/core to RxJS, mandating every app depends on it. This way, developers who want to use RxJS can still enjoy a higher level of interoperability, while others are free to ditch RxJS if they so choose.

With this function, the previous code would be seamlessly transformed in the following, while retaining the same capabilities:

```
@ViewChild('containerElement') containerElement: ElementRef<HTMLDivElement>;
clicked = outputFromObservable(fromEvent(this.containerElement, 'click'));
```

So now we can say that we have achieved both parent-to-child and child-to-parent component intercommunication separately. But what about the cases when we want both combined—the approach that is better known as two-way binding? Let's explore what modern Angular has to offer.

MODEL PROPERTIES

In the past, to create a two-way binding we had to create a pairing of `@Input`/`@Output` properties with a clever syntactic trick (naming the `@Output` the same name as the `@Input` but suffixed with "Change"). A two-way binding looked a lot like the following code:

```
@Input() property: string;
@Output() propertyChange = new EventEmitter<string>();
```

This way, in the templates that used this component, we could take advantage of the Angular template's syntactic sugar and do the following:

```
<app-component [(property)]="someProperty"/>
```

However, with signals, this becomes irrelevant, and a new way of creating two-way bindings has been added in Angular v17.2, which is the model signal. To define a model signal, we just need to use the `model` function:

```
property = model();
```

This will create a signal that is also an input, and every time its value changes, it will emit that new value to the parent component as if it were an output. This means we can just bind to it in templates just the same way we did in the previous example with a "traditional" two-way binding.

Finally, before we go on to signal-based components, we have one last thing to discuss.

SIGNAL-BASED VIEWCHILDREN AND CONTENTCHILDREN

As we know, sometimes we need to grab a reference to some HTML elements (or other components) from a given component's template. This is usually accomplished via `@ViewChild` and `@ContentChild` (if the elements we seek are inside the content projected via `<ng-content>`) or their plural counterparts (@ViewChildren and `@Content-Children`) in case we want to get multiple elements/components. From the previous few subsections, it becomes evident that Angular is moving away from decorators and toward signal-based functions. The same scenario is playing out here as in Angular v17.3: functions with similar names have been introduced to replace the aforementioned decorators:

```
@ViewChild('container') containerDiv: ElementRef<HTMLDivElement>;
```

Instead of doing this, we can use the much simpler `viewChild` function:

```
containerDiv = viewChild<ElementRef<HTMLDivElement>>('container');
```

Notice that while this looks purely cosmetic to just remove the decorators, in this case we won't just get an `ElementRef` but a signal of `ElementRef`. This means we can create computed signals from view children and also apply effects with them as tracked dependencies. This becomes especially useful with `viewChildren`, which now lets us know when new elements have been added to the `QueryList` and when some have been removed. This was previously only possible with a setter function and another property that we would set whenever the list changed, but it now works out of the box. Similar functions named `contentChild` and `contentChildren` are also now available to use with projected content.

With this set, we are now ready to move on to a discussion of signal-based components and the prospect of going completely zoneless.

SIGNAL-BASED COMPONENTS AND ZONELESS APPLICATIONS

In chapter 7, section 7.5.1, we mentioned that the Angular team proposed signal-based components that are meant to overhaul the current change detection mechanism. Let's see how it will potentially work.

With the proposed approach, developers will be able to mark their components as signal-based via a flag in the component's metadata. This will result in the following modifications to the component's behavior:

- Component will not be part of Zone.js-based change detection.
- Component will be change-detected only when some of its *signal* properties change.
- It will be completely safe to invoke functions in the template.
- All of its inputs will be signals.
- Change detection will be view-based (more on this later).

This will be a huge improvement over the current setup. Essentially, if we mark all the components in the application as signal-based, we can easily ditch Zone.js and continue as usual. This also means adopting a more reactive approach to building Angular applications and a departure from "magical" update mechanisms.

Of course, this change itself raises some questions; let's try to address them next. The first question might be: what will happen to non-signal-based components? (We refer to them as zone-based components.) As the Angular team promises, we can use zone-based components in conjunction with signal-based ones. In that case, we will be unable to remove Zone.js; however, this will allow us to iteratively transition an existing Angular project to zoneless.

The next question we might have is: how will change detection work then? The answer is that in signal-based components, Angular will listen to signal updates (and signal updates *only*) and then perform checking based on a corresponding view (this is view-based change detection). Views are either a template of a component or an `ng-template` inside of it. All structural directives automatically create `ng-templates`. The following listing shows a small example of a component template with different views annotated.

Listing 10.17   Template with multiple views

```
<div>
  <p *ngIf="condition()">          ◄───────────   View of the
    <ul>                        ◄────────────┐    component itself
      <li *ngFor="let item of items">   ◄──┐ │
        {{item().name}}                     │ │    View created with
      </li>                                 │ │    the NgIf directive
    </ul>                                   │
  </p>                                      │      View created with
</div>                                      │      the NgFor directive
```

Each view has its own context and contains a number of bindings; for instance, in this example, the view created by the `NgFor` directive has a binding on the item signal. In signal-based components, Angular will keep track of views and which signal is being used in which view, meaning that when it receives a notification about some signal's change, it can proceed to immediately check (and maybe update) the views that contain bindings to that particular signal (and those views *only*!). This will be a massive improvement over the current setup, with the only tradeoff being having to convert all properties to signals.

> **TIP**   Binding to ordinary properties (not signals) in the template might still work; however, those bindings will get updated only when some other signal changes its value. The Angular team is considering disallowing binding to ordinary properties in signal-based components altogether.

As mentioned, signal-based components are still a work in progress, meaning in v18 we are still unable to even preview them. However, with the current understanding of how things will be, we know that it will not affect the code itself and will be more similar (but not exactly the same) as a new change detection strategy. The following listing shows an example of a hypothetical signal-based component that uses all the features we just discussed.

Listing 10.18   Hypothetical signal-based component with model bindings

```
@Component({
  selector: 'app-root',
  standalone: true,                              Binds to a signal in a
  template: `                                    two-way fashion
    <div>
      <input placeholder="Search for product..." [(ngModel)]="query"/>   ◄─┐
      <ul>
        @for (product of filteredProducts(); track product.id) {
          <li>
            {{product.name}}
          </li>
        }
      </ul>
    </div>
  `,
})
```

```
export class App {
  private readonly productService = inject(ProductService);
  type = input<number>();
  query = signal('');
  allProducts = computed(() =>
    this.productService.getProductsByType(this.type()));
  filteredProducts = computed(() => {
    return this.allProducts.filter(product =>
    product.name.includes(this.query()))
  });
}
```

Signal input to read from a URL parameter view component-router input binding

Computed signal derived from an HTTP call observable

Computed signal filtering products based on user's input

As we can see, with this approach, we can describe quite complex interfaces and relations in a declarative and eloquent fashion, without the need to even write methods, and enjoy the benefits of zoneless change detection.

> **WARNING** All the features mentioned in this section are hypothetical and not available as of Angular v17. They have been proposed by the Angular team and will almost certainly undergo changes until they become publicly available. Read more in the Angular signals RFC (https://mng.bz/mRYy) on signal-based components.

Finally, another aspect of existing Angular projects that might be affected is the pipes. Pipes have been historically used to circumvent a limitation of zone-based change detection, that being the inability (or rather it not being welcomed) of invoking functions in templates. However, with zoneless change detection and the advancement of the inject function, pipes might no longer be necessary to reuse pieces of logic within different templates.

Next, let us discuss the most concrete advancement in the Angular change detection story, which we can already try out in v18: the new change detection scheduler that allows us to (experimentally) go zoneless right now.

10.3.5 Zoneless scheduler for change detection

Now that we understand Zone.js and the internal mechanisms of change detection, we can notice that zones act as schedulers for change detection, rather than performing the change detection itself (which is still a function of Angular and will not change or go away even with the zoneless approach).

It logically follows that, to go zoneless, Angular first needs to introduce another scheduling mechanism. This has been successfully achieved in v18. Starting from this version, under the hood, Angular will actually employ two mechanisms at once: the conventional zone-based scheduler and the new zoneless one in parallel. This new scheduler will start change detection cycles depending *only* on some particular events

- `ChangeDetectorRef.markForCheck`—This is the method that is used by the async pipe to trigger change detection.
- `ComponentRef.setInput`—We used this previously to pass on changed inputs to dynamically render child components.

- Changing a value of a signal that is used in a template.
- Event listener callbacks.
- Attaching new views that are already dirty (as a result of one of the previous points).

As we can see, these requirements mean that if we had to turn off zone-based change detection, the only way of triggering change detection (and consequently updates to the UI) is either by using observables/signals or manually. However, we should again note that, currently, this new scheduler works *in parallel* to Zone.js, meaning nothing is going to break if we upgrade an existing application to v18.

We can try out a completely zoneless experience by simply enabling experimental zoneless support with a simple function in the application configuration (the app.config.ts file at the root of the project):

```
bootstrapApplication(AppComponent, {providers: [
  provideExperimentalZonelessChangeDetection(),
]});
```

As we can see, the function name itself contains the word "experimental," which should act as a hint for us to avoid moving such changes into production-ready applications, as this will fully disable Zone.js and might very possibly result in bugs until we change our application in ways that fully conform to the list of requirements mentioned previously. However, this should not discourage us from starting early and adopting these requirements to be ready for a fully zoneless future.

PREPARING FOR ZONELESS

Outside of the points we mentioned earlier, there are some other ways in which we can inadvertently become reliant on Zone.js, and that is mainly through the NgZone injectable. This injectable provides functions to work with Zone.js through an Angular wrapper, and some of those functions are *not* compatible with zoneless. These functions are NgZone.onMicrotaskEmpty, NgZone.onUnstable, NgZone.isStable, and NgZone.onStable. If we are using any of these functions in our application, we must start by removing references to them, as the tasks performed by them will become unnecessary with zoneless. It is also important to note that NgZone.run and NgZone.runOutsideAngular are zoneless-compatible and there is no need to remove references to them. Thankfully, most common Angular applications (especially enterprise ones) very rarely use these functions; the most widely used is runOutsideAngular anyway, so this step should be relatively easy for most Angular developers.

Another step to consider is to make sure our server-side functionality stays intact. The way that Angular SSR works is that it essentially emulates the rendering process that happens on the frontend (with HTTP calls and everything else) and then converts the results to HTML to send back to the client in a process called *serialization*.

To know when the app is ready to be serialized, Angular SSR internally relies on Zone.js to know when the app is stable (for example, all necessary HTTP requests have been completed to render the final UI). However, sometimes with zoneless, there might be cases where we want to postpone that to await an async task, like a navigation redirect (a useful example is when the app refreshes the user's credentials and then redirects to a dashboard page).

In these cases, we need to have access to a mechanism that can manually tell Angular to wait with the serialization; starting from v18, a specific injectable called `Experimental-PendingTasks` has been added, which gives us exactly that sort of functionality and helps fix any problems with SSR. It can be easily used with any async task:

```
const tasks = inject(ExperimentalPendingTasks);
const cleanup = tasks.add();
await someAsyncTask();
cleanup();
```

This way, Angular will hold off the serialization until the cleanup function is called, helping us avoid any problems or race conditions bugs. The "experimental" prefix again gives us a hint not to rush with deploying this specific approach to production.

With these simple steps, in addition to converting to signals/observables, we can make sure that, in the future, when zoneless becomes the golden standard, our existing application can easily become more performant and lightweight by ditching Zone.js completely. Finally, to wrap the book up, let's discuss some other updates to the Angular ecosystem and have some musings on the direction that the framework will be taking.

10.4 In other news

As of version 18, Angular is undergoing a process that the core team and contributors refer to with the bombastic word "renaissance," which is warranted; after all, we just dedicated an entire book to all the new changes and approaches that have emerged from v13 to v18. This renaissance is marked by a very important landmark that is unrelated to code, which is the launch of the new Angular documentation website and the new home for all things Angular: angular.dev (https://angular.dev/).

The new website is scheduled to become the primary resource for learning about Angular, with new tutorials, rewritten documentation, and built-in playgrounds, where we can test out Angular code snippets without the need to bootstrap a whole new application.

This new documentation also includes a revised and improved road map (https://angular.dev/roadmap) of future additions to the framework; some of them, like stable deferred loading or zoneless applications are already covered in this chapter. Some other potential improvements that are worth noting are

- *Partial hydration*—Instead of hydrating the entire page, SSR applications might become able to hydrate only the parts of the DOM that are in the viewport, resulting in even faster time-to-interactive metrics
- *Improvements for debugging*—In particular, it might become possible to debug Angular applications that run inside iframes and also debug signals.

- *Class struggle*—Potential new component/directive/pipe authoring format, possibly without classes; still in the discussion stage.
- *Improvements to Angular material*—Support for new CDK primitives, improved tooling, and more.

As we've seen throughout this book, both the Angular team and the wider community put great care into the development of this beloved framework, which leads us to believe that no matter what, Angular steps into a very bright future.

Summary

- Angular introduced a built-in template syntax for control flow.
- Instead of structural directives like `NgIf`, `NgFor`, and `NgSwitch` we can now use `@if`, `@for`, and `@switch`.
- From v17, it is possible to lazy-load standalone components directly from the template with `@defer`.
- Deferred loading can be customized to show a placeholder, loader content, and error content.
- Deferred loading can be enhanced with prefetching and specific loading triggers.
- Angular is making steps toward a zoneless future.
- `OnPush` components that use signals will now benefit from more optimized local change detection.
- Angular has introduced a new documentation website and a road map for amazing future improvements.

index

ngOnInit method 76, 113–114
NgOptimizedImage 96–100
  adding lazy loading and setting width/height 97
  prioritizing image loading 98
  srcsets and image loaders 98–100
ng serve command 221, 223
NgSwitch directive 249–252
ng update command 8
NgZone injectable 274
NgZone.isStable function 274
NgZone.onMicrotaskEmpty function 274
NgZone.onStable function 274
NgZone.onUnstable function 274
NgZone.run function 274
NgZone.runOutsideAngular function 274
NotificationService 168–169
notifications$ observable 169
notificationsOpen signal 167
npm install express command 217
NullInjector 51, 69

O

object-oriented programming (OOP) 4
Observable class 121
observables
  converting signals to 149
  converting to signals 147–149
  signals vs. 134
    everything is synchronous 134
    reading value does not affect application 134
    unsubscription will be automatic 134
    value can always be read 134
    value can be changed on the fly 134
  unsubscribing from 106–115
    DestroyRef 108–111
    problems with 107
    reasons for 107
    takeUntilDestroyed operator 111–115

of function 115, 159
onDestroy method 110
onDestroy$ observable 108
OOP (object-oriented programming) 4
OperatorFunction 116, 121
@Optional decorator 69
Optional decorator 69
optional flag 72
@Output decorator 268–269
outputFromObservable function 269
output function 268

P

partial hydration 275
PermissionsService 111
phase option 227
pipe function 121–122
pipe method 116, 121
@placeholder block 256–257
prerendered static websites 239
prerendering 233–235
private authService: AuthService 31
ProjectDetailsComponent 266
projectId property 76
properties, every property can be a signal 174
provideClientHydration() function 230
provideClientHydration() method 220
provideHttpClient function 67
provideRouter function 10, 33
providers array 24, 32, 51
providers property 32

R

reactive programming 104–105
  computed signals 138–143
reactive values 140
refactoring, unit testing and 180
refreshView method 162
required inputs 75
requireSync option 158
resolvers, migrating 67
reusability, improved 59
root injector 51
RouterTestingModule 189

routing
  default export components in 101
  standalone components 31–34
routing parameters, binding to input properties 81
rxjs-interop package 111
RxJS (Reactive Extensions for JavaScript) 4, 103
  advanced interoperability with 170–173
  custom operators 61
  more traditional Angular applications
    every property can be a signal 174
    looking for derived values 174
    primitive RxJS 174
  problems with 126–129
    async vs. sync and glitches 128–129
    stateless nature of Observables 126
    steep learning curve 126
  reactive programming 104–105
  reasons for using 106
  RxJS-heavy Angular applications 173
    BehaviorSubjects 173
    RxJS-based custom state management 173
    RxJS interoperability on a local scale 174
  signals and interoperability with 147–151
    converting observables to signals 147–149
    converting signals to observables 149
  signals and synchronizing with 158
  signals vs. 126–130
  solution for 129–130
    creating new reactive values from existing ones 130
    everything is synchronous 130
    interoperating with RxJS 130